Descartes

and the *Meditation*

D0084479

A superior piece of work…I can't think of any other work that sets for itself as ambitious a task or that does as well with anything like it.
Roger Ariew, Virginia Polytechnic Institute and State University

It is written at just the right level, and is extremely clear…everything is presented fairly and in a way that genuinely engages the issues. This is the best current introduction to the *Meditations*.
Stephen Gaukroger, University of Sydney

This is a splendid piece of work, clearly and engagingly written. It will be accessible and helpful to students, but also to professional philosophers.
Vere Chappell, University of Massachusetts

René Descartes is generally accepted as the "father of modern philosophy," and his *Meditations* is among the most famous philosophical texts ever written.

In this Routledge Philosophy GuideBook, Gary Hatfield guides the reader through the text of the *Meditations*, providing commentary and analysis throughout. He assesses Descartes' importance in the history of philosophy and his continuing relevance to contemporary thought.

Descartes and the Meditations will be essential reading for all students of philosophy, and for anyone coming to Descartes for the first time.

Gary Hatfield is Adam Seybert Professor in Moral and Intellectual Philosophy at the University of Pennsylvania. He is the author of *The Natural and the Normative: Theories of Spatial Representation from Kant to Helmholtz* and the editor of *Kant: Prolegomena to Any Future Metaphysics*.

Routledge Philosophy GuideBooks

Edited by Tim Crane and Jonathan Wolff
University College London

Routledge
Taylor & Francis Group

LONDON AND NEW YORK

Routledge Philosophy GuideBook to

Descartes

and the *Meditations*

Routledge

■ Gary Hatfield

First published 2003
by Routledge
2 Park Square, Milton Park, Abingdon, Oxon OX14 4RN

Simultaneously published in the USA and Canada
by Routledge
270 Madison Avenue, New York, NY 10016

Reprinted 2004, 2006, 2007, 2009, 2010

Routledge is an imprint of the Taylor & Francis Group, an informa business

© 2003 Gary Hatfield

Typeset in Times by Taylor & Francis Books Ltd
Printed and bound in Great Britain by the MPG Books Group

British Library Cataloguing in Publication Data
A catalogue record for this book is available from the
British Library

Library of Congress Cataloging in Publication Data
A catalog entry for this book has been requested

ISBN 978-0-415-11192-8 (hbk)
ISBN 978-0-415-11193-5 (pbk)

To Holly, Sam, and Tiny

Contents

Preface

No single text in philosophy is more widely read than Descartes' *Meditations*. Long a mainstay of the philosophical curriculum, it has served as a stalking horse for philosophers of every stripe. Although new to succeeding generations of beginning students, the work is comfortably – or, in some cases, discomfortingly – familiar to those students' teachers, and to the broader culture of letters.

This familiarity creates an interpretive barrier. Even novice readers may soon feel that they "know" what the central arguments and conclusions of the work are, where its philosophical significance and force lie. There are the skeptical challenge, the famous *cogito* in reply, the criterion of clear and distinct perception as guaranteed by a non-deceiving God, the circle, the mind–body distinction, and the resulting problem of mind–body interaction.

Indeed, these elements are there in the *Meditations*. Yet they are only part of the picture, only vehicles to an end that, in philosophical interpretations from the middle decades of the last century, was largely overlooked: Descartes' use of the work to promote a new general science of nature (French scholarship, and earlier English-language scholarship, did attend to this factor). As Descartes wrote to Mersenne in letters that are now frequently cited (and are quoted more fully in Chapter 1), his *Meditations* contains "all the foundations" of his physics, which "destroy" the principles of Aristotle (by yielding a radically different conception of matter and its properties, and of mind and the operation of the senses). Deeper insight can be gained into the work by remembering that its arguments and conclusions are primarily in the service of this project. Thus the skeptical doubt is put in place in order to help the reader to attain distance from the ordinary conception of nature, so that a new conception might more easily be grasped; the *cogito* is not intended to "prove" the meditator's existence (as if this were in doubt), but provides a key to the metaphysical method by which further truths can be known; and so on.

Another feature of the usual approach to the text of the *Meditations* has dulled the senses of generations of readers, making some portions of the text virtually disappear as the eye scans the page: the treatment of the text as a string of detachable arguments, embedded in some stage setting – the division into six "days" of concentrated thought – that serves, from this perspective, as so much filler. Recently, however, several commentators have analyzed the philosophical force of the work in relation to its literary genre as a work of *meditations*. Descartes adapted the literary form of the spiritual exercise to his own philosophical purposes. Just as spiritual exercises involve purging the senses and intellect, receiving divine illumination, and uniting the will with God, so Descartes' cognitive exercises involve skeptically purging the cognitive faculties, achieving intellectual illumination through the use of the "light of nature," and training the will to affirm only those metaphysical propositions that are perceived with clarity and distinctness by the intellect. When read in this way, stretches of the text that seemed to be doing no philosophical work, especially passages at the beginnings and endings of each Meditation, take their place in contributing to the philosophical force of his rich and compact book by guiding the reader in a process of discovery aimed at doing more than simply deriving conclusions from premises through valid arguments. The meditative process was to help the reader to discover ideas of the essences of things, ideas allegedly obscured by over-reliance on the senses.

In this way, Descartes' project to establish a new conception of nature and his choice of the meditative mode of writing are united in another aspect of the *Meditations* that deserves special attention: a reliance on what Kant would later call the "real use" of the intellect to establish the work's primary metaphysical conclusions. Descartes' arguments for the foundations of his physics, for his corpuscular theory of the senses, against Aristotelian "real qualities," and for the mind–body distinction share dependence on appeals to a purely intellectual conceiving of the essences of matter and mind. Descartes adopted the meditative mode of writing as an effective means to train readers in the proper use of their intellectual faculty. And indeed, in explaining the importance of the skeptical doubt and the need to spend days or even weeks in meditation, Descartes indicated that his readers must learn to "withdraw the mind from the senses" in order to perceive the primary truths of metaphysics. (The three main points listed in the preceding paragraphs have appeared in my "The Senses and the Fleshless Eye: The *Meditations* as Cognitive Exercises," in A. Rorty (ed.), *Essays on Descartes' Meditations*, pp. 45–79, and "Reason, Nature, and God in Descartes," in S. Voss (ed.), *Essays on the Philosophy and Science of René Descartes*, pp. 259–87.)

I have sought to weave these interpretive themes into a work that situates Descartes within his historical context without sacrificing attention to the philosophical depth of the *Meditations*. The basic context is set in Chapter 1, although more is added throughout, especially in Chapter 9 on Descartes' new science. I have aimed to provide clear statements of the major arguments and argumentative strategies of the *Meditations*, and to sketch major lines of interpretation and reconstruction, while providing my own reading. The basic structure of the work, its textual strategy, and its own front matter are treated in Chapter 2. The subsequent six chapters treat each of the six Meditations in full; a topical breakdown of these Meditations may be found in the subheadings of Chapters 3–8, listed in the table of contents. Of course, a book of this scope cannot be exhaustive, but it does offer a reading of each topical section in every Meditation. Chapter 10 examines Descartes' legacy.

I should note that in providing a philosophical context for Descartes, I have considered philosophical positions as they were understood and represented in his day. Thus, he engaged Aristotelian philosophy as presented by various scholastic philosophers, several of whom are named in Chapter 1. Their positions may or may not coincide with the thought of the historical Aristotle, as we would interpret him today. Therefore, this book does not seek to compare Descartes' philosophy directly with that of Aristotle himself.

My attempt throughout has been to understand Descartes' arguments, to see where he thought they got their force, and to evaluate them in light of objections from his own time and from more recent philosophical critics, and in light of my own interpretation. It has not been possible to mention all objections, or to respond in detail to every one that is mentioned. Moreover, in a systematic work, what comes later builds on what has come earlier; therefore, as we move through the *Meditations*, we accept some conclusions for the sake of further argument, despite the presence of unresolved objections to them (whether mentioned or unmentioned). The aim is not to give the impression that there are no objections or that they are not serious. Far from it. I hope that readers will evaluate the arguments as I reconstruct them, will seek to develop alternative construals, and will come to their own conclusions about the strengths and weaknesses of the arguments.

I have aimed to make the work accessible to general readers and students in introductory courses on the history of modern philosophy while giving it sufficient depth to be useful in more specialized courses on Descartes or on rationalist philosophy. I also intend it to be useful and stimulating to scholars of Descartes' work and to philosophers more generally.

The experience of presenting the meditational reading of the text (first offered in the fall of 1980 at Harvard University) and other aspects of the interpretation to generations of students has been instructive. Among the many students who have stimulated my ongoing thinking about Descartes, I must especially acknowledge Hannah Ginsborg and John Carriero at Harvard, Stephen Menn at Johns Hopkins, and Alison Simmons at Penn. In preparing the work for publication, the assistance and commentary of Yumiko Inukai have been invaluable. Comments on all or part of the manuscript by Allison Crapo, Karen Detlefsen, Sean Greenberg, Steve Kimbrough, Susan Peppers, Holly Pittman, and Alison Simmons have been of much help. Michael Ayers deserves special thanks for detailed comments on and challenges to the penultimate draft. I gratefully acknowledge the encouragement and patience of Tim Crane and Jo Wolff, and the useful comments provided by referees for the press. Academic leave from the University of Pennsylvania greatly aided my writing of the book. Michael Ryan of Special Collections, and Bob Walther as philosophy bibliographer in the University Library, have genuinely aided this and other work in the history of philosophy. Last but not least, Holly, Sam, and Tiny were constant companions, cheer-leaders, and sources of inspiration.

Abbreviations and citations

Citations to Descartes' works are made using the pagination of the modern standard edition of the original Latin and French, Charles Adam and Paul Tannery (eds.), *Oeuvres de Descartes*, revised edition (Paris: Vrin/C.N.R.S., 1964–76). This edition is usually designated by "AT" plus the volume and page number. Since all citations in the text of the present book are to the pagination in AT, I have dropped those initials and have given volume and page numbers only, as in (7:21) for volume 7, page 21.

The pagination of AT is shown in the margins of most translations of Descartes' works. For the major philosophical works, I've followed the translations of John Cottingham, Robert Stoothoff, and Dugald Murdoch (eds.), *Philosophical Writings of Descartes*, 2 vols. (Cambridge: Cambridge University Press, 1984–85), standardly referred to as CSM. Where CSM provides only selections, or no translation at all, additional translations are listed below. For Descartes' letters, I've used Cottingham, Stoothoff, Murdoch, and Anthony Kenny (eds.), *Philosophical Writings of Descartes, Volume 3, Correspondence* (Cambridge: Cambridge University Press, 1991), standardly referred to as CSMK. Because I have provided AT numbers, I do not provide references to CSM and CSMK, or to other translations, in the text.

All my citations using AT numbers can be located using numbers printed in the margins of these or other translations (with two exceptions, noted below). On the few occasions where I have found it necessary to alter the translation from the listed source (which I've done as conservatively as possible), I've marked the citation with an asterisk (*). In the few cases where I cite a passage for which there is no translation, the citation is italicized.

Although the context often indicates the work cited, the AT volume and page numbers can serve as a sure guide, as follows:

AT vol./page	Work
1–5	Correspondence
5:144–79	Conversation with Burman
6:1–78	*Discourse on the Method*
6:79–228	*Dioptrics* (also known as *Optics*)
6:229–366	*Meteorology* (also known as *Meteors*)
7	*Meditations*, with Objections and Replies
8A	*Principles of Philosophy*, Latin edition
8B:341–69	*Comments on a Certain Broadsheet*
9A:198–217	Note, and Letter to Clerselier, French edition, *Meditations*
9B:1–20	Author's letter to French edition, *Principles*
10:151–69	Correspondence with Beeckman
10:213–48	Early writings (private thoughts)
10:359–469	*Rules for the Direction of the Mind*
10:495–527	*The Search for Truth*
11:1–118	*The World, or Treatise on Light*
11:119–222	*Treatise on Man*
11:223–86	*Description of the Human Body*
11:301–488	*Passions of the Soul*

I have cited the *Meditations* in the pagination of AT, vol. 7, in the original Latin. The translations of the *Meditations* (with Objections and Replies) and *Search for Truth* appear in CSM, vol. 2. The Early Writings, *Rules*, and selections from the *Discourse* and essays, *Principles*, and *Passions* (along with other works) are in CSM, vol. 1. A literal and accurate translation of the front matter and six Meditations, with facing-page Latin, is provided by G. Heffernan (ed.), *Meditations on First Philosophy = Meditationes de prima philosophia* (Notre Dame: University of Notre Dame Press, 1990).

For *The World* and *Treatise on Man*, I have followed the complete translations in Stephen Gaukroger (ed.), *The World and Other Writings*

(Cambridge: Cambridge University Press, 1998). The *Meteorology* appears only in Paul J. Olscamp (ed.), *Discourse on Method, Optics, Geometry, and Meteorology* (Indianapolis: Bobbs-Merrill, 1965); this edition does not show AT numbers. Most of my citations to the *Principles* may be found in CSM, which gives selections only for Parts 2–4; for a complete translation, consult V.R. Miller and R.P. Miller (eds.), *Principles of Philosophy* (Dordrecht: Reidel, 1983), which also does not provide AT numbers; CSM, vol. 1, provides a guide to the AT numbers by translating the titles of every numbered article in Parts 2–4.

I've followed CSMK for the conversation with Burman, which provides selections; for a full translation, see J. Cottingham (ed.), *Descartes' Conversation with Burman* (Oxford: Clarendon Press, 1976).

References to additional discussion or alternative interpretations, and citations providing factual support, are collected at the end of each chapter. Secondary works are referred to by author, or author and short title, after their first mention. A selected list of recent English-language works on Descartes may be found at the end of this volume.

PART I

OVERVIEW AND SYNOPSIS

Chapter 1

Descartes' project

In 1641, at the age of 45, Descartes published the *Meditations on First Philosophy*. First philosophy is another name for metaphysics, the study of the basic principles of everything there is. Descartes understood metaphysics to ground all other knowledge, of the self, of God, and of the natural world; and he intended his *Meditations* to enable its readers to discover the one true metaphysics for themselves. It was a very ambitious work.

The *Meditations* describes itself as a work on "God and the soul" (7:1). And indeed it argues that God exists and that the soul or mind is distinct from the body. In preparation for these arguments, it raises and then overturns skeptical challenges to the very possibility of knowledge. On the surface, it appears to be a work about the possibility of knowledge concerning theological topics.

But if we look more deeply, we find that Descartes' aims were far from traditional. In letters to his friend Marin Mersenne, he secretly confided (3:298) that this work contained "all the principles" of his physics (3:233). His talk of God and the soul was interlaced with metaphysical foundations for a revolutionary new physics or natural philosophy. His aim was to overturn the prevailing theory of the natural world, which put humankind at the center of things, and replace it with a radically new vision of nature as a grand but impersonal machine. Because he wanted his revolutionary intentions to remain hidden from first-time readers, no part of his book is labelled "principles of physics" or "theory of the natural world." We shall have to uncover his radical agenda for ourselves – an agenda that had tremendous influence on the subsequent history of philosophy and science.

To understand what Descartes wanted to do in the *Meditations*, we need to place that work in the context of his life and other writings. His intellectual career did not begin with aspirations in metaphysics but in mathematics and natural philosophy. His earliest efforts in those fields encouraged him to believe that he had discovered a special method. His thoughts on method changed and developed as he gained interest in metaphysics. These changes contributed to his ambitious vision for the *Meditations*.

After reviewing Descartes' intellectual projects and their results in this chapter, we will consider the structure and method of the *Meditations* as a philosophical text in the next. In Part II, we will examine the six Meditations, one by one. Finally, in Part III we will consider his revolution in science as supported by the *Meditations*, and sum up his philosophical legacy for us today.

Education

Descartes' education in a Jesuit school introduced him to the philosophical tradition he reacted against in his own philosophy, the Aristotelian tradition as interpreted by the scholastic philosophers of the Roman Catholic universities of Europe. As it happens, the Jesuits were excellent teachers of mathematics, and the rigor of that discipline inspired Descartes' initial thoughts of rebellion in philosophy. Not long after completing his schooling, he discovered some mathematical results for which he is justly famous. But from his schooldays the model of clarity found in elementary mathematical works had made him want to challenge philosophy. He decided that by comparison with such clarity, philosophy was badly in need of reform, and he was the person for the job.

Descartes was born in 1596 in the Poitou region of France, near Tours in the small town of La Haye (now named "Descartes"). His father, the son of a physician, was a member of the landed gentry and a councillor in the parliament at Rennes. His mother, who came from a family of land-owning merchants, died in childbirth thirteen months after Descartes was born. The young René lived with his maternal grandmother, together with his older brother and sister. As was common for the sons of the gentry, he went to boarding school, attending the Jesuit college at La Flèche, in Anjou, from 1607 to 1615. The college had been established in 1604 by Henry IV, the former leader of the Calvinist Huguenots, who nominally converted to Catholicism in 1593 to undermine Catholic opposition to his kingship. In 1594, following an assassination attempt by a Jesuit student, Henry expelled the order from Paris and closed their colleges in other French cities. After reconciliation in 1603, he donated the palace and grounds at La Flèche to the Jesuits for a new college.

The Jesuits are a Roman Catholic religious order, known formally as the Society of Jesus, founded in Spain in 1539 by Ignatius of Loyola. Their mission was to improve the spiritual character of humankind, with a special emphasis on education. The order founded new colleges and universities and assumed control of many existing schools in France and elsewhere throughout the seventeenth and into the eighteenth century.

Jesuit schools, renowned for their quality, drew students of various backgrounds and aspirations, including prospective clergy, students preparing for law or medicine, and future civil servants, military officers, and merchants. The first six years of study focused on grammar and rhetoric. Students learned Latin and Greek and studied selections from classical authors, especially the ancient Roman orator Cicero, whose works were read as models of style and eloquence but also contained surveys of philosophical positions. Many of Descartes' fellow students left after the first six years, some entering society and some transferring to university, where after completing the arts curriculum they could continue directly into the higher faculties of law, medicine, or theology. Those who remained at La Flèche, including Descartes, completed the mathematical and philosophical portion of the arts curriculum in their final three years. Descartes was apparently satisfied with his choice of school, for later in life he advised an inquiring father that none offered better philosophical instruction, even for those wanting to transcend traditional philosophy (2:378).

The early modern arts curriculum was not confined to the medieval "seven liberal arts." Those seven arts consisted of the "trivium" (grammar, rhetoric, and logic), which except for logic were covered in the first six years ("grammar school"); and the "quadrivium" (geometry, arithmetic, astronomy, and music), taught at La Flèche in the final three years. The primary curriculum for the arts degree, earned in the final three years of instruction, consisted in the branches of philosophy: logic, natural philosophy (also called physics), metaphysics, and morals.

The official Jesuit curriculum required that philosophical instruction follow Aristotle. The study of logic, physics, metaphysics, and morals drew upon Jesuit commentaries on Aristotle's texts, or on independent treatises (including simplified textbooks) that covered the Aristotelian subject areas. These commentaries and treatises sometimes departed significantly from Aristotle and the major medieval Christian interpreters, such as Thomas Aquinas and John Duns Scotus, although most of them contained core areas of agreement. Descartes knew such commentators both from school and from later reading; he explicitly mentioned (3:185) Francisco Toledo, Antonio Rubio, and the Coimbran commentators (who included Peter Fonseca). He also knew the work of Francisco Suarez (7:235) and admired the philosophy textbook of Eustace of St. Paul (3:232), a member of the Cistercian Order and so not a Jesuit. He studied Aristotelian philosophy intensively during his final three years of college, and up to 1620 (3:185).

All the same, Descartes' studies in philosophy were not limited to the Aristotelian variety. The early study of Cicero introduced him to ancient atomists, Plato and Aristotle, skeptics, and Stoics. The Aristotelian commentaries of Toledo, Rubio, the Coimbrans, and others discussed a variety of positions, including atomistic physics and Platonic theories of knowledge, as well as the various Neoplatonic, Islamic, and Latin commentators on Aristotle. Although rejecting Platonic theories of knowledge, they described in some detail the view that knowledge arises from the purely intellectual apprehension of Forms distinct from the sensory world. Descartes' mature theory of knowledge was closer to Plato than to Aristotle. But while he was in school the conflicts among philosophical positions made them all appear merely probable; since none achieved the "certainty" and "self-evidence" of mathematics (6:7), he treated them all as if false (6:8).

Jesuit school mathematics comprised the abstract branches (geometry and arithmetic) and various applied branches, including not only astronomy and music (from the quadrivium), but also optics and perspective, mechanics, and civil or military architecture. In Descartes' time, the ancient sciences of astronomy and optics were undergoing radical revision. The sixteenth-century astronomer Nicholas Copernicus opposed the previous geocentric astronomy by hypothesizing that the Earth moves around the Sun. A moving Earth would violate Aristotle's physical principle that all earthly matter naturally strives to reach the center of the universe, making the Earth a unique central globe around which all other heavenly bodies revolve. Galileo Galilei, using the newly invented telescope, discovered moons around Jupiter in 1610, challenging Earth's uniqueness. Descartes took part in a celebration of this discovery at La Flèche in 1611. Johannes Kepler published works in mathematical optics in 1604 and 1611 that contradicted ancient theory by showing that the eye forms an image on the retina; Descartes was familiar with these results by the 1620s.

After La Flèche, Descartes studied law at the University of Poitiers, graduating in 1616. His father wanted him to pursue law, so that the family could gain a title of nobility (which they finally received in 1668), but Descartes was reluctant, and after turning twenty-one he enlisted in the army.

Gentleman soldier and mathematical scientist

In 1618, Descartes joined the forces of Maurice of Nassau, Prince of Orange, general of the army of the United Provinces (the Dutch

Netherlands), who had been supported intermittently by the French in struggles against the Spanish Netherlands. When Descartes joined the army at Breda, the United Provinces were in the ninth year of a twelve-year truce with Spain. Breda was located just north of the border with the Spanish-held provinces of the Netherlands (present-day Belgium) and was the residence of Maurice as well as his mathematicians and engineers. In July, Maurice led part of the army north to Utrecht and its environs to intercede for one Calvinist faction against another. As part of the defensive force arrayed against the Spanish, Descartes stayed in Breda and did not see military action.

While garrisoned outside Breda, Descartes met the Dutch natural philosopher Isaac Beeckman, an event that changed his life. The two first conversed on 10 November 1618 in front of a placard stating a mathematical problem. Descartes was already interested in applied problems in mathematics and may well have been studying military architecture. Both men were happy to find someone else who spoke Latin and knew mathematics. Beeckman was soon challenging Descartes with problems in mathematics, musicology, kinematics, and hydrostatics. These problems encouraged Descartes to think of material things as composed of small round spheres, or atoms, of matter. Some short writings remain (*10:67–74*) in which Descartes took this "atomistic" approach (later rejected in favor of infinitely divisible corpuscles). In December 1618 he completed his first book, the *Compendium on Music*, written in Latin and dedicated to Beeckman (published posthumously in 1650).

A new method

Early in 1619, Descartes solved the long-standing mathematical problem of trisecting an angle, using a proportional compass of his own devising, and he discovered algebraic solutions to several classes of cubic equations. This work gave him new insights into the relation between geometrical constructions and algebraic equations. His proportional compass was constructed of rigid straight edges that hinged and slid over one another to create fixed proportions (in a continuous manner, as the device opened and closed). Descartes saw that his compass could represent algebraic equations, including cubic equations (involving a cube root in relation to other terms, such as $x^3 = ax^2 + b$). By treating the lengths of the arms and cross-pieces as values of the constants and unknowns in an equation, he could treat the curves traced by their interaction as values of equations expressing those constants and unknowns. These techniques for treating algebraic equations as relations among straight lines became the basis for analytic geometry.

Descartes excitedly proclaimed to Beeckman on 26 March 1619 that he now envisioned a "completely new science" for solving "all possible equations" (10:156–7). He contrasted his project with the *Ars brevis* ("Compendium on Method") of Ramon Lull, a thirteenth-century Majorcan knight turned monk. Lull claimed that his method, which manipulated words or concepts organized under headings, could solve problems of any kind. Descartes considered it a sham (6:17, 10:164–5). His own new method would be limited to relations of quantity. By combining lines representing continuous or discrete quantities, it would solve "all possible equations involving any sort of quantity" (10:156–7).

There is no evidence that Descartes had originally intended to find a new method of any sort. He and Beeckman were working on very specific problems. "Mathematical sciences" such as optics and astronomy had existed from ancient times, as had many of the problems in pure mathematics that Descartes solved. His discoveries typically extended previous mathematical methods involving proportions, making them more general. But this initial breakthrough foreshadowed a lifetime of fascination with method (shared by his contemporaries), eventually extending beyond mathematics to philosophy and metaphysics.

Descartes' early work in mathematics did not rely on the syllogistic logic he learned in school. Mathematics typically was not formulated using syllogistic logic. Geometrical works stated axioms, definitions, and postulates, from which theorems were proved. Proofs took the form of instructions for constructing figures using compass and straight edge. The rules of inference included "common notions" such as "If equals be added to equals, the wholes are equal" but did not involve the statement of specifically logical axioms. At this time, there was no thought that logic formed the core of mathematics (that was a nineteenth-century idea). Algebra and arithmetic proceeded by using equations constructed with arithmetic operators. Equations were not part of the structure of syllogistic logic. (Syllogisms and mathematical demonstration are discussed in the Appendix.) Descartes considered the syllogism too cumbersome for original reasoning, though useful for presenting known results (e.g., 6:17). Sometimes syllogisms were used in presenting mathematical results, although Descartes did so only rarely (10:70), and not in his famous *Geometry*.

A mission in life

Despite his achievements in mathematics, Descartes remained uncertain where "fate" would lead him (10:162). He wrote to Beeckman in April 1619 that he planned to join the army in Germany (10:162), where developments were leading toward the Thirty Years' War. Calvinist Protestants in Bohemia (now in the Czech Republic) had challenged the authority of their Catholic prince, Ferdinand, who had become Holy Roman Emperor in March. On arriving in Germany, Descartes joined the Catholic army of Maximilian I (Duke of Bavaria, ally of France, and supporter of the new emperor) and was present in Frankfurt-on-Main for Ferdinand's coronation in September. In the meantime, the Protestant Frederick V had been crowned king of Bohemia by the Calvinist nobles, and war was brewing.

Descartes was returning to the army in Bavaria after the coronation when winter caught him in Neuburg, a peaceful Catholic principality on the Danube north of Munich. While there, he settled on a new course in life. In the *Discourse on the Method* he recalls his interrupted travel and reports that "finding no conversation to divert me, and otherwise, fortunately, having no cares or passions that troubled me, I stayed all day shut up alone in a stove-heated room where I had complete leisure to converse with myself about my thoughts" (6:11*). His reflections convinced him that he should extend the clarity of his new science of proportion to the other sciences (6:20–1). He would now seek clear and distinct connections among ideas in other fields to match the perspicuity of algebra and geometry (6:19–20). Because the principles of other sciences "must all be derived from philosophy" (including natural philosophy), he resolved first "to try and establish some certain principles" in that field (6:21–2).

His decision to reform the sciences was partly inspired by three dreams during the night of 10 November 1619. We know their content primarily through Adrienne Baillet's 1691 biography of Descartes (but see 10:216). The dreams were complex, involving whirling wind, a melon, acquaintances he passed without greeting, thunder, sparks, pain in the side, disappearing books, and the title of a poem by Ausonius, "What road in life shall I follow?" Descartes interpreted them as commanding him to reform all the sciences, that is, all organized knowledge. As we've seen, he decided to begin with philosophy. By his own account, it was nine years before he discovered a new foundation for philosophy (6:30).

His early notebooks offer some hints about his philosophical ideas near the time of the dreams. He favored a sense-based epistemology. ("Epistemology" means theory of knowledge, which in Descartes' day encompassed descriptions of the cognitive faculties of the mind, such as the senses or intellect.) Contrary to his later views, he wrote that "man has knowledge of natural things only through their resemblance to the things which come under the senses" (10:218). Indeed, he thought it best to conceive even "spiritual things" by making use of "certain bodies which are perceived through the senses, such as wind and light" (10:217). As he explained, "wind signifies spirit," and "light signifies knowledge" (10:218). The comparison of spirit with wind or fine matter was similar to the ancient philosophies of Democritus, Epicurus, and the Stoics.

Descartes reports that in the stove-heated room he worked out the provisional moral code set down in Part Three of the *Discourse*. A source for part of the code has recently been discovered. A copy of Pierre Charron's *Traité de la sagesse* ("Treatise on Wisdom"), found in Neuburg, was inscribed to Descartes by a Jesuit father during the winter of 1619. Charron was a philosophical skeptic, who said he knew nothing. He recommended that in one's state of ignorance, one should simply obey the laws and customs of the country in which one lived. Descartes' first moral precept is a version of this advice, "to obey the laws and customs of my country" (6:22–3).

Although familiar with the revival of philosophical skepticism, Descartes was not inclined toward becoming a skeptic. He treated many of his opinions as doubtful, as skeptics also do. But his aim was to eradicate incorrect opinions by retaining only those that were certain. In uprooting his errors, he says, "I was not imitating the skeptics, who doubt only for the sake of doubting, and pretend to be always undecided; on the contrary, my whole aim was towards certainty" (6:29*). True skeptics don't simply have doubts about whether they know some particular item of knowledge. They seek to use various arguments to place themselves in a state of sustained doubt, in which they suspend judgment about any theoretical knowledge going beyond mere appearances. Descartes was not troubled or challenged by such skepticism. He used the skeptical technique of suspending judgment in order to bracket, for further investigation, areas of potential knowledge now lacking the clarity and evidence found in mathematics.

The method made general

The *Discourse* reports that, upon leaving his warm room, for "the next nine years" (1619–28) he did nothing but "roam here and there in the world, trying to be a spectator more than an actor in all the comedies that play there" (6:28*). In fact, he did not merely roam. During 1620, he continued to work on scientific and mathematical problems. He may have visited Ulm (west of Neuburg on the Danube, in present-day Wurttemberg) and consulted with the mathematician Johannes Faulhaber, who taught at the military college. He may also have been present at the Battle of White Mountain in November, when Frederick was defeated and forced into exile at The Hague, where Descartes later (in 1642) befriended his daughter, the Princess Elizabeth (only two years old in 1620). After visiting France in 1622 he spent two years in Italy, 1623–25. Upon his return (or just prior to leaving in 1622), he fought a duel (disarming but sparing his foe) and perhaps composed his lost treatise on fencing near that time. He continued to study philosophy, for he later recalled examining works by Tomaso Campanella around 1623 (2:659) and not being much impressed. In any case, by 1630 he knew of the Italian anti-Aristotelian innovators of the time, including, besides Campanella, Sebastian Basso, Giordano Bruno, Bernardino Telesio, and Lucilio Vanini (1:158).

During these nine years, he worked intermittently on a book on "universal mathematics," which was to present his new method. The uncompleted manuscript, published in Latin in 1701 as the *Rules for the Direction of the Mind*, contained twenty-one out of a projected thirty-six Rules. In it, he did indeed seek to extend a method like that in mathematics to "any subject whatsoever" (10:374*). He now claimed that all mathematical sciences could be recast as a single discipline with "order or measure" as its subject matter (10:378), to be investigated using his new science of proportion. He further claimed that all the sciences in general depend on certain "pure and simple natures," which any investigator should seek first (10:381). This search for simple natures or simple ideas lay at the heart of his generalized method, extended beyond mathematics.

The generalized method of the *Rules* was later summarized in the *Discourse*, now distilled into only four rules:

The first was never to accept anything as true if I did not have evident knowledge of its truth: that is, carefully to avoid precipitate conclusions and preconceptions, and to include nothing more in my judgments than what presented itself to my mind so clearly and so distinctly that I had no occasion to doubt it.

The second, to divide each of the difficulties I examined into as many parts as possible and as may be required in order to resolve them better.

The third, to direct my thoughts in an orderly manner, by beginning with the simplest and most easily known objects in order to ascend little by little, step by step, to knowledge of the most complex, and by supposing some order even among objects that have no natural order of precedence.

And the last, throughout to make enumerations so complete, and reviews so comprehensive, that I could be sure of leaving nothing out. [6:18–19]

The first rule states a general standard of clarity and certainty. The second and fourth read as a summary of procedures that might be followed in solving a problem in algebra (e.g., dividing the problem into various simpler equations and checking over one's work); but they also portray a more general strategy of fully analyzing problems into their elements, so that nothing relevant is overlooked. The third states a more general principle of method, to start with simple and easily known objects and to think of the complex objects as knowable through the simple ones.

Both the *Rules* and the *Discourse* assert that knowledge in all fields can be resolved down to certain "simple natures" (10:381) or "simple things" (6:19) known with mathematical clarity and self-evidence. What are these simple natures? Rule Six says that the qualities of such natures include being "independent, a cause, simple, universal, single, equal, similar, straight, and other qualities of that sort" (10:381), but it does not offer examples of the natures themselves. Rule Eight outlines the steps for solving a problem in optics and alludes to the notion of a "natural power" without revealing what such a power is (10:395). Rule Twelve finally provides examples of three sorts of simple nature: things known by the mind about the mind, such as the notions of knowledge, doubt, ignorance, and volition or willing; things known as present in bodies, such as shape, extension, and motion; and things common to minds and bodies, such as existence, unity, and duration (10:419). This at least suggests a basic division of the simple natures into mental and bodily or corporeal (we might now say "physical"). But in that work Descartes does not claim that bodies have *only* the properties of spatial extension, such as shape and motion, as he would claim later.

Descartes' hope for extending the clarity and certainty of mathematics to other topics depended on finding simple constituents everywhere. In elementary mathematics, we follow the method of the *Rules* when, in adding large numbers, we resolve the computation into smaller ones whose truth we can grasp intuitively, such as $2 + 3 = 5$. The generalization of this method requires that other fields be reducible to correspondingly simple ideas and entities. If complex things are in fact constituted through combinations of basic entities, we might comprehend those things by isolating in our thought the simple ideas of such entities and then combining them so as to reflect the composition of things in the world. A nice method, if we can find the simple ideas, and if they and their combinations actually fit the way the world is.

When Descartes returned to France in 1625, he was freed of his father's demand that he enter civil administration as an attorney. He subsequently remained in Paris until 1628, joining a group of mathematicians and intellectuals that included Marin Mersenne, another advocate of mathematical descriptions of nature, and Guillaume Gibieuf, a theologian at the Sorbonne. During this time, he discovered the sine law of refraction and performed experiments in optics. Rumor of his method spread among French intellectuals, and he endeavored to finish the *Rules*. But he abandoned the work in 1627–28, near the end of the section on algebraic solutions to "perfectly understood" problems and prior to writing any of the projected section on problems "not perfectly understood" (10:429). Perhaps he gave up when the limitations of his scheme to represent all mathematical problems through relations among line segments became apparent. In any event, the thrust of his investigations now turned toward metaphysics and a new science of nature as a whole.

Metaphysical turn

In 1628 and 1629, Descartes again reformulated his intellectual agenda. Late in 1627, he attended a public lecture by a chemist named Chandoux, which had been arranged by the Papal Nuncio in Paris. The lecturer criticized Aristotle's natural philosophy and proffered a chemically based natural philosophy. Those in attendance all applauded, except Descartes. Cardinal Bérulle – the founder of the Parisian Oratory and a disciple of Augustine of Hippo's Neoplatonism – wanted to know why Descartes disapproved. In answering, Descartes praised the speaker's rejection of Aristotle's philosophy but chastised him for offering merely probable opinions in its place. He proclaimed that he himself possessed a universal method for separating the true from the false with certainty. Bérulle called upon him to give the fruits of his method to the world (1:213; see *Meditations*, 7:3).

As it happens, Descartes devoted the rest of his life to intellectual pursuits. He eventually published four major books – covering geometry, optics, the physical world, the human body and human emotions, and metaphysics – and others were left unpublished when he died in 1650. In the course of his development, he retained his method of searching for simple notions, but his account of the cognitive basis for his method changed.

Prior to his return to the Dutch Netherlands late in 1628, his work had focused on mathematics (pure and applied) and method. Now he undertook for the first time a sustained investigation of metaphysical topics. During his first nine months in the Netherlands he worked on nothing else. In April 1630, he wrote to Mersenne about the results of this work. He said he had discovered "how to demonstrate metaphysical truths in a manner which is more evident than the demonstrations of geometry" (1:144*). For someone who previously regarded mathematics as providing the ultimate standard of certainty, this statement marks a significant change. The letter also reports that metaphysical investigations concerning God and the self (the soul or mind) had led him to discover "the foundations of Physics" (1:144). Although it is unclear whether Descartes was at this time closely familiar with the Augustinian philosophical theories embraced by Bérulle, in saying that he came to knowledge of first principles by turning first to God and the soul, he echoed Augustine's procedure in the *Confessions* (ch. 7). We shall soon see evidence that by 1629 he had rejected the sense-based epistemology of 1620 and adopted a position closer to the Platonic theory that primary truths are known through purely intellectual (non-sensory) contemplation.

The same letter announces the radical metaphysical thesis (later published in the Objections and Replies to the *Meditations*) that "the mathematical truths, which you call eternal, have been established by God and are entirely dependent on him, just as are all his other creations" (1:144–5). By this he meant that the mathematical truths are free creations of God, dependent on God's will, and that God could have willed them otherwise. In other words, God might have made it that the three angles of a triangle do not equal two right angles, or that $2 + 3 \neq 5$ (further discussion in Chapter 9). This position differed both from the scholastic Aristotelian view that the eternal truths are grounded in the essence of God, either in his very being or in his intellect, and from the properly Platonic view that the eternal truths are independent of God and are grounded in eternal Forms that determine the rational structure of thought and all existent things – which copy (or dimly reflect) those Forms.

During these nine months, Descartes drafted an early version of his metaphysics (see 1:350) containing the "first meditations" that the *Discourse* (6:30–40) dates to this time, and to which it ascribes the basic ideas found later in the *Meditations*.

A unified physics

Descartes' metaphysical musings were interrupted in summer 1629 by a scientific problem. In April, Christopher Scheiner had observed an impressive set of false suns, or parhelia, near Rome. A report circulated among natural philosophers. When Descartes learned of it, he immediately set to work to explain this optical phenomenon. Parhelia are now known to be caused when ice crystals in the upper atmosphere reflect and refract the sun's light. Descartes advanced the theory that the highest clouds are made of ice crystals and snow, which circular winds melt and refreeze so as to form a solid, transparent ring of ice that acts as a lens to produce the parhelia (6:355).

Although this solution is fanciful (a solid lens is not formed in the sky), the attempt to explain this complex natural phenomenon drew Descartes into general physics more fully than before. He soon wrote to Mersenne that completion of his work on parhelia would be delayed about a year, since "instead of explaining a single Phenomenon, I am determined to explain all the Phenomena of nature, that is, the whole of Physics" (1:70*). One year became three. Since at this time "physics" meant the study of all of nature, including living things, Descartes had indeed expanded his project greatly, beyond optics and atmospherics to include all chemical, mineralogical, geological, biological, and even psychological phenomena.

The project developed into a major work, which Descartes modestly entitled *The World*. It was to have three parts: a treatise on light (which would contain a general physics), a treatise on man (covering human physiology), and a treatise on the soul or mind. Only the first two parts are extant (the third was either never written or has been destroyed). These two parts contain a new comprehensive vision of material nature.

In Descartes' youth, the accepted opinion remained that the Earth holds a unique place at the center of the universe, with the Sun and planets traveling around it. Natural processes, such as growth and decay, or even the freezing and thawing of water, were considered to take place only on or near the Earth. Some theories posited a crystalline sphere to carry the Moon around the Earth, and to separate the sublunary region of change from the immutable heavens. On this view (explained more fully in Chapter 9), terrestrial and celestial physics are fundamentally different. In overturning this picture, Descartes went far beyond the Copernican hypothesis that our Sun lies at the center of the universe with the Earth moving about it. He contended that the Earth is one among many planets, revolving around many different suns distributed throughout the cosmos. He further proposed that the whole universe is made of one kind of matter, which follows one set of laws. He invented the concept of a single universe, filled with matter having a few describable properties and governed by a few laws of motion.

While others, including ancient atomists and Stoics, had sketched part of this new picture, Descartes' vision of a unified physics governed by a few laws of motion was far richer and more detailed. Its combination of breadth and unity was unprecedented in his earlier work with Beeckman, or in the works of Copernicus, Galileo, or Kepler. This unified vision set the framework for Newton's subsequent unification of mechanics and astronomy. To explain Descartes' expanded vision we can look to the metaphysical researches of 1629, which yielded "foundations of Physics." These foundations supported his picture of a universe governed throughout by a few natural laws and underwrote his claim to know the nature of all the material substance in the universe.

In a chapter of *The World* entitled "The Laws of Nature of this new world," Descartes related the laws of motion to the activity of God. He composed the entire work as a fable, in which God creates a new universe "like ours" (and clearly intended actually to be ours) beyond the boundaries of the Aristotelian universe of his schoolbooks (11:31–2). In this "new" world, God creates a single uniform matter that has only the properties of size, shape, and motion (11:33–4), and he imparts a certain fixed quantity of motion to this matter. Because God is immutable, he preserves the same quantity of motion in the world from creation onward. Descartes explains how an immutable God can govern the motions of a changing world:

> If God always acts in the same way and consequently always produces the same effect, many differences in this effect occur, as if by accident. And it is easy to accept that God, who is, as everyone must know, immutable, always acts in the same way. Without going any further into these metaphysical considerations, however, I will set out here two or three of the principal rules by which we must believe God to cause the nature of this world to act, and these will be enough, I believe, to acquaint you with all the others. [11:37–8]

He then sets out three rules or "laws of nature," which depend "solely on God's conserving each thing by a continuous action" (11:44*). These laws, which include a near counterpart to Newton's law of inertia, are examined more fully below (Chapter 9).

Besides these three laws, Descartes recognizes no other laws in his world "but those that most certainly follow from the eternal truths on which mathematicians have generally supported their most certain and most evident demonstrations: the truths, I say, according to which God Himself has taught us He disposed all things in number, weight, and measure" (11:47). Allusion to the Biblical phrase "but thou hast ordered all things by measure and number and weight" (Wisdom of Solomon, 11.20) was commonplace, but Descartes now explains that God "taught us" these truths by implanting them in the mind or soul.

> The knowledge of these truths is so natural to our souls that we cannot but judge them infallible when we conceive them distinctly, nor doubt that if God had created many worlds, they would be as true in each of them as in this one. Thus those who know how to examine the consequences of these truths and of

our rules sufficiently will be able to recognize effects by their causes, and, to express myself in scholastic terms, will be able to have *a priori* demonstrations of everything that can be produced in this new world. [11:47]

The relevant scholastic meaning of the term "*a priori*" in this context is "reasoning from cause to effect." Such reasoning need not rely on experience of the causes and effects, for in this context what is "natural" to our souls is innate. We have seen that Descartes considered the eternal truths of mathematics to be free creations of God. Perhaps a further metaphysical insight of 1629 was that God, in freely decreeing those truths, also made them true in the world he created and implanted knowledge of them in the human mind, thereby explaining our capacity to discern the true foundations of physics by discerning the mathematical essence of matter (as Descartes believed he was the first to do).

After three years of work, Descartes had produced (at least) the first two parts of his *World*, the general physics and the treatise on man. The second of these ambitiously offered (or promised) entirely mechanistic explanations of human physiology and parts of human psychology. In connection with this work, Descartes visited butchers' shops to watch animals being slaughtered and took home animal parts for dissection (1:263, 523; 2:525). The resultant theories are discussed in Chapters 8 and 9.

Late in 1633, Descartes learned that Galileo had been condemned by the Roman Catholic Inquisition for defending the Copernican hypothesis that the Earth moves around the Sun. Since he affirmed that hypothesis in his *World*, he suppressed the work. He was loyal to the Church but also concerned at being made "a criminal" for affirming the theory; he considered burning all his papers (1:270–1). The extant parts of the work were published posthumously in 1664 (in French), as *The World, or Treatise on Light*, and the *Treatise on Man*.

The *Discourse* and the method

After the Galileo affair, Descartes did not give up his project of reforming the sciences. In 1637, he tested the response to his new ideas by offering a sampler, the *Discourse on the Method* together with essays on *Dioptrics*, *Meteorology*, and *Geometry*. These works were also written in French, making them accessible to literate people outside the universities, including artisans, people at court, and "even" women (1:560). (Descartes held that all human beings, irrespective of gender, possess the same intellectual power [see 6:1–2].) At this time, Latin was the universal language of learning in European universities, and the language of nearly all philosophical works, but some philosophical and scientific authors, including Francis Bacon and Galileo as well as Descartes, had begun to publish in their native languages (English, Italian, and French).

Descartes used the *Discourse* to introduce his program of scientific work to the public, to sketch some metaphysical results, and to ask for money to support the empirical observations needed to decide among his own rival scientific hypotheses (6:65). (Although publication was anonymous, the identity of the author was soon known.) The metaphysical discussions, found in Part Four, include the skeptical dream argument, the famous *cogito* argument ("I think, therefore I am"), an argument that mind and body are distinct, a proof for the existence of God, and an argument that the clear and distinct perceptions of reason are true (6:31–40). These arguments will be considered primarily through their fuller (and sometimes significantly different) counterparts in the *Meditations*.

After the *cogito* argument appeared in the *Discourse*, Mersenne and others (2:435, 3:247) asked about its similarity to a passage in Augustine's *City of God* (Bk 11, ch. 26). As we will see in reading the *Meditations*, Descartes' philosophy has affinities with Augustine's. Nonetheless, Descartes replied to his correspondents that he was (in 1637–38) unfamiliar with Augustine's works (*1:376*, 2:535). He promised to consult them, which he had done by 1640 (3:247). Assuming that in 1637 he did not know Augustine's works directly, he might have become familiar with their content through the Augustinians Bérulle and Gibieuf. (Although Bérulle died in 1629, Descartes maintained contact with Gibieuf [1:16–17, 153; 3:184, 237].) Another argument in the *Discourse* – starting from his ability to conceive of something more perfect than himself and concluding that only an actually perfect being, God, could have given him this ability (6:33–5)

– also echoes Augustine. Descartes might have gleaned this argument from his Augustinian contacts or read in Cicero a similar argument due to the ancient Stoic Chrysippus.

The essays attached to the *Discourse* were supposed to exhibit the results of his method, and in fact they offered several bits of his physics (although not the whole of his *World*). The *Dioptrics* sketched his physics of light, explicated the laws of reflection and refraction, described the gross anatomy and physiology of the senses and eye (including the formation of the retinal image), gave explanations for the perception of light, color, size, shape, and distance, and described lenses for correcting vision and for telescopes, as well as a machine for cutting them. The *Geometry* presented his solution to an ancient problem in mathematics, the "Pappus locus problem" – to describe a set of points (a locus) in relation to four (or more) given lines, such that from the points four lines can be drawn to intersect the four given lines at equal angles, with the newly drawn lines standing in a certain given ratio among themselves. In working out his solution, Descartes developed the basis for algebraic or "analytic" geometry, including what later became the Cartesian coordinate system. (He soon abandoned "abstract geometry" in favor of geometry as used in natural philosophy [2:268].) The *Meteorology* began from certain "suppositions" or hypotheses that stated his basic assumptions in natural philosophy – that "the water, earth, air, and all other such bodies that surround us are composed of many small parts of various shapes and sizes, which are never so properly disposed nor so exactly joined together that there do not remain many intervals around them; and that these intervals are not empty but are filled with that extremely subtle matter through the mediation of which, I have said above, the action of light is communicated" (6:233*). Using these assumptions, the work offered explanations for atmospheric, mineralogical, and visual phenomena, including the bands of the rainbow. (Descartes later wrote [1:559] that this explanation of the rainbow provided the only full example of his method in the *Discourse* and essays.) Taken together, the *Dioptrics* and *Meteorology* offered a mechanistic, corpuscular explanation of light, color and other "secondary qualities" (as they were later called) in terms of the motion of particles and the effect of those motions on perceivers. Color as experienced became a perceiver-dependent sensation, by contrast with Aristotelian "real qualities" transmitted from the object to the perceiver's mind.

Although the suppositions in the *Meteorology* laid out the fundamental entities in his physics, in the *Discourse* and essays Descartes did not openly reject other explanatory entities. In particular, he did not explicitly deny the existence of the active principles or substantial forms, and real qualities, of Aristotelian physics. He did, however, signal that such things had no place in *his* physics (6:239). Furthermore, while claiming that he could "deduce" his physical assumptions from his metaphysics, he did not provide the deduction (6:76). For now, the corpuscularian principles of his physics would simply be "proved" through effects, that is, through their ability to explain a wide variety of phenomena, including new empirical observations (see also 1:423–4, 563; 2:199).

Descartes' metaphysics as summarized in Part Four did not mention the claim, crucial for his physics, that the essence of matter is extension. The promised metaphysical foundations for his physics surely must include that claim, as well as the role of God as conserving the quantity of motion in the world.

In 1638, Descartes explained to a Jesuit at La Flèche, Antoine Vatier, that he had omitted the metaphysical proof for his physics because it required the use of skeptical arguments that he "did not dare" put before a general audience – stronger arguments than the dream argument that he had published. These stronger arguments presumably include the hypothesis that God might be a deceiver, which appears in the *Meditations* (7:21). He explained to Vatier that the stronger skeptical arguments were needed to help the reader to "withdraw the mind from the senses" (1:560). The previous year, he told Mersenne that in the *Discourse* he had not fully developed the needed skepticism about the senses because the work was in the vernacular; but he recalled that "eight years ago I wrote in Latin the beginnings of a treatise on metaphysics in which this argument is conducted at some length" (1:350). It is clear, then, that the metaphysical treatise of 1629 used skepticism to divert the mind from sensory matters. Earlier, we saw that the initial metaphysical investigations of 1629 permitted him to discover "the foundations of Physics" (1:144).

We will need to look to the *Meditations* themselves, the successor to the treatise of 1629, to learn more about how one can discover the foundations of physics by withdrawing from the senses.

The *Discourse* invited readers to send their objections to the publisher (6:75), and Descartes was soon writing letters to defend his physical suppositions, his omission of substantial forms and real qualities, and his metaphysics, including mind–body dualism (e.g., 1:353, 2:38–45, 197–201). The Jesuit mathematician Pierre Bourdin attacked the *Dioptrics* in public disputations in Paris during 1640, and Descartes responded with a letter sent via Mersenne (*3:105–19*). He became increasingly concerned about the Jesuit response to his work (3:126, 184, 752), for he wanted them to support, and even to teach, his new philosophy (1:454–6, 2:267–8, 4:122).

The *Meditations*

Soon after the *Discourse* was published, Descartes' correspondents (1:564) began to press him for the metaphysical foundations for physics, as well as the complete version of his physics that had been mentioned. Although at first he was unwilling to comply, in 1639 he promised to publish his metaphysics (2:622), which became the *Meditations on First Philosophy*, published in Paris late in 1641. The work consisted of the six Meditations together with Objections by philosophers and theologians and Descartes' Replies.

As a named field of study, "first philosophy" was invented by the ancient Greek philosopher Aristotle. It included study of the highest being, which Aristotle called "god." Because first philosophy extended beyond physics, Aristotle's followers called it "metaphysics," which literally means "that which is beyond physics." Aristotelian metaphysics studied being in general, that is, the basic properties of everything there is. Aristotle's medieval followers disagreed on whether metaphysics could provide the first principles specific to the other sciences, but they agreed that metaphysical principles are the last things learned, since they must be "abstracted" from experience and are the most abstract principles of all. Descartes, by contrast, held that metaphysics contains first principles specific to the other sciences, that these principles could be known *a priori* (without appeal to experience), and that they should be discovered first, to guide further investigation. In a later work he compared all knowledge to a tree, with metaphysics as the roots, physics as the trunk, and medicine, mechanics, and morals as limbs (9B:14).

Although in publishing his metaphysics Descartes was fulfilling a promise to provide foundations for his physics, he did not advertise that fact in the published work, and he asked Mersenne to keep quiet about it. Furthermore, the first edition carried the subtitle "In Which the Existence of God, and the Immortality of the Soul Are Demonstrated," and the dedicatory Letter presented the work as focusing on these two topics, as areas in which philosophy could support religion (7:1–2). As the Synopsis observes, the work does not in fact offer a demonstration of immortality (7:12–13); the subtitle to the second edition (of 1642) accurately reflects this fact by describing the book as one "In Which the Existence of God, and the Distinction of the Human Soul From the Body, Are Demonstrated."

Despite what the Letter says (7:2), the main aim of the work was not to support religious truths in the face of "unbelievers." As we have seen, Descartes revealed its primary aim in writing to Mersenne that "the little Metaphysics I am sending you contains all the Principles of my Physics" (3:233*). And yet it remains the case that no part of the *Meditations* openly promulgates principles of physics. Descartes explained this fact in another letter to Mersenne:

> I will say to you, just between us, that these six Meditations contain all the foundations of my Physics. But, please, you must not say so; for those who favor Aristotle would perhaps have more difficulty in approving them; and I hope that those who will read them will unwittingly become accustomed to my principles, and will recognize the truth, before they notice that my principles destroy those of Aristotle. [3:297–8*]

He was worried about the approval of "those who favor Aristotle." Partly this meant the approval of Church authorities, who might otherwise block publication given the close connection at this time between Aristotelian philosophy and Christian theology (among both Catholics and Protestants). We have just seen that he hoped the

Jesuits, who favored Aristotle, would eventually be willing to teach his philosophy.

Such political strategizing does not tell the whole story. As we will see in Chapter 2, Descartes had good methodological reasons, connected with his "analytic" method and with the textual organization of the *Meditations* into six Meditations, for not directly confronting his largely Aristotelian audience by introducing his fundamental principles up front. Moreover, although his emphasis on God and the soul in the dedicatory Letter surely was intended to win favor from theologians, we have seen that Descartes earlier described contemplation of God and the soul as leading him toward the foundations of his physics. The connections among his various claims about God and the soul, skepticism toward the senses, and physics will become apparent in Chapter 2 as we examine the methodological structure of the *Meditations*.

Subsequent works

Descartes began but left unfinished a dialogue entitled *The Search for Truth* (perhaps written while he waited for the *Meditations* to appear). The dialogue included a scholastic philosopher (Epistemon, or "knowledgeable"), an untutored man of good sense (Polyander, or "everyman"), and a stand-in for Descartes (Eudoxus, or "famous," although etymologically suggesting "good opinion"). It reprises arguments from the *Meditations* (up to Meditation 2).

Although Descartes considered the metaphysical investigations portrayed in the *Meditations* and *Search* to be important, he did not think readers should devote constant attention to them. In 1643, he wrote to Princess Elizabeth of Bohemia (daughter of Frederick V) "just as I believe that it is very necessary to have properly understood, once in a lifetime, the principles of Metaphysics, because they are what gives us knowledge of God and our soul, I also believe that it would be very harmful to occupy one's intellect frequently in meditating upon them, because this would impede it from properly attending to the functions of the imagination and the senses" (3:695*). Those functions guide practical action and aid the investigation of nature.

In the very letter informing Mersenne that he was sending him a draft of the *Meditations*, Descartes told him he was planning a textbook covering his entire philosophy, including the long-awaited physics (3:233, 272). He hoped that his Latin *Principles of Philosophy* would replace the prevailing Aristotelian curriculum in colleges and universities, at least in metaphysics and physics. His plan initially called for publishing the textbook together with an Aristotelian one, Eustace of St Paul's *Summa philosophiae* ("Compendium of Philosophy"), with annotations revealing the comparative advantage of his views (3:232). But he soon abandoned that plan, believing that his principles so obviously destroyed any opposing ones that direct refutation was unnecessary (*3:470*).

When the *Principles* appeared in 1644 it had four parts. The first reviewed the metaphysics of the *Meditations*. The second explicitly revealed the fundamental principles of physics, including the equating of matter with extension, the denial of a vacuum, and his three laws of motion. The third described the formation of solar systems and the transmission of light. The fourth concerned the formation of the Earth and the explanation of various physical phenomena. He had intended to add fifth and sixth parts, covering biological phenomena, including plants, animals, and the human animal, but he ended up simply appending to the fourth part a discussion of the human senses and sensory nerves (8A:315–23).

During the 1640s Descartes engaged in polemic over the religious orthodoxy of his philosophy. The trouble began with disputations organized and published at the University of Utrecht in 1641, in which an early follower of Descartes, Henry le Roy (or Regius), defended mind–body dualism and the mechanistic view of matter and rejected Aristotelian substantial forms. The Calvinist theologian Gisbert Voet (or Voetius) replied that mind–body dualism makes a human being into an accidental collection of two different kinds of thing, rather than a genuinely unified being, and that denying that the human soul is the substantial form of the body might result in denying altogether that humans have a soul. In January 1642, Descartes advised Regius to reply that human beings are unified beings composed of body and soul (3:508) and to refrain from denying substantial forms outright; it would be enough to say that they are not needed in mechanistic explanations (3:501–7). Regius' response to Voetius was confiscated by the municipal authorities of Utrecht upon publication. Descartes now entered the fray directly, defending Regius in the second edition of the *Meditations* (Letter to Dinet). The controversy widened, and in 1643 Descartes published a 200-page book in Latin, *Letter to Voetius* (8B:1–194). He narrowly avoided condemnation by the Calvinist authorities. When Regius broke ranks and published a brief attack on the *Principles* in 1647, Descartes responded with *Comments on a Certain Broadsheet* in 1648, reaffirming mind–body dualism and his proofs of God's existence.

In the meantime, Descartes' works were being vigorously discussed at the University of Leiden. In 1646, theology professor Jacob Trigland complained that other professors were allowing students to defend Descartes' philosophy, which he considered blasphemous and atheistic. Adrian Heereboord, a professor of logic who subsequently authored several books on Cartesian philosophy, defended Descartes in public disputations and orations. In May 1647, Descartes protested the charges against him in letters to the university curators (5:1–15, 35–9). Despite continued disputes and complaints, Leiden became a center for teaching, studying, and writing Cartesian philosophy and remained so for over fifty years.

At this juncture, Descartes had realized his ambitions in metaphysics and general physics, but not in medicine or morals. He had boasted earlier that he would discover a health regimen to extend his own life by a century (*1:507*), although as he grew older he moderated such claims (2:480, 4:329). In the mid-1640s, he returned to his physiological studies with the aim of covering everything from embryology to human psychology. In 1647–48, he worked on but left unfinished his *Description of the Human Body* (published posthumously in 1664, in French). The final work published in his lifetime, *The Passions of the Soul* (1649, in French), contained Descartes' theory of the emotions and his moral psychology. It responded to queries from Princess Elizabeth, who had also plied him with metaphysical questions concerning mind–body union and interaction.

In mid-April 1648, the young Frans Burman, son of a Protestant minister, visited Descartes in his house in Egmond (Dutch Netherlands) armed with questions about his published works. He posed eighty questions about specific passages, forty-seven on the *Meditations* alone, the rest mainly on the *Principles* and *Discourse* (in Latin translation). He apparently took notes on Descartes' replies during the interview and four days later prepared a manuscript record of the discussion, aided by Johann Clauberg. Although this record was written by Burman, not Descartes, it affords valuable information on Descartes' own interpretation of key arguments in the *Meditations*.

In 1649, Descartes accepted the invitation of Queen Christina of Sweden to become a court philosopher in Stockholm. He died of pneumonia early the next year (11 February 1650). His followers published many of his letters (1657–67), which contained philosophical, mathematical, and scientific discussions, as well as pharmaceutical and medical advice for his friends.

Reception and influence

Descartes drew both followers and opponents in the second half of the seventeenth century. His philosophy was condemned by the theological faculties at Louvain and Paris, by the Jesuits, and by the Augustinians of the Parisian Oratory. His works were banned from teaching even at Leiden and Utrecht, but the ban was routinely ignored by the magistrates who pronounced it, and by the numerous Cartesian professors they appointed. Despite such controversy, his name was soon added to lists of great philosophers, from which it has never disappeared. His *Discourse* and *Meditations* remain among the most widely read of all philosophical texts.

Over the centuries, opinions have changed about what is valuable and controversial in Descartes' philosophy. Such change should be expected, for the assessment of past thinkers is often influenced by current knowledge and interests.

Throughout the seventeenth century Descartes' scientific concepts exerted the widest influence. His vision that the material world is composed of small corpuscles of homogeneous matter, and that all the properties of material things can be explained through the interaction of such corpuscles, captured the imagination of many followers. Textbooks of Cartesian physics were published, as were medical works in Cartesian physiology. His physics was taught at universities in the Dutch Netherlands, England, Sweden, and Italy, and in public lectures in France. From 1699, Cartesians were admitted to the Royal Academy of Sciences in Paris, the primary home of French scientific thought. The young Isaac Newton was reading and criticizing Descartes' *Principles* in 1664 as he formed the philosophical outlook that framed his later work. Descartes' account of momentum and impact was studied in relation to those of Newton and G.W. Leibniz well into the eighteenth century. At Newton's own Cambridge the Cartesian *Treatise on Physics* of Jacques Rohault was taught into the 1740s; in France and Germany, Cartesian physics was debated for twenty years beyond that.

Descartes' rationalist project of discerning the foundations of physics and philosophy through reason alone was disputed by other seventeenth-century philosophers, who believed that all knowledge arises through sensory experience. Among his empiricist opponents, the French atomist Pierre Gassendi shared the mechanistic conception of matter, but he held that matter is constituted from indivisible atoms as opposed to the infinitely divisible extension of Descartes, and he affirmed the existence of a vacuum, which Descartes considered to be impossible. The Irish chemist Robert Boyle remained agnostic on atoms versus infinite divisibility (and on the vacuum), as did the philosopher John Locke (who, however, argued for the vacuum); they joined Descartes in affirming a corpuscular philosophy against the Aristotelians, while rejecting his rationalism. The English philosopher Thomas Hobbes adopted corpuscular mechanism but rejected Descartes' dualism in favor of the materialist theory that thoughts are nothing but matter in motion. Descartes' Aristotelian opponents were also empiricists of a sort, as they held that sensory experience is required for knowledge; but they also held that the intellect is able to extract the real essences of things through sensory experience, in this way differing from the other empiricists mentioned. In any case, partly as a result of Descartes' efforts and those of the new empiricists, scholastic Aristotelian philosophy was fading throughout the seventeenth century.

Writing in the second half of the seventeenth century, Benedict Spinoza and Leibniz shared Descartes' rationalist approach to metaphysics but reached different metaphysical conclusions. Spinoza held that there is only one substance, of which mind and body are aspects. Leibniz held that there are many individual substances, all mind-like, so that even the constituents of matter are simple substances that perceive or represent the world from a material perspective without themselves being truly extended.

In the course of the eighteenth century, interest in the particulars of Descartes' scientific vision faded (even as the mechanistic approach to nature waxed), but discussion of his skeptical arguments and his emphasis on reason over sensory experience continued. The Scottish philosopher Thomas Reid blamed Descartes for abetting the skeptical philosophies of George Berkeley and David Hume. (Whether Berkeley and Hume really were skeptics remains a matter for debate.) Reid thought that Descartes' claim to know the contents of his own mind best of all, and the related claim that the immediate objects of knowledge are "ideas" in the mind, effectively cut the mind off from the world by placing it behind a "veil of perception." He and others, including the empiricist Hume, rejected Descartes' claims that our intellectual ideas directly reveal things as they are in themselves.

Near the end of the eighteenth century, Kant summed up the history of philosophy as a struggle between rationalism, which he ascribed to Plato and Leibniz, and the empiricism of Aristotle and Locke. He believed that both positions were partly wrong and partly right. In his view, rationalism fails because the intellect cannot in fact transcend the senses and grasp the essences of things in themselves (whether mind, matter, or God). The empiricists are right that all knowledge arises with sensory experience, but they fail to acknowledge that some of our knowledge – mathematical, natural scientific, and metaphysical – requires a non-empirical framework. Kant believed that principles extracted from this framework, such as the causal law, could be known to hold within sensory experience but could not be used to go beyond sensory experience (e.g., to infer the existence of a god as creator). His criticism effectively ended rationalist metaphysics.

In the nineteenth century, Descartes was treated as a great historical philosopher who influenced both science and metaphysics. His substance dualism was rejected in favor of various substance monisms (positing only one type of substance), the most common of which was the dual-aspect theory that the mental and material are two aspects of one underlying substance. The English biologist Thomas Henry Huxley praised Descartes' role in the history of physiology, and particularly his view that animal bodies, including the human body, are complex machines.

In the middle of the twentieth century, three aspects of Descartes' work received the greatest attention: his skeptical arguments, his *cogito* argument, and his argument for a mind–body distinction. His new physics was largely ignored in English-language writings after mid-century, although it was known earlier and was emphasized in French and German scholarship. In the last quarter of the century, the history of philosophy underwent a renewal, so that historical texts were interpreted and evaluated on their own terms. This meant asking what past authors had considered important in their philosophy and evaluating their arguments in relation to their actual aims, rather than simply using their texts as foils for recent philosophical positions. Attention returned to Descartes' project of using metaphysics to found a new theory of nature. His doctrine of mind–body unity and his physiological and psychological theories shared equal billing with his mind–body dualism. It became widely recognized that Descartes was not a skeptic but had used skeptical arguments instrumentally, with the aim of achieving metaphysical knowledge.

Reading Descartes today

Descartes' philosophical teachings are so influential that they cannot be avoided, whether one agrees with them or not. The skeptical doubt, the *cogito*, and mind–body dualism continue to function as landmark positions in the geography of present-day thought. Although few now accept his substance dualism, he is often invoked in the philosophy of mind. Some admire and some disparage his realism about the mental. Others blame him for many modern ills, contending that his dualism caused thinkers to devalue the body and emotions.

In this guidebook, we want to get past stereotypes and reputation in order to look at Descartes anew. We have learned that he was an original scientist, mathematician, and metaphysician, who laid the basis for analytic geometry, published the first unified celestial and terrestrial physics, and proposed new theories of mind, body, and their interaction. These new theories framed Descartes' work on the philosophy and psychology of sense perception and the role of the body in emotion. It is in the context of this larger picture that we will read Descartes' *Meditations*.

There are many reasons for reading Descartes today. Because his positions serve as landmarks, it is useful simply to find out what he said. Moreover, the depth of his argumentation is formidable, even if one disagrees with his premises and conclusions. The *Meditations* was constructed to bring readers to see the conclusions of the arguments for themselves. For this purpose, Descartes adapted a literary form common to the seventeenth century, the meditative mode of writing. His adaptation of form to content is worthy of appreciation in its own right.

In analyzing Descartes' text and arguments, the student will gain skill in analyzing and evaluating texts and arguments more generally. Such skill is one main product of philosophical study, but in order to interpret the text and evaluate the arguments, we will need to understand what Descartes said. To read with comprehension will require learning about the intellectual context within which Descartes wrote, including the Aristotelian philosophers who were his first opponents and initial audience.

In the end, our aims are to understand and evaluate Descartes' project in relation to his context, to appreciate his philosophical influence, and to see what we still find compelling in his work.

References and further reading

There are two recent intellectual biographies of Descartes, S. Gaukroger, *Descartes: An Intellectual Biography* (Oxford: Oxford University Press, 1995), and G. Rodis-Lewis, *Descartes: His Life and Thought* (Ithaca, NY: Cornell University Press, 1998). I have generally followed Rodis-Lewis's dates for events in Descartes' early life. On p. 44, she describes the inscribed copy of Charron's book in support of her thesis that the *Discourse* was strongly (i.e., accurately) autobiographical. The point about obeying the laws of one's country is in

Pierre Charron, *Of Wisdom*, bk 2, ch. 8 (rare early translations of this work exist, but no full translation in the past century). Descartes' dreams are examined in G. Sebba, *The Dream of Descartes* (Carbondale: Southern Illinois University Press, 1987). Baillet's full biography, *Vie de Monsieur Des-Cartes*, is available only in French (originally published in 1691; reprint, New York: Garland, 1987; an abridged edition was translated into English in 1693); the dreams are described in vol. 1, pp. 81–6. Various condemnations of Descartes' philosophy are translated in R. Ariew, J. Cottingham, and T. Sorell (eds.), *Descartes' Meditations: Background Source Materials* (Cambridge: Cambridge University Press, 1998).

The question of Descartes' knowledge of and relation to St Augustine's thought has been much discussed, on which see Gaukroger, p. 207; Rodis-Lewis, p. 69; and also S. Menn, *Descartes and Augustine* (Cambridge: Cambridge University Press, 1998). On Cicero's statement of Chrysippus' argument for the existence of a god, see *De natura deorum*, III.x.

W.R. Shea's extensive scientific biography of Descartes, *The Magic of Numbers and Motion* (Canton, Mass.: Science History Publications, 1991), reviews the limitations to the mathematical representational scheme of the *Rules* that may have led to its abandonment (pp. 140–2).

General books on Descartes' philosophy that take his scientific interests into account include A.B. Gibson, *Philosophy of Descartes* (London: Methuen, 1932), N.K. Smith, *New Studies in the Philosophy of Descartes* (London: Macmillan, 1953), and B. Williams, *Descartes, The Project of Pure Inquiry* (London: Penguin, 1978). The reception of Descartes' thought at Leiden and Utrecht, including the religious controversies, is examined by T. Verbeek, *Descartes and the Dutch: Early Reactions to Cartesian Philosophy, 1637–1650* (Carbondale: Southern Illinois University Press, 1992). On Newton's early reading of Descartes (and other sources), see J.E. McGuire and M. Tamny, *Certain Philosophical Questions: Newton's Trinity Notebook* (Cambridge: Cambridge University Press, 1983). Additional references on Descartes' science and its reception are provided in Chapter 9.

General overviews of philosophy in the seventeenth century may be found in M.R. Ayers and D. Garber (eds.), *Cambridge History of*

Seventeenth-Century Philosophy (Cambridge: Cambridge University Press, 1998), and G.H.R. Parkinson (ed.), *The Renaissance and Seventeenth Century Rationalism* (London: Routledge, 1993). The *Cambridge History* contains numerous biobibliographies on major and minor seventeenth-century figures. S. Emmanuel (ed.), *Blackwell Guide to the Modern Philosophers: From Descartes to Nietzsche* (Malden: Basil Blackwell, 2001), provides introductory discussions for major seventeenth- and eighteenth-century philosophers, including Descartes, Hobbes, Spinoza, Malebranche, Reid, and Kant. Kant's summary history of philosophy occurs in the final chapter of his *Critique of Pure Reason*, translated by P. Guyer and A. Wood (Cambridge: Cambridge University Press, 1998). On the history of the term "metaphysics" (which was not invented by Andronicus of Rhodes, Aristotle's ancient editor, despite a widely repeated story to that effect), see T. Ando, *Metaphysics: A Critical Survey of its Meaning* (The Hague: Martinus Nijhoff, 1963).

Chapter 2

Reading the *Meditations*

The *Meditations* is a piece of writing. We are interested in it as philosophical writing, which means that we want to understand its conclusions, grasp its vision, and locate the source of its philosophical force. How does a work gain philosophical force? Surely this must vary depending on the aims and methods of the work, which in turn will vary from thinker to thinker and age to age. The modern standard for producing philosophical conviction is the argument. In its bare-bones structure, an argument is set out in numbered steps, called premises, which lead logically to the conclusion. A logical argument is such that if its premises are true and the conclusion follows logically from them, then the conclusion must be true. (On logical argument and Descartes' relation to it, see the Appendix.)

Descartes certainly used arguments, and we will examine many of them. Partly we will be interested in the logical structure of his arguments (even if, as we saw in Chapter 1, he did not consider it important to present arguments explicitly in a formally valid structure). However, no matter how flawless the logic, to establish the truth of its conclusion an argument's premises must be true. How is the truth of a premise established? Some premises might be established by previous argument, but not all, on pain of circularity or infinite regress. Some might be accepted on the basis of sensory experience. Others might be taken as rationally self-evident.

Discovering a firm basis for his premises, or first principles, was especially important to our author. He believed that true principles, once discovered, would serve to guide further reasoning by the clarity of their own content. As modern readers looking back at Descartes' work, we will want to understand how he endeavored to reveal such clarity to his audience. And we will sometimes reconstruct his reasoning in formally valid arguments as a way of understanding for ourselves how his principles were supposed to lead to further conclusions.

In the *Meditations*, Descartes was especially concerned to establish first principles in metaphysics. Many of the principles he favored were not accepted by his philosophical contemporaries. Moreover, most of his contemporaries, as empiricists of one sort or another, held that all knowledge arises from the senses. But Descartes believed that the special premises he wished to establish, concerning the nature of reality, could not be based in sensory experience. He was faced with the difficult problem of getting a hostile audience, committed to an opposing epistemology, to see the force of his first principles. The *Meditations* was constructed to meet this challenge.

Method in the *Meditations*

In Chapter 1, we saw that Descartes listed four rules of method in his *Discourse* (6:18–19). Boiled down, these amount to (1) accepting as true only what is known so clearly and distinctly as to be beyond doubt; (2) resolving problems into the simplest parts possible; (3) moving from the simple to the complex; and (4) thoroughly reviewing and checking one's work. This is a method appropriate to a great mathematician. Indeed, we have seen that, from 1619 on, Descartes sought to extend the certainty characteristic of mathematics into philosophy.

The *Meditations* uses a method of doubt to find what is indubitably known, as in rule (1). It seeks to resolve problems into basic or simple parts (2), first searching for a single indubitably known thing, then for the basic constituents of all things, and subsequently moving on to more complex knowledge (3). Finally, it includes reviews and checks throughout (4).

Seventeenth-century thinkers were fascinated with the notion of method. They wanted to know how new knowledge can be discovered and how existing knowledge can be presented and justified to someone who doesn't already accept it. By the 1620s, Descartes was renowned for possessing a new method of the first sort, before publishing even a single word of his philosophy. We can infer that he was also interested in methods of exposition, for he used several, including autobiographical narrative in the *Discourse*, fable in *The World*, dialogue form in the *Search for Truth*, and textbook format in the *Principles*.

In crafting the *Meditations*, Descartes drew on still other methodological devices. He took the "analytic method" from mathematics, adapted the literary form of the meditation from religious writings, and used the Objections and Replies to stage his own version of a scholastic disputation.

Analytic method

Descartes described the analytic and synthetic methods near the end of his second Replies to Objections (7:155–6). The synthetic method starts from definitions, axioms, and postulates and moves on, in an unbroken chain of demonstrations, to prove theorems. Euclid's geometry is the classic example. The reader can be compelled to assent by showing how the current step follows from what has been given. The analytic method, by contrast, takes nothing as previously given. It starts from a particular problem and works backward, as it were, until some simple and evident truths by which the problem could be proved or solved are reached. Those following the method are supposed to see the simple and evident truths for themselves along the way. In both methods, Descartes insisted, the arguments or demonstrations depend solely "on what has gone before" (7:155) – meaning that nothing is assumed that has not been explicitly introduced or shown to follow from what has been introduced. But with the synthetic method, the chain of explicit demonstrations can begin with axioms and postulates that are simply assumed or accepted on authority. With the analytic method, the reader will become convinced only if he or she achieves appropriate insights into crucial premises, or first principles, along the way. (Descartes believed that in the analytic method he had reconstituted the secret method of discovery of the ancient Greek mathematicians [10:373].)

Descartes thought that the synthetic method, with its requirement that the definitions, axioms, and postulates receive prior acceptance, would not be an effective way to argue for his new metaphysics. It was fine for elementary mathematics; the opening statements in Euclid might be sufficiently evident that they would be granted by all – or at least they were so widely accepted that students could feel secure in adopting them. But in metaphysics he saw a different situation. There, various writers were in disagreement, even on the basics (e.g., whether the natural world could exist on its own or must be created, whether matter is continuous or made of discrete parts, and so on). The dominant Aristotelian metaphysics was, in his view, deeply flawed. To the extent that his readers were inculcated with an opposing but flawed metaphysics, they would resist his new principles.

For these reasons, he believed the method of analysis was needed, to lead readers to consider metaphysical first principles for themselves. But he did not claim that the method would be universally effective. For an inattentive or lazy reader, it would not compel assent, for it did not offer an unbroken chain of demonstration from previously given premises. Rather, its aim was to help the reader to retrace the path of discovery, intuitively grasping the needed principles at each step. When using the method of analysis, "if the reader is willing to follow it and give sufficient attention to all points, he will make the thing his own and understand it just as perfectly as if he had discovered it for himself" (7:155).

The six Meditations were constructed to focus the reader on the required points. They use the method of doubt to clear his or her mind of previous opinions, leading to a first truth in the *cogito* argument. The basis for this first truth is then sought "analytically" (in

Meditation 3), by asking what could explain the given indubitable knowledge. The reader can then use the discovered basis to find additional first truths. Further reflections on this basis, as dependent on innate ideas, follow (7:51, 68).

The Meditations *as meditations*

Descartes did not think that his metaphysical principles would meet resistance simply because his readers already held other beliefs. Rather, he considered certain core beliefs, opposed to his metaphysics, to be the ordinary and natural result of human cognitive development. Human infants are immersed in the body (see 8A:35). They rely on their senses for preservation, and for the most part the senses serve them well in this regard. From such successes, children mistakenly come to believe that the senses immediately inform them not only of what is useful in external objects but also of their ultimate nature (7:83). Later on, adults have forgotten how these early opinions were formed, so they unreflectively hold that bodies are simply composed out of the properties manifest to the senses, including colors, sounds, tastes, odors, and tactile qualities such as hot and cold (the Aristotelian "real qualities"), as well as others such as size, shape, and motion.

This description shows how childhood prejudices could lead one to become an Aristotelian philosopher. With their sense-based theory of cognition, orthodox Aristotelians held that immaterial beings such as God, since they do not fall under the senses, can be cognized only obscurely in this life. In their view, such cognition must proceed through analogy with created things; for example, we observe that any change in sensible things requires a cause, so, by analogy, we posit a supreme cause as creator of the whole world. By contrast, Descartes (like the Platonists) held that a clear and distinct idea of God could be gained only by turning away from the senses and the created material world and relying on purely intellectual contemplation.

To reach his Aristotelian audience (as also the new empiricists), Descartes needed to overcome the belief that all knowledge and thought are based in the senses. In essence, he had to retrain his readers to turn from the senses toward purely intellectual ideas.

Otherwise, the analytic method of the *Meditations* would not work. To effect this retraining, he adopted a second methodical device: he composed his work using the literary form of the meditation.

In Descartes' day, the meditative method was well developed in religious writings known as spiritual exercises. Ignatius, founder of the Jesuits, had composed a set of exercises, and Descartes participated in meditations or spiritual exercises at La Flèche. Such exercises were intended to train the meditator's mental faculties. Works in this genre followed a standard order. First, one retreats from the world of the senses in order to meditate upon religious images (with Ignatius), or to clear the mind of images in order to experience union with God (as in Augustine). Then one trains the will to avoid the error of sin. In this process, the exercitant sequentially focuses on the relevant cognitive faculties: first the senses, then the imagination and intellect, and finally the will.

Descartes' *Meditations* is not spiritual, but cognitive and epistemic. ("Epistemic" means having to do with knowledge and its grounds.) It aims to produce metaphysical knowledge, not to induce a religious experience. In it, one turns away from the world by denying the reliability of the senses (First Meditation), clears the mind of sensory images in order to experience the mind itself and to find there the idea of God (Second and Third Meditations), and then seeks to regulate the will so as to avoid error in judgment (Fourth Meditation). Once the meditator's mind has been properly trained, Descartes presents the ideas and arguments that provide the basic premises for further points in his metaphysics, including his theory of material substance, his mind–body dualism, and his new theory of the senses (Fifth and Sixth Meditations). The concluding remarks of the first four Meditations especially reveal Descartes' use of the meditative genre, when he speaks of training his will to pretend that the material world does not exist (7:22), of fixing a result in memory (7:34), of contemplating God (7:52), and of controlling the will (7:62).

Objections and replies as disputation

To convince the widest variety of readers of his new metaphysics, Descartes creatively adapted another form of literature. Medieval scholastic works sometimes took the form of disputations, in which the opinions of various sides, pro and con, were reported on a given topic. Disputations took place in universities at public meetings, and they might subsequently be published. Descartes engaged in such disputations at La Flèche. As an extension of this practice, in the *Discourse* he promised to reply by letter to any objections that were sent to him. With the *Meditations*, he arranged for both objections and replies to be published with the original work. Together with Mersenne (who chose several of the objectors, and composed his own objections), he distributed copies of the *Meditations* to some leading philosophers and theologians, whose objections were appended to the six Meditations with Descartes' replies.

Descartes used his Replies to Objections for various purposes. Partly, he wanted to test himself against strong objections and show that he could meet them. In a philosophical culture accustomed to disputation, that would provide powerful support. He also wanted to show that he could avoid theological difficulties, so he made sure to have theologians represented among the objectors. (He originally proposed that objections be solicited only from theologians [3:127, 183], although he had himself already shown the manuscript to a philosopher, his follower Regius at Utrecht [3:63].) Perhaps most importantly, the Replies allowed him to elaborate his positions using standard philosophical terminology and modes of argument, and to introduce matters not discussed in the body of the work (such as his doctrine on eternal truths).

Overview and front matter (7:1–16)

The *Meditations* consists of the opening Letter to the Faculty of Theology at the Sorbonne, a Preface to the reader, a Synopsis, the six Meditations, Objections and Replies, and (added after the first edition) letters to Dinet and Clerselier. The six Meditations were written first as a self-contained treatise, which was completed by March 1640. Shortly thereafter, and continuing into 1641, this treatise was circulated to elicit objections (first by Descartes in the Netherlands, and subsequently by Mersenne). In the latter part of 1640, Descartes composed the "front matter," consisting of the Letter, Preface, and Synopsis.

Letter to the Sorbonne (7:1–6)

Descartes wrote to Mersenne that prior to publication he wanted his work to be "seen and approved by various Doctors [of Theology]," including "the Sorbonne as a body" (3:126–7*). In September, he wrote (3:184–5) that he would dedicate the book to the Faculty of Theology at the Sorbonne, the most respected theologians in France. He was hoping for their support in an anticipated battle with the Jesuits (3:126, 184, 752). He wanted them to examine the work and either give their approval or provide him with objections, to which he would reply (3:239–40). Four members of the faculty considered the work; their approval, given in August 1641, was noted on the title page of the first edition.

In the Letter, Descartes suggests that the Sorbonne should take the work under its sponsorship or "protection" because of what (ostensibly) are its two principal theses: the existence of God and the distinction of soul from body (and hence the soul's natural immortality). These are, he explained, the two things of greatest religious significance that could be proved by "natural reason" – that is, by the human mind working on its own. They are "prime examples of subjects where demonstrative proofs ought to be given with the aid of philosophy rather than theology" (7:1).

This Letter is notable for claiming that the arguments of the *Meditations* are needed to convince "unbelievers" of the existence of God and the soul. Those who believe in God, it says, are happy to do so on the authority of the Bible, and also to accept the authority of the Bible because it comes from God. But "this argument cannot be put to unbelievers because they would judge it to be circular" (7:2). Descartes has therefore examined all rational proofs for the existence of God and the separability of soul from body in order to present the best available (7:3–4). That is what he, as a philosopher, can do for religion.

But if he was providing rational proofs, why should he have sought "protection" under the "authority" of the theologians of the Sorbonne? Descartes addresses that question by comparing attitudes toward mathematics and metaphysics. Everyone is taught to accept mathematical proofs as uncontroversial, even though only a few people actually understand them. But in philosophy, everyone believes that the questions can be argued in various ways. In mathematics, the basic ideas are easily understood, whereas in metaphysics they are not. To follow Descartes' metaphysical arguments, the reader must possess "a mind completely free from preconceived opinions and one that can easily withdraw itself from involvement with the senses" (7:4*). In case his readers did not succeed in this difficult task, Descartes was willing to enlist institutional authority – especially against other organized groups, such as the Jesuits.

We saw in Chapter 1 that Descartes was not completely forthright in saying that the book was intended primarily to offer proofs to unbelievers; he wanted it to convince his readers (surreptitiously) of the foundations of his new physics. Indeed, from as early as 1629 (1:85), Descartes had expected the main objections to his philosophy (from Jesuits and others) to arise over his physics or natural philosophy (1:271, 285, 324, 455–6, 564) – including his account of sensory qualities and his affirmation of the Earth's motion – not his views on God or the soul (although they were later criticized too). Did he, then, simply include the material on God and the soul as a shield from criticism, or to attract help from the Sorbonne? Was he simply appeasing a religious age?

Some interpreters think that Descartes cared only about his physics and was simply seeking to appease religious authority on prudential grounds (after what had happened to Galileo). Indeed, Hiram Caton argues that Descartes was actually a materialist and an atheist, who camouflaged his true intentions with talk of God and immortality. According to Caton, Descartes sought to undermine his own demonstration of God's existence by hinting at its weakness in the Letter, where he mentions the circularity involving God and Scripture. This hint was supposed to prefigure the circularity of Descartes' use of clear and distinct perception to prove God's existence, and his appeal to God to establish that clear and distinct perception yields truth. (This charge of circularity is discussed below.)

Despite Descartes' confession to Mersenne (3:233, 298) that he was not fully honest in presenting the *Meditations*, there is nothing to indicate he was insincere in proving God's existence and mind–body distinctness. Such topics were part of the theoretical work of philosophy at this time. They were not simply matters for religious belief (or disbelief) but were part of philosophy and subject to rational scrutiny. If we assume that Descartes was a religious believer, we should also realize that his primary philosophical aim was not to promote religious belief but to establish foundations for his physics. We should expect the discussions of God and the soul to contribute to this metaphysical goal.

In thinking about these questions, it is important to distinguish religious matters from philosophical discussions of God and the soul. Descartes avoided what he considered to be purely theological questions (1:153, 4:119, 5:176, 7:428), such as whether the world was created in six days (5:168–9), "mysteries" of religion such as the Trinity (3:274), the existence of miracles (2:557–8, 3:214, 11:48), the role of the will in relation to sin (7:15), and so on. In purely religious matters, he favored divine illumination through the "light of grace" over natural reason, which meant that he left such matters to revelation as interpreted by the Church or accepted by individuals (3:426, 7:147–8, 8B:353–4, 9A:208). He criticized others for mixing religion and philosophy (2:570) or trying to derive philosophical truths from the Bible (2:347–8, 8B:353). As regards God and the soul, he addressed aspects that he considered knowable by reason alone. The concept of a supreme god and the question of whether the soul is immaterial had been part of Greek philosophy, prior to the medieval synthesis of Greek thought with the Judeo-Christian–Islamic tradition. Descartes considered the notion of a supreme being to be a proper topic for "natural" reason, that is, reason independent of divine revelation. One might with hindsight suspect that his theory of God was influenced by the surrounding religious culture, but that does not alter the fact that his intent was to address only those aspects of God known by reason alone. Similarly, he thought that the soul might be studied as a part of the natural world by means of reason. Indeed, for philosophical purposes, he equated soul (Latin *anima*) with mind (*mens*) and preferred the latter term (7:161, 356). He did, as needed, try to show that his philosophy was *consistent* with Catholic (and, in the Netherlands, Calvinist) doctrine (3:349, 5:544). This was prudent, for his personal safety and the acceptance of his works by educational and political authorities depended on it. In some cases, these doctrinally consistent explanations were tortured (e.g., on bodily surfaces [7:250–1, 433–4]), but he was not prepared to change his core philosophical positions to gain acceptability (3:259). If he feared punishment, he was willing not to publish (1:271–2).

A good case can be made that Descartes needed the arguments about God and the soul to secure the foundations of his physics. Famously, he raised the possibility of a deceiving God in the First Meditation as his strongest reason for doubt, which, if answered, would yield the most certain knowledge. He used this hypothesis in conjunction with his analytic method to search for first principles. In physics proper, he appealed to God as the operator behind his laws of motion, acting to conserve the quantity of motion in the universe. This role was foreshadowed near the end of the Third Meditation. As for the soul or mind, in the seventeenth century nearly every philosopher considered the mind to be part of nature and so to fall within the discipline of physics (which treated all of nature). Consequently, in examining human beings in his physics, Descartes needed to account for the mind, its relation to the body, and its role in various bodily functions, including sensation.

Preface to the reader (7:7–10)

The Preface offers a hint as to the intended breadth of Descartes' work and attempts to forestall quick objections. It affirms that the *Meditations* will cover not only God and the soul but also "the foundations of First Philosophy in its entirety" (7:9). The work will provide a complete version of the metaphysical arguments only sketched in the *Discourse*. But, furthermore, it will cover *all* the "foundations" (Latin *initia*, literally, elements or first things, hence first principles or foundations) of metaphysics, beyond God and the soul. As he wrote to Mersenne, it would examine "all the first things to be discovered by philosophizing" (3:235; also 3:239).

Descartes used the Preface to address the objections he received to the summary arguments of the *Discourse*. The argument for mind–body distinction in that work has every appearance of being fallacious. When this was pointed out, Descartes claimed that the earlier work provided only a truncated version of an argument that would now be presented in full. A second objection, concerning the argument for God's existence, allows Descartes to introduce his distinction between an idea of God considered simply as a state of a human mind and the content of that idea – a distinction crucial to the argument as presented in the Third Meditation. He dismisses other objections as "lifted from the standard sources of the atheists" (7:8–9).

Perhaps in an attempt to forestall new objections, he repeats a point from the Letter. Modestly predicting that the new, deeper, more complete arguments of the *Meditations* would not gain a wide audience (although in fact he was already recasting them in textbook form), he offers a warning to the casual reader: "I am not an author for anyone who might read this book except those who are willing and able to meditate seriously with me and to draw their minds away from the senses and, at the same time, all preconceived opinions" (7:9*). He encourages readers to attend to the order and connection of his arguments without dwelling on individual sentences. The *Meditations* is intended to present the "very thoughts" that allowed him to arrive at the truth, to find out whether others would find such thoughts convincing (7:10). Those not convinced might examine the Objections and Replies, where, he suggests, he has responded to virtually every serious objection that might be raised. (Although not in fact foretelling every serious objection, they do record many of the most important problems with Descartes' arguments.)

Synopsis (7:12–16)

Late in December 1640, Descartes sent to Mersenne an "abstract" or "synopsis" of the *Meditations* (3:271). This Synopsis summarizes the six Meditations while also addressing specific queries from Mersenne.

Several weeks earlier, Mersenne had asked Descartes why the proof for mind–body distinctness had to wait until the Sixth Meditation, and why there was no proof of the soul's immortality (3:266). (The *Discourse* had hinted at such a proof [6:59–60].) The Synopsis explains (7:13) that the proof of mind–body distinctness depends on knowing that clear and distinct perceptions are true (Meditation 4) and discovering the nature of corporeal things (Meditations 2, 5, 6).

As for immortality, Descartes explains that by proving the soul is distinct from the body and need not perish with it, he allows for it without proving it. A proper proof would have to explain how a human body can perish by losing its configuration, even though matter (or body in general) cannot perish (subject to God's preservation, as described in Meditation 3); and how a human mind, because it is a "pure substance," preserves its identity across all changes of its "accidents" (properties that may change from moment to moment) and so does not perish (7:14).

These clarifications take up nearly half of the Synopsis (7:12–14), which otherwise provides a convenient summary of the points in the work "concerning God and the soul" (to Mersenne, 3:268), including the use of the skeptical doubt as a means to understand intellectual (immaterial) beings such as God and the soul (7:12, 14). Descartes apparently hoped that the Synopsis would be helpful to those concerned to certify his religious orthodoxy.

The *Meditations* proper (7:17–90)

Although Descartes described the six Meditations to Mersenne as a "treatise" (3:183), we have seen that it was not structured as an ordinary philosophical treatise, in which an author directly presents arguments and discoveries. It was written as meditations. He explains in the Second Replies that he wrote "Meditations" – rather than "Disputations," or "Theorems and Problems" as in mathematics – because of his desire to follow the analytic method (7:157). This choice of genre carries implications for our interpretation of the first-person pronoun (in English, "I") in the six Meditations themselves.

First person in the Meditations

In the front matter and the Replies, the first-person pronoun clearly refers to René Descartes, author of the work. The referent for this pronoun is not so obvious in the body of the work. The work is presented as describing a sequence of thoughts that Descartes has had, characterized in the Preface as "the very thoughts" that brought him to see the metaphysical truths he now presents (7:10). At the same time, the six Meditations most certainly do not record the thoughts that Descartes had in the course of a few days in his stove-heated room (in 1619), since his metaphysics was initially developed only nine years later. It is certain that his thoughts continued to develop after he had composed his unfinished metaphysical treatise of 1629, and after he had presented a sketch of his arguments in the *Discourse* in 1637. And when he wrote the *Meditations*, he did not actually believe some of the things he said in the First Meditation, such as that up to that instant he had believed the senses to be the primary basis of knowledge (7:18); surely, when writing the first part he had already formulated the quite different attitude toward the role of the senses found later in the work.

The *Meditations*, then, unlike the *Discourse*, is not properly auto-biographical. So how shall we understand the "I"? We might view the six Meditations as a story that Descartes has constructed in the first person to represent in the fictional setting of six "days" of meditating the very sequence of thoughts by which he had discovered his metaphysics – or at least a sequence of thoughts that, in accordance with the analytic method, would show how the discovery can be made. The "I" of the six Meditations would function as narrator and protagonist in a metaphysical morality play (with one or two other characters: God or the malign demon). The reader could then "take the moral" of the story through empathy with the narrator.

This construal properly distinguishes the "I" of the six Meditations from Descartes, their author. It also permits the "I" to serve as a placeholder for every reader (or any human being), an intention signaled by occasional use of the first-person plural ("we say," "let us," etc. [7:21, 30, 32]). But it does not fully capture the active role that the reader is to take in becoming the "I." When Descartes says that he wants only readers who will "meditate seriously" with him (Preface, 7:9), we may read this as an instruction to approach his metaphysical meditations like religious exercises – as guiding the reader to experiences each must have for him or herself. This means that we, as readers, are to engage his arguments and exercises fully and directly, thereby undergoing, as much as possible, a cognitive progression that permits us to grasp the things that Descartes has already discovered. The reader must not simply follow a narrative in his or her imagination, but must employ all her cognitive resources to relive the process of doubt and discovery described in the work.

When naming the "I" in the main body of the work, we will often speak of "the meditator" rather than of Descartes as author. (For distinctness of reference, we can imagine the meditator as female.) At the same time, as author, Descartes did in fact construct the work's exercises and arguments with certain didactic aims in mind. Hence, in describing the philosophical strategy behind various arguments or devices, Descartes, and not the meditator, should be invoked. Moreover, as the work progresses the meditator's conclusions come to express Descartes' own metaphysical positions. By the end of the work, the distance between Descartes as author and meditator as convert should diminish to nothing.

Overview of the metaphysical treatise

The individual Meditations are of various lengths, the first being the shortest, the sixth the longest. A rough idea of their contents, and hence of the order of Descartes' argument, can be gleaned from their titles (Table 1). The general order is clear. Descartes begins by having the meditator engage in a process of doubt (Meditation 1). She finds that the existence and nature of her own mind are better known to her than are material things (2). The meditator then considers two proofs for the existence of God (3), learns to guide her judgment so as to find truth and avoid falsity (4), considers the essence of material things and examines another proof of the existence of God (5), and discovers a real distinction between mind and body and proves the existence of material things (6).

However, the sequence of topics expressed in the Meditations' titles does not fully describe the main arguments and conclusions of the work. The titles of Meditation 2, and perhaps 3, 5, and 6, reached their final form late in the process of composition, after the first three sets of objections were in hand (3:297). They conform with Descartes' goal of publicizing his efforts concerning God and the soul. But they do not draw attention to the contents of the work as a treatise on general metaphysics, undertaken to establish something "stable and likely to last" in the sciences (7:17). Nor do they draw attention to the

Table 1 Topical analysis of the *Meditations*

Med.	Title	Epistemological topics	Metaphysical topics
1	What can be called into doubt	Sensory fallibility Mathematics dubitable	
2	The nature of the human mind, and how it is better known than body	Indubitable "I" (cogito) Mind cannot be imaged Knowledge of body via intellect	Nature of thinking thing Body as extension
3	The existence of God	Truth rule, clear and distinct perceptions are true Natural light vs. teachings of nature Idea of God innate God is no deceiver	Causal principle Metaphysics of ideas God's existence and attributes Preliminary distinction between geometrical and other sensory qualities
4	Truth and falsity	Analysis of judgment: intellect and will Analysis of cognitive error Reaffirmation of truth rule (God is no deceiver)	Cognitive error and the problem of evil Freedom of the will
5	The essence of material things, and the existence of God considered a second time	Innate ideas of essences Knowledge of God needed to banish doubt	Essence of matter is extension Ontological argument for God's existence
6	The existence of material things, and the real distinction between mind and body	Intellect vs. imagination Role of senses and intellect in knowing bodies Analysis of sensory error	Mind as distinct substance; with intellectual essence External objects exist Mind–body union Status of sensory qualities Psychophysiological correlations

main methodological and epistemological moments, as the meditator battles back from the general doubt of Meditation 1. These further topics are summarized in Table 1 under two separate headings.

Further topics: methodological and epistemological

In a work ostensibly intended to demonstrate some truths about God and the soul, the author might not choose to highlight the methods used for those purposes. It might then seem natural that, other than asking his readers to concentrate on the arguments (in the Preface), Descartes did little by way of discussing his method up front. (The most extensive discussions occur in the Replies to Objections.)

Nonetheless, as we have seen, he thought carefully about the methodological structure of his work. Furthermore, at the beginning of the First Meditation he characterizes the work as having an epistemological aim. It will seek to evaluate and undermine the foundations of the meditator's previous claims to knowledge and find new foundations (7:17). From these comments and the Synopsis, the meditator can know that, even if epistemological topics such as "doubt" and what is "known" are mentioned only in the titles of Meditations 1 and 2, the whole work is aimed at achieving certain knowledge. Furthermore, she has been apprised in the Synopsis that a specific rule for gaining such knowledge, involving the truth of "clear and distinct perception," will be introduced in the later Meditations.

The First Meditation employs the celebrated method of doubt. The meditator is instructed to doubt all her previous beliefs. To achieve this aim, she is offered various arguments to undermine what she considered to be the sources of her previous knowledge. She casts doubt on the senses and comes to doubt the existence of the material world by means of the deceiving-God hypothesis. She uses the latter hypothesis to call into doubt even the "transparent" truths of mathematics (7:20–1).

Descartes did not employ his method of doubt as part of a general skeptical outlook. He was using it as a tool in his search for knowledge. Famously, its first result concerns the meditator's own existence as a thinking thing, achieved through the *cogito* reasoning. This important item of knowledge serves as a basis for subsequent knowledge. Exactly how it does so requires some philosophical interpretation, and we will consider several possibilities in Chapter 4. But one way in which the *cogito* result helps – as Descartes has the meditator observe at the beginning of Meditation 3 (7:35) – is by providing an example of what it takes to know anything. The meditator can then work backward, in accordance with the method of the analysis, to find its underlying basis.

In this way, Descartes leads the meditator to extract his famous rule for finding the truth: that clear and distinct perceptions are true. Although this rule is first asserted early in the Third Meditation, the Synopsis says that it is established in the Fourth (7:12, 14). And, indeed, much of the Third Meditation concerns whether the hypothesis of a deceiving God, which at least seems to call the rule into question, can be removed. The use of the rule in evaluating and rejecting the deceiving-God hypothesis has led some readers to charge Descartes with circular reasoning. In our examination of Descartes' epistemology, we will want to pay close attention to the question of whether he needed to provide – and if so, how he might have provided – further support for his truth rule beyond the argument at the beginning of Meditation 3. One candidate for validating the rule would be to have it guaranteed by a non-deceiving God. But appeal to such a guarantee is what led to the charge of circularity (discussed later in this chapter).

Descartes frames the epistemology and methodology of the six Meditations in the vocabulary of cognitive faculties. From the outset, he speaks freely of such faculties, including the senses, imagination, memory, and intellect or reason. In analyzing acts of judgment in Meditations 3 and 4, he adds the will as a separate mental faculty. All six Meditations contain points about the operation, reliability, and comparative roles of various mental faculties. Discussion of such faculties had been found in philosophical analyses of knowledge since antiquity. Descartes could expect his readers to understand his terminology. Readers today may be less familiar with this sort of talk.

Part of Descartes' epistemological project was to convince the Aristotelians and the new empiricists that their theory of how the cognitive faculties function to yield knowledge was erroneous. As previously mentioned, Aristotelians and empiricists held that sensory materials of one sort or another are required in every cognitive act. But Descartes maintained that some acts of cognition – indeed, those that hold the key to metaphysical knowledge – occur through the intellect alone.

His disagreement with the Aristotelians and new empiricists hinged on his claim that the "pure intellect" can operate independently of the senses and imagination. In the terminology of mental faculties, "imagination" has a technical meaning. To imagine something is to form an image of it, as when, with eyes closed, we might think of our pet cat by picturing to ourselves what he looks like. Such images are concrete. They show the cat in some particular position, usually in relation to a surface (on a favorite perch, or on the floor crying to be fed), perhaps with eyes open or closed, tail in the air or tucked next to the body, and so on. Although many thoughts involve such images, Descartes contended that other thoughts, even about the same objects, contain no images at all. These are the perceptions of the pure intellect, which extend to God, the mind as a substance, and geometrical essences. The distinction between imagination and pure intellect, discussed at length early in the Sixth Meditation (7:71–3), was fundamental to Descartes' epistemology, as the interchanges with Hobbes and Gassendi in the Objections and Replies make clear (7:178, 181, 183, 358, 365, 385). According to Descartes' rationalist epistemology, the essences of even material things are known not through sensory experience but by contemplating ideas that are available to the intellect innately, independently of sensory experience.

A final aim of Descartes' epistemological program was to re-evaluate the role of the senses in knowledge. In the Sixth Meditation the senses are rehabilitated, although with a different role in philosophical knowledge than the meditator had accepted in the First. Descartes argues that the primary function of the senses is to allow detection of potential bodily benefits and harms in the surrounding environment. They do not provide materials used for discovering the essences of natural things; that function is left to the intellect alone. But the senses can provide knowledge beyond the locally pragmatic. They can be used in natural philosophy to help to ascertain facts about the material world, such as the true size of the Sun (7:80).

Further topics: metaphysical results

Although Descartes had been famous for his interest in method, from 1629 on his main interest in pure philosophy lay in metaphysics. The metaphysical results of the *Meditations* constitute the desired fruits of his new method. As he advertised to the Sorbonne, some main results concern God, the soul or mind, and its distinction from body. These depend on further metaphysical concepts and principles, which are introduced as needed. And they hold further implications for the notion of the whole human being (composed of mind and body) and for the ontology of sensory qualities as part of the foundation for Descartes' physics. ("Ontology" is the study of the nature of "being," that is, what exists or has reality; the ontology of sensory qualities involves an analysis of those qualities in objects and in relation to our perception of them.)

The main arguments concerning God occur in Meditations 3 and 5. Descartes offers three separate proofs for God's existence and fills out the metaphysics of God by ascribing such attributes to him as infinity, independence, omniscience, and omnipotence. He seeks to establish metaphysically that God is the creator and preserver of everything (7:45). We will examine these arguments, and the metaphysical concepts they rely on, in Chapters 5 and 7.

The Fourth Meditation asks how a perfect God could create anything evil or subject to fault. The answer relies on the Neoplatonic (Augustinian) metaphysics of good and evil. Descartes argues that evil literally does not have existence (it has no "being"). Rather, some things are simply less good than others. God is infinitely good, but everything else falls short in some way. Descartes uses this Augustinian analysis of evil to explain how a perfect God could create imperfect humans. As part of this explanation, he analyzes the notion of free will in humans. In making us free, God allowed us to make our own errors. Here we find Descartes using tenets from theological metaphysics to further his own project.

Metaphysical topics concerning God are prominent in Meditations 3–5, but in the end, they serve as support for the final metaphysical aims of the work, concerning the essences of mind and body, the relations of mind and body in the whole human being, and the proper understanding of matter and its sensory qualities. These topics are taken up in the Second and Third Meditations, and they form the entire subject matter of the Sixth. One important result is the claim that the essence of matter is extension – a finding that had significant implications for Descartes' physics (examined in Chapter 9). Another is that the mind is an "intellectual substance" (7:78), the essence of which is thinking.

The title of the Sixth Meditation announces the "real distinction" between mind and body and promises a proof for the existence of bodies. In fact, the Meditation is largely devoted to mind–body union and interaction, and the theory of the senses. It thoroughly investigates the embodied mind, including the functions of sensation and appetite (7:75–7, 80–1, 83–9), and it allots nearly equal space to the metaphysics of the sensory qualities (7:74–7, 82–3). Some of this material belongs as much to natural philosophy as to metaphysics, such as the extensive discussion of the operation of the nerves to produce sensations. Several points in the argument appeal to sensory evidence (7:80, 86, 87). Although these discussions are framed by the metaphysical thesis that mind and body are different kinds of substance, the extended discussion of sensory and nervous function marks a transition from metaphysical foundations for physics to some first results in natural philosophy itself.

Objections and Replies (7:91–561)

When Descartes had completed the body of the *Meditations*, he showed it to some philosophical allies in the Dutch Netherlands, including his follower Regius, and to a Catholic theologian named Johannes Caterus. Regius corrected the punctuation and spelling and sent several objections, which Descartes answered brusquely by return letter (3:63–5). By contrast, he placed Caterus' objections at the end of his manuscript, with replies. In November 1640, he sent the six Meditations, Letter (and probably the Preface), and these first Objections and Replies to Mersenne, followed by the Synopsis (3:238–9, 271).

Mersenne collected the rest of the objections by circulating the material to philosophers and theologians in France. Completed objections and replies were included in the manuscript sent to further objectors. (Explicit or tacit references among the Objections and Replies may be found at 7:127, 200, 208–11, 213, 348, 414, 417.) The first six Objections and Replies appeared in the first edition, published late in 1641 in Paris under Mersenne's supervision. The seventh set, by the Jesuit Bourdin, appeared in the second edition (Amsterdam, 1642) with a letter from Descartes to Father Dinet (7:563–603), head of the French Jesuits. Descartes himself oversaw publication of the second edition (3:448).

The objectors represented innovative as well as conservative viewpoints. The innovators included the English materialist Hobbes, who moved to France in 1640 (third set), the French priest and Epicurean philosopher Gassendi (fifth set), and Mersenne himself (who contributed to the second and sixth sets, along with some theologians, philosophers, and geometers). The theological objectors included, besides Caterus and Mersenne's helpers, the French Catholic theologian Antoine Arnauld (fourth set). The most conservative objector was Bourdin. In 1644, Gassendi published the Fifth Objections and Replies separately, along with additional *Counter-Objections*. Descartes responded with a Note and a Letter to Clerselier (9A:198–217), published with Clerselier's French translation of the Objections and Replies in 1647 (the body of the work was translated by the Duke of Luynes).

Despite their differing viewpoints and chosen emphases, there were some topics to which all objectors responded. All save Bourdin raised questions about the proofs for the existence of God, and all questioned the proof of mind–body distinctness. Hobbes and Gassendi contended that organized matter might think; the second, fourth, and sixth objectors, although not asserting that hypothesis, challenged Descartes' success in ruling it out (7:122, 198, 422). Caterus and Bourdin posed general objections to the argument for a real distinction (7:100, 503–9).

The Objections and Replies stand outside the meditational form of the six Meditations. They provide commentary and disputation that illuminates and extends the original text, and they introduce as a new point his doctrine that the eternal truths are God's free creations (7:380, 432, 435–6; discussed in Chapter 9). Their explications of technical vocabulary can be especially helpful. The concept of substance, mentioned directly only in the Synopsis and Third Meditation (7:12, 40), is explained more fully in the Second and Third Replies (7:161, 176); it is elaborated using the crucial notion of a "complete being," or something capable of existing on its own, in the First and Fourth Replies (7:120–1, 219–31). The second, third, fifth, and seventh sets explain the methodological use of skepticism and doubt (7:129–30, 144–6, 171–2, 257–8, 454–82). At the request of the second set of objectors, Descartes appended to the Second Replies the Geometrical Arguments (7:160–70), restating his main metaphysical proofs in geometrical fashion, with formal definitions, axioms, and postulates.

Following the argument

Part II of this guidebook is directed at the arguments and conclusions of the six Meditations, examined one by one. Descartes has warned that the arguments should not be considered in isolation, since their order and connection are crucial. Having reviewed the main conclusions, we can be mindful of where the arguments are headed.

Various readers continue to disagree about the overall point of Descartes' enterprise, and the significance and role played by each argument. What shall we think of a work that has already been studied for several hundred years with no final agreement on its structure and purpose? Interpretive uncertainty is usual with great texts. A good strategy for a first-time reader is to attend to the overall purpose and structure of the text while remaining open to a variety of interpretive hypotheses. As you consider or even form such hypotheses, you should also note objections against Descartes' arguments so construed. Then read his work again, looking for support for one or another interpretation, and checking to see if the objections hold up. Great philosophical texts repay such effort with increased insight and understanding, and Descartes' works are no exception.

The principle of charity

Philosophers sometimes appeal to the "principle of charity" as an aid in reading philosophical texts. According to this principle, one avoids attributing silly mistakes to authors such as Descartes and seeks to interpret their works so as to have them make "good philosophical sense." The latter phrase means that we should attempt to find a reading of the text that renders its various statements consistent with one another and that provides a coherent and forceful interpretation of the arguments therein. One standard for such interpretations is that they render the text as making points we would agree with now, or that seem the most interesting.

How far shall we take such advice? The principle may be followed a good way. For instance, although it is possible that Descartes made mistakes in reasoning or contradicted himself, overly hasty attributions of contradictions or weak arguments to him may simply reveal our own limitations and ineptitude. The principle of charity advises us not to take the easy way out by quickly deciding that a text is incoherent or contains deplorably weak arguments. When philosophers contradict themselves, such contradictions are often deep – they reveal fundamental tensions in a philosopher's systematic enterprise. We might miss these deeper points by abandoning our interpretive effort too soon. Furthermore, some metaphysical arguments may appear weak to us now because of advances in science since they were written, or because the prevailing attitude toward religious belief has changed. But if we dismiss such arguments out of hand simply because we disagree with their conclusions, we lose any chance of gaining a comprehensive view of the structure, variety, and history of philosophical positions and arguments.

Nonetheless, the principle of charity can be taken too far. By interpreting past arguments so as to maximize their agreement with current wisdom, we run the risk of repeatedly reading our own favorite positions into past texts. Moreover, while we should seek coherent and forceful readings because they are of greater philosophical interest, this does not require that past authors always come out "right." If we always see only "correct" positions in past texts, we will mask genuine differences between now and then, and we will fail to see how the problem space of philosophy has changed. A coherent argument for a position we now consider wrong can be of interest for what it teaches us about philosophical positions and arguments and their forcefulness. The strong principle of charity, which would have us read past philosophers as saying things we would want to say now, is too restrictive and distorting.

Reading contextually

The strategy of reading past philosophers in their own historical and philosophical context affords a further standard for assessing their arguments. Philosophy typically addresses problems and topics of importance in its time, and it usually takes as its primary audience other philosophers, who bring with them the assumptions and convictions of that time. In order to understand why philosophers construct their arguments in a certain way, we will usually need to know which positions they intend to overturn, and the assumptions shared by author and opponent. Such knowledge may enable us to see how an argument that we would now reject could have seemed forceful in the past.

The interpretation of past philosophy can be interesting simply for the insight it gives us into unfamiliar ways of thinking. But that is not its primary philosophical benefit. Philosophy attempts to get at the fundamental issues in the intellectual pursuits of a given age. These issues change over time, but in some ways they remain the same. Questions about the possibility of knowledge, about the rational grounds for thinking that a supreme being exists, and about the place of the mind in nature have been asked in one form or another since the time of the ancient Greeks. The common assumptions and the range of plausible positions have changed from age to age, even while some things stayed (nearly) the same. We want to notice both what is similar and what is different between our ways of thinking and that of Descartes. In this way, we can appreciate more fully both our framework of thought and his.

The overall problem space of philosophy changes more slowly than the particular positions that are offered as solutions to (or dissolutions of) the problems themselves. Aspects of Descartes' thought still influence philosophical and scientific thought today. These include perspectives on perception as a source of knowledge, the place of mind in nature, the relation of mind to the body or brain, and the basic explanatory categories of physical science and psychology.

A historically sensitive reading of Descartes can detect the changes and continuities in philosophical responses to these topics. Often, understanding how a problem has come to be posed in its present form will help us to rethink both problem and answers.

Interpretive threads

As we saw in Chapter 1, since their publication Descartes' writings have been the subject of various interpretations. The *Meditations* has often been the focus. We can recognize three main approaches to the *Meditations* in recent years: epistemological, metaphysical, and cognitive.

Epistemological readings

Some read the *Meditations* as primarily a work in epistemology or theory of knowledge. According to this view, Descartes' foremost concern was to determine the possibility and limits of knowledge, considered generally. His epistemic goal was to see whether certainty can be achieved about anything. His primary result was to find that his immediate knowledge is limited to his own mental states. His problem was then to see whether he could move beyond those states to know anything else. As a pure epistemologist, he would be indifferent to the outcome and ready to abandon any claim to extramental knowledge if his investigation led to that conclusion.

Descartes' use of the method of doubt and his emphasis on certainty are consistent with an epistemological reading. For that reason, we will remain attuned to what he says about the basis of knowledge, and to the content and limits of what can be known. At the same time, we have strong evidence that Descartes did not write his book simply to discover whether knowledge is possible. From the start he conceived the *Meditations* as the first full presentation of his metaphysics. He was not trying to discover *whether* anything can be known but intended to show *how* knowledge is possible and to offer *proofs* for metaphysical first principles.

Metaphysical readings

Metaphysical readings acknowledge these goals and therefore focus on the metaphysical results of Descartes' work. These results include the *cogito* conclusion and the arguments concerning the existence and essence of God, the essences of matter and mind, the mind–body relation, and the nature of sensory perception. On this view, Descartes examined the scope and limits of knowledge so that he could show that his metaphysical findings were certain and unshakeable; but his use of the method of doubt played no substantive role. The doubt was simply a filter for certainty.

A cognitive and metaphysical reading

A third type of reading, which will be favored here, joins Descartes' theory of knowledge – or, better, his theory of the cognitive faculties – with his quest for a new metaphysics. According to this sort of reading, Descartes sought to bring his readers to an awareness of cognitive resources latent in their own minds, which they could then use to see the first principles of metaphysics for themselves.

As we have seen, the *Meditations* contains frequent mention of various cognitive faculties or powers of mind, including the senses, imagination, memory, intellect, and will. For much of the twentieth century, talk of such faculties was considered illegitimate and therefore as unsuited to a "charitable" interpretation of an author such as Descartes. This supposed illegitimacy was frequently expressed by repeating a joke from the seventeenth-century playwright Molière about the Doctor who explained that opium puts people to sleep because of its "dormitive" or sleep-inducing virtue. The joke depends on the idea that it is empty and pointless to *explain* the ability to induce sleep by positing a sleep-inducing ability. However, Descartes (and others) did not fall into the trap of seeking to explain human intellectual ability by saying that the intellect has the faculty of intellection. Faculty terms were classificatory. Intellect, will, memory, etc. are identifiable kinds of mental activity, each with its own characteristics, which are subject to further description and classification. Talk of faculties offers a classification of the powers of the mind (1:366).

By taking seriously the faculty talk in the *Meditations*, we can see that the apparently "epistemological" parts of the work functioned to reveal significant facts about the mind's cognitive faculties. Descartes was particularly interested in analyzing the roles of the senses and the pure intellect. The Aristotelians had assigned the intellect an important role in knowledge, of discerning the "universal," or common nature, shared by all the instances of a natural kind (e.g., the common nature that makes each horse a horse). But in doing so, the Aristotelian intellect always had to operate on an image (also known as a phantasm) originating from the senses. As has been mentioned, Descartes held that the intellect can operate independently of the senses. Because this would have been news to the Aristotelians, he had to work hard to convince them of it. Meditations 2–6 all emphasize the discovery and proper use of the pure intellect, with the method of doubt preparing for and aiding this discovery (see 7:130–1). Once the meditator becomes accustomed to the clear and distinct perceptions of the intellect, metaphysical conclusions fall thick and fast in Meditations 3–6. On this reading, Descartes seeks to reform the theory of cognition in preparation for discovering and defending a new metaphysics.

Specific questions, alternative paths

Beyond these large questions about the overall aim of the *Meditations*, others arise about specific arguments and conclusions. We will sometimes consider competing construals of an argument as we proceed through the text, and each reader should try to decide which version is most philosophically compelling, while also fitting Descartes' text.

One important question concerns the role of consciousness in Descartes' philosophy. The *cogito* argument in the Second Meditation focuses attention on the conscious thoughts of the meditator. Elsewhere, Descartes affirms that every act of thinking possesses consciousness (7:246). But in the Third Meditation he emphasizes the representational character of thought, and in several places he characterizes the mind as an intellectual (or perceiving) substance (e.g., 7:12, 78). This raises the question (addressed in Chapters 4 and 8) of which, if either, is more fundamental in Descartes' conception of thought: consciousness, or intellection and representation.

Another decisive interpretive question concerns the problem of the "Cartesian circle," first raised by Arnauld (7:214). The problem is that Descartes apparently appeals to God's existence and perfection to legitimize the criterion of clear and distinct perception, and he also uses that very criterion to prove the existence and perfection (hence goodness) of God. This procedure seems circular, in that a specific criterion of truth is used to establish the argument that legitimizes that very criterion. Given the centrality of the criterion of clear and distinct perception in establishing Descartes' metaphysical results, this charge of circularity is potentially devastating.

We will consider several approaches to the circle in Chapters 5–7. For now, I will illustrate the sorts of interpretive choice open to readers by mentioning two approaches yielding different conclusions about circularity. On one reading, Descartes does not use an appeal to God to legitimize clear and distinct perception itself. Rather, he achieves his initial confidence in clear and distinct perception by reflecting on the *cogito* reasoning at the beginning of the Third Meditation. He then uses such perception to investigate and remove the hypothesis of the deceiving God, left over from the First Meditation, by establishing that God is no deceiver. Hopefully, because God is not used to vindicate the criterion itself, the circle can be avoided.

On another reading, Descartes wants or needs to prove that the mind is properly attuned to a mind-independent reality. He calls upon God, as creator of the human intellect as well as the very natures of things, to guarantee that the intellect is attuned to those natures. This divine guarantee underwrites the claims of transcendent metaphysics to know the natures of things as they are in themselves. It seems difficult to avoid the circle on this reading. If we followed a strong principle of charity, we might rule out this reading on the face of it. But we will not do that. Our approach will be to consider both Descartes' successes and failures. If the conclusion that he fell prey to the circle is to be rejected, it will not be on the basis of simple charity. It will require a reading that makes good philosophical sense contextually and fits the text well.

Be active when reading

One of the most satisfying aspects of reading good philosophy is the joy of working out your own view of what is good and what is important in a particular work. I suggest that you use this guidebook and the hints it contains to come to your own reading of the text. As you formulate this reading, try also to consider how you would convince someone with a different reading that yours is a good one. In the end, whether you agree with Descartes or not, in reading his text you will raise new questions for yourself, and consider new answers, on such topics as the nature of mind and body, and the possibility of metaphysical knowledge.

References and further reading

Introductory works aimed primarily at Descartes' *Meditations* include G. Dicker, *Descartes: An Analytical and Historical Introduction* (New York: Oxford University Press, 1993), A. Kenny, *Descartes: A Study of His Philosophy* (New York: Random House, 1968), and J. Cottingham, *Descartes* (New York: Basil Blackwell, 1986). Dicker offers a primarily epistemological reading, Kenny a metaphysical one, and Cottingham a cognitive and metaphysical one. The more advanced works of M. Guéroult, *Descartes' Philosophy Interpreted According to the Order of Reasons* (Minneapolis: University of Minnesota Press, 1984–85), and M.D. Wilson, *Descartes* (London: Routledge & Kegan Paul, 1978), provide metaphysical readings. E. Curley, *Descartes Against the Skeptics* (Cambridge, Mass.: Harvard University Press, 1978), offers a cognitive and metaphysical reading. References to further epistemological readings are given in Chapter 4.

A. Rorty (ed.), *Essays on Descartes' Meditations* (Berkeley: University of California Press, 1986), contains many helpful essays; the first three, by Rorty, Kosman, and Hatfield, examine the meditational structure of Descartes' work (which Hatfield places in an Augustinian context). D. Sepper reviews work on that topic in "The Texture of Thought: Why Descartes' *Meditations* Are Meditational, and Why It Matters," in S. Gaukroger, J. Schuster, and J. Sutton (eds.),

Descartes' Natural Philosophy, (London: Routledge, 2000), pp. 736–50. R. Ariew and M. Grene (eds.), *Descartes and His Contemporaries: Meditations, Objections, and Replies* (Chicago: University of Chicago Press, 1995), focuses on the objections and replies. For the view that Descartes was an atheist, see H. Caton, *The Origin of Subjectivity: An Essay on Descartes* (New Haven, Conn.: Yale University Press, 1973).

For the mainstream scholastic Aristotelian doctrine that all thought requires an image, see Thomas Aquinas, *Summa theologica* (London: Blackfriars, 1964–81), Part 1, question 84, articles 7–8; on the doctrines that in this life God's essence cannot be known by natural human cognition because all thought is based in the senses, and that his existence and role as creator can be thought of and known only through analogy, see Part 1, question 12, articles 11–12, and question 13. These passages are available in A.C. Pegis (ed.), *Introduction to Saint Thomas Aquinas* (New York: Modern Library, 1948).

Works examining method in Descartes include L.J. Beck, *Metaphysics of Descartes: A Study of the Meditations* (Oxford: Clarendon Press, 1965) and *Method of Descartes: A Study of the Regulae* (Oxford: Clarendon Press, 1952), and D.E. Flage and C.A. Bonnen, *Descartes and Method: A Search for a Method in Meditations* (London: Routledge, 1999). M. Miles, *Insight and Inference: Descartes's Founding Principle and Modern Philosophy* (Toronto: University of Toronto Press, 1999), examines Descartes' method from the perspective that his philosophy actually was focused on the soul and God and only secondarily directed toward the new science.

On the methods and uses of the history of philosophy, see J. Ree, M. Ayers, and A. Westoby, *Philosophy and Its Past* (Sussex: Harvester Press, 1978), R. Rorty, J.B. Schneewind, and Q. Skinner (eds.), *Philosophy in History: Essays on the Historiography of Philosophy* (Cambridge: Cambridge University Press, 1984), and A.J. Holland (ed.), *Philosophy, Its History and Historiography* (Dordrecht: Reidel, 1985).

THE ARGUMENTS OF THE SIX MEDITATIONS

Chapter 3

Withdrawing the mind from the senses

Meditation 1: What can be called into doubt

The First Meditation introduces Descartes' famous skeptical arguments, challenging the accuracy of the senses, the existence of the external world, and even the truths of mathematics. To support these challenges, Descartes advanced the celebrated dream argument and developed the deceiving-God and evil-deceiver hypotheses.

Although these skeptical arguments can be studied in isolation, we are interested in them as steps toward the larger aims of the *Meditations*. In evaluating them, we will take their overall purpose into account. Descartes uses them in searching for certain knowledge and as part of the analytic method of the *Meditations* (explained in Chapter 2).

The title directs the meditator toward what can be "called into doubt." In this context, to "call" something into doubt means to give reasons for being uncertain about it. It does not require proving it false or believing in the opposite.

As we have seen, Descartes thought that some of the meditator's beliefs were in error and needed changing (just as he had previously revised his own beliefs). The doubt begins a process of replacing error with truth. According to the Synopsis, its purpose is threefold: (1) "freeing us from all our preconceived opinions"; (2) "providing the easiest route by which the mind may be led away from the senses"; and (3) eventually making it "impossible for us to have any further doubts about what we subsequently discover to be true" (7:12; also 7:171–2). In other words, the doubt is undertaken to get rid of old, bad opinions and to withdraw the mind from the senses so as ultimately to achieve indubitable, or absolutely certain, truths.

So far so good, but we need to be more specific. Does Descartes want the meditator to revise all her previous beliefs, or only some of them, especially in philosophy and metaphysics? Does the Meditation explain why the mind should be withdrawn from the senses? Does it offer any reason to believe that doubting will lead to indubitable truth, or to any truth at all? Does it call into doubt everything that can or should be doubted? Let us keep these questions in mind as we proceed.

Project (7:17–18)

The opening paragraph gives a specific reason for undertaking the doubt. Descartes asks the meditator to believe that in childhood she (as he, and everyone else) has accepted a large number of falsehoods and has subsequently constructed a "whole edifice" on them, of a "highly doubtful nature." Because these childhood beliefs continue to color adult thought, a general doubt is needed:

> I realized that it was necessary, once in the course of my life, to demolish everything completely and start again right from the foundations if I wanted to establish anything at all in the sciences that was stable and likely to last. [7:17]

Descartes makes the interesting suggestion that if we have reason to suspect that we have a large number of false beliefs, we should attempt to overturn *all* our beliefs. Is this a reasonable way to proceed? That depends on one's purpose. Descartes' stated purpose is to achieve something stable and lasting in the sciences. Later on, he reminds the meditator that she is not reviewing her beliefs insofar as they guide practical action, but for the sake of theory (7:22). What kind of theory? As the main title of the work says, a metaphysical theory, that is, a theory of the nature of reality.

Still, supposing we suspect that our metaphysics might be wrong, is it obvious that we should try to doubt all our opinions? Why shouldn't we instead partition off our metaphysical beliefs, hold them as uncertain, and re-examine them as opportunity arises or new evidence presents itself? Descartes did not adopt this strategy. He believed it important to challenge all previous beliefs. In the Seventh Replies, he compared the process to removing the bad apples from a full basket by overturning the basket to survey its contents (7:481). The analogy suggests that bad beliefs might be hidden by, or might hide, good ones, just as good and bad apples alike can be buried deep in a basket.

When he composed the *Meditations,* Descartes was already convinced that the true metaphysics is hidden from the human mind by childhood prejudices that naturally arise from immersion in the senses. He also believed, and has the meditator affirm (7:22), that the senses serve as the basis for many useful and true beliefs – such as where the food is in the kitchen, or that a moving vehicle is about to run us down. His concern about the senses was not that they are always wrong, but that they are not the right source for metaphysical knowledge. Descartes was convinced that the truths of metaphysics can be gained only through what philosophers later called *a priori* reason – and what he called the pure use of the intellect, independent of the senses. To appreciate the purely intellectual truths of metaphysics, we must turn away from the senses entirely. The general doubt is needed to suspend old beliefs that might hinder this process.

Returning to the basket analogy, the doubting exercise will not end with our simply surveying our previous beliefs to find the good ones and return them to the basket. Rather, Descartes thinks that in removing some bad apples, we will uncover some new types of apple, not seen before. As he explains to Hobbes in the Third Replies, the doubt is needed "to prepare my readers' minds for the study of things which are related to the intellect, and help them to distinguish these things from corporeal things" (7:171–2). In the First Meditation, Descartes is not yet in a position to convince unsuspecting readers of this point. And yet he wants them to follow him in a process that will yield new metaphysical cognitions, if they "withdraw the mind from the senses." Since he can't produce direct evidence of the need for such withdrawal prior to their having the new cognitions, he in effect asks his readers to go along without, at this point, having provided a fully convincing reason for doing so.

At the same time, he offers a worthy prize: something "stable and likely to last" in the sciences. The promised prize might make these initial steps seem worth the effort.

Sensory foundations (7:18)

In seeking to undermine previous beliefs, Descartes does not direct the meditator to inspect all her beliefs one by one, as in the apple-basket analogy. Rather, once "the foundations" are undermined, everything else will follow; therefore "I will go straight for the basic principles on which all my former beliefs rested." These foundations are the senses: "Whatever I have up till now accepted as most true I have acquired either from the senses or through the senses" (7:18).

When he wrote the *Meditations*, Descartes no longer held that the most fundamental truths are derived through the senses. But other philosophers did. It was a standard tenet of Aristotelian philosophy (also shared by the new empiricists) that "there is nothing in the intellect that was not first in the senses." In this epistemic scheme, the intellect requires sensory materials for its operation, even to think about God or other immaterial beings. Remember the Aristotelian position that there is "no thought without an image." This restriction extended even to thought of "common natures," such as the nature shared by all horses, or by all members of any natural kind; although the mind abstracts what is "common" to all horses, it must always use an image in thinking about this nature. Sensory images (or phantasms) are the basis of every thought. The project of withdrawing the mind from the senses is un-Aristotelian from the start. (A Platonist would welcome Descartes' radical withdrawal; we will consider his relation to Platonism in Chapter 7.)

A focus on the senses is natural to all human beings early in life (7:75, 157), but unless countered, Descartes believed, it causes the truths of metaphysics to remain obscure.

Sensory fallibility (7:18–19); Dream argument (7:19)

The first argument for doubting the senses arises from their occasional deceptiveness. The meditator reasons: "from time to time I have found that the senses deceive, and it is prudent never to trust completely those who have deceived us even once" (7:18). An example of such deception, supplied in the Sixth Meditation (7:76), is a square tower appearing to be round when viewed from a distance. Is it really reasonable to distrust those who have misled us only once, no matter how trustworthy they have been on other occasions? In the present circumstances, because the meditator seeks stable knowledge in the sciences, the standard of certainty is set high: it is absolute certainty. Consequently, even the smallest chance of deception is enough to discredit the witness. And yet, perhaps we know friends who have misrepresented their judgment of our culinary skill (when invited to taste our most recent effort) but who would not deceive us in matters of life or death, or about something affecting our livelihood. Even if we demand certainty, circumstances may tell us when our informant is to be trusted.

Similarly with the senses. Even if the senses deceive us about things that are small or far away, they seem trustworthy for things near at hand. As the meditator asks, can we really doubt the things we see close up and in good lighting? Can we doubt that we are seated here by the fire, reading this book? Only someone deranged would doubt the senses on such occasions; such a doubter seems as insane as those who think "that their heads are made of earthenware, or that they are pumpkins, or made of glass" (7:19). Descartes does not propose that the meditator seriously consider, as a ground for doubt, the possibility that she is mad. In equating doubt about things seen up close in good light with madness, he is offering her a reason to dismiss such doubts. The *Meditations* is constructed for sane readers who are willing to accept the reason given for undertaking the process of doubt – to gain lasting knowledge – and engage the process accordingly.

The argument from sensory fallibility having been rebutted, trust in the senses is again undermined by a more general argument that stays in effect until the Sixth Meditation. As the meditator now recalls, we sometimes do have vivid experiences of touching objects right in front of us, even though the objects are not actually present and perhaps do not exist. In dreams, we can have the experience of seeing things up close, yet (since we are actually in bed) those things are not there. One might dream she is reading this book, sitting by a fire next to a favorite lamp. The vividness alleged to mark sensory reliability can occur in dreams. The meditator therefore concludes "that there are never any sure signs by means of which being awake can be distinguished from being asleep" (7:19). (If you doubt this argument, propose a sure sign of your own and then ask whether you could ever merely dream that it occurred.)

In presenting the dream argument, Descartes must assume that we know what he is saying when he mentions dreaming and being awake. It may therefore seem as if he must presuppose that the distinction between waking and dreaming is valid, and that some experiences *really are* veridical waking experiences, and some dreams. Of course, if he needed to be able to tell the two apart, he would already have grounds for overturning the dream argument by distinguishing waking experience from dreams. But his point is that in at least some cases, the experiences involved in dreams are seemingly indistinguishable from waking experience. To convey this point to the reader, he need not prove that there are actual cases of waking experience; it is enough if the reader is simply able to understand what he is talking about (however she does so) when he has her consider that the experiences she calls dreams are sometimes indistinguishable from those she calls waking. Moreover, Descartes would not need to prove that there is in fact no such thing as waking experience, since he is not trying to prove to the reader that she is always dreaming. Rather, he is initially trying to instill doubt about whether she possesses a sure mark of sensory validity on any given occasion.

The argument, if accepted, establishes that we might be mistaken on any given occasion about the actual presence of a whole scene or episode. But if sensory experience can be deceptive on any given occasion, can we ever be certain of anything we perceive by means of the senses? Can the dream argument now be extended to call all our sensory experiences into question? Once its initial conclusion has been accepted, it seems possible to generalize the scope of the doubt by supposing that all our experiences are like dreams. Perhaps the contents of our experiences never "match" a present reality (by hypothesis, we have already undercut any specific evidence to the contrary). That is, the meditator muses, perhaps not only is she not now extending her hand and shaking her head (because she merely dreams those actions), but maybe "I do not even have such hands or such a body at all" (7:19). This suggests a more radical proposal, that we cannot rule out a general discrepancy between the contents of our experience and the very structure of the world.

Painter's analogy (7:19–20)

The meditator now considers a counter-argument to this radical proposal. Descartes has her ask how the content of dreams could arise. She reasons that even if we cannot be certain that any *particular* experience presents us with existing objects, "it must surely be admitted that the visions which come in sleep are like paintings, which must have been fashioned in the likeness of things that are real, and hence that at least these general kinds of things – eyes, head, hands and the body as a whole – are things which are not imaginary but are real and exist" (7:19–20). The comparison with paintings suggests that just as painters use models, our dreams must at the very least be based on prior acquaintance with really existing objects to supply the constituents of our dream content.

Painters typically did use models for imaginary scenes and non-existent monsters. The monstrous forms in Hieronymus Bosch's *Garden of Earthly Delights* (*c*. 1505) are composed from various animal parts – for example, fish-headed or rodent-headed demons with human-like bodies. So perhaps dreams would have to be based on previous experiences of heads and hands, even if the dreamer herself couldn't be sure that *she* had a head and hands (which assumes she could experience such things without having eyes or other senses –

something Descartes didn't pause to explain). At this stage, the dream argument would undermine knowledge of the particular structure of the world but would leave in place the supposition that there must exist models for the parts of things found in our dreams.

But Descartes suggests an even more radical thought. Perhaps painters can paint things that do not simply "jumble up the limbs of different animals" or the parts of other things; they might come up with images that are "completely fictitious and unreal" (7:20). Some of the architectural forms in Bosch's painting might fit that description, and we certainly know of such forms from the twentieth-century paintings of Wassily Kandinsky and Robert Motherwell. Their forms do not look like animals, buildings, or any object in nature.

If painters can produce wholly fictitious forms, then perhaps our dreams could too, in which case we could not claim that our dream images inform us about various kinds of form in the world. We could not be sure whether any form, such as a rodent head, is modeled on reality or is a fictitious creation. Would such an image tell us anything? The meditator surmises that in a painting at least the colors must be "real" – that is, the pigments used to make the painting are real, hence pigments exist. Perhaps there are even more basic features of the medium of images that reveal basic aspects of reality. These would be the "real colors from which we form all the images of things, whether true or false, that occur in our thought" (7:20). (They would not be material pigments, or material media of any kind, since Descartes is only using an analogy with painting to characterize dream images – which are not composed of paint!)

The meditator now runs through some very Cartesian thoughts about what these "real colors" might be. By simply musing on the fundamental features of images, the meditator arrives at a list of what Descartes in fact believed to be the fundamental features of material reality: "corporeal nature in general, and its extension; the shape of extended things; the quantity, or size and number of these things; the place in which they may exist, the time through which they may endure, and so on" (7:20). Images are intrinsically spatial, so the spatial structure of extension (generalized to extension in three dimensions to account for the "depth" of sensory or dream images), shapes, sizes, and relative locations of things are basic aspects of images or imaginary scenes, no matter how fantastic. Time is added to reflect the temporal dimension of experience (in dreams or in presumed sensory experiences). The meditator concludes that spatial extension and temporal duration are the basic elements of any sensory-imaginal representation.

According to one possibility, these very general features of images are just what an empiricist would be left with if forced by the dream argument to abandon knowledge of specific objects and retreat to the most general features of experience. Even an Aristotelian could follow the retreat this far (as long as the images from which to abstract these general features were granted). At the same time, there is a fundamentally Cartesian aspect to these remaining features. For Descartes does not include colors among the "real colors" of images. That is, even though visual images and visual dreams always include color with space and time (even if one were to dream in black and white, those count as colors!), Descartes resolves images down to only spatial and temporal properties. This foreshadows his later position, adumbrated in the Third Meditation and supported in the Fifth and Sixth, that, contra the Aristotelians, color is not a basic or primitive property of bodies. Here, he simply produces this result as the "natural" outcome of reflections on the medium of images. He has not in any way argued for this outcome; if it seems natural to the meditator at this stage, she is on her way to becoming a Cartesian. If not, she can in any case proceed to the next ground for doubt.

The meditator now doubts knowing the existence of any specific object forms. She must therefore doubt the findings of those sciences that concern particular kinds of existing thing. Descartes lists physics, astronomy, and medicine. What is left? Only "arithmetic, geometry and other subjects of this kind, which deal only with the simplest and most general things, regardless of whether they really exist in nature or not" (7:20). Geometry describes the properties of shapes, whether any such shapes actually exist or not. It sets for us the domain of possible shapes that could exist in reality without telling us whether any such shapes actually do exist. So, at this point, our only remaining knowledge is of the most general constraints on the forms that things could take. Still, the existence of a world containing such forms has not been denied. At this most extreme moment in the dream argument, all knowledge of particular kinds of thing has been under-mined, but the existence of a material world in general has not been explicitly doubted. (At 7:28 and 7:77, the comparison with dreams yields doubt about the material world's existence, but these passages occur after such radical doubt has been introduced on other grounds.)

The passage provides two examples of these "simplest and most general things" that remain undoubted: the addition of 2 and 3 to make 5, and the fact that a square has four sides. The meditator asserts that these things are true "whether I am awake or asleep," and indeed that "it seems impossible that such transparent truths should incur any suspicion of being false" (7:20). At this point, she may think that she has arrived at something "stable and lasting" in the sciences, the truths of mathematics. Could anything be more certain than those? Descartes now endeavors to call even these most basic truths into question.

Deceiving God (7:21); Mathematics dubitable (7:21)

Descartes now has the meditator recall a "long-standing opinion" which provides grounds for calling even the transparent truths of mathematics into doubt – the opinion "that there is an omnipotent God who made me the kind of creature that I am." The belief that there is an omnipotent God is not by itself a reason for doubt, but Descartes has the meditator consider the hypothesis that the all-powerful God is bent on deceiving her. Faced with this hypothesis, it may seem that no human belief can be placed beyond doubt.

Deceiving-God hypothesis

The deceiving-God hypothesis plays an important role in the later Meditations. It is a powerful ground for doubt. Therefore we shall want to pay careful attention to how it is framed and what it casts into doubt. To that end, we will first examine two different versions of the hypothesis, which yield somewhat different grounds for doubt, before asking which version Descartes used.

An all-powerful deceiver might make us go wrong on either of two scenarios. First, if God were out to deceive us on particular occasions, then surely he could succeed at any time and, perhaps, about anything. Call this the *intervention hypothesis*:

IH: God intervenes to give us false thoughts.

That is, God affects our minds at any given moment to give us the thought that something is true when it is false (or vice versa).

Second, if God made us, perhaps he made us with a mental defect that produces false thoughts. Call this the *defective design hypothesis*:

DDH: God made us in such a way that we produce false thoughts.

On this hypothesis, since God is assumed to have created and equipped our minds, a deceiving God might have made us so that we often, or always, produce false thoughts, no matter how careful we are.

Either hypothesis can be used against both sense perception and intellect or reason. On IH, God could cause us to have all the sensory experiences we have now without there being any world at all. George Berkeley, the eighteenth-century Irish philosopher, held that to be the case (while denying he was a skeptic). IH is similar to the more recent "brain in a vat" hypothesis, in which we imagine each of us to be a brain suspended in a vat of nutrients, with wires attached to our sensory and motor nerves. Teams of mad scientists use super computers to give us sensory stimulation consistent with a complex world, taking into account the activity of our motor nerves (those that would lead to our muscles, if we had any) to produce experience consistent with our moving about at will. (However, the brain-in-the-vat hypothesis is importantly different from the deceiving-God hypothesis, since the God of Descartes' hypothesis is not a computer and would be understood to intervene instantaneously, at any degree of complexity, and without material instrumentality.)

Alternatively, IH could be used to call reason into question, by supposing that God intervenes sometimes, or always, when we are adding sums or counting the sides of squares, and makes us go wrong. This would be similar to the mad scientists using implanted electrodes to give a jolt to the brain that made us go wrong when reasoning.

Similarly, DDH can be used to call the senses, reason, or both into question. God might have designed our senses so that they produce a completely distorted view of the world. The world might be presented as having colors, as spatially extended and temporally ordered, when it has none of those properties. Or we might be constructed so that we see all objects as having those properties, when only some of them do. DDH calls reason into question on the supposition that God made us so that we sometimes, or always, go wrong in our reasoning. (These cases might be compared with the hypothesis that each of us is an experiment in artificial intelligence, made with either defective sensors or defective logic routines, or both.)

Descartes' use of the hypothesis

Given these several possibilities, how did Descartes use his deceiving-God hypothesis? Let us consider two passages that follow immediately upon remembrance of the opinion of an omnipotent God. In the first, the corporeal or material world is called into question:

> How do I know that he [the omnipotent God] has not brought it about that there is no earth, no sky, no extended thing, no shape, no size, no place, while at the same time ensuring that all these things appear to me to exist just as they do now? [7:21]

In this passage, IH is used to question (at least) the senses. God "ensures" that we experience the very appearances that we do in fact experience, while all the time there is no spatially extended universe at all. Here, for the first time, the very existence of the material world as a whole is explicitly called into question.

What about the "transparent truths" of mathematics, which were to be the target of the deceiving-God hypothesis? At the very least, they no longer serve as knowledge of the "real colors" of the world. For, recall that on the "real colors" view arithmetic and geometry describe the basic features of a universe that is unknown in its particulars. But if such a universe does not exist (as IH applied to the senses allows), then arithmetic and geometry do not apply to it. Does the fact that there is no world to which mathematics (or at least geometry, which is spatial – arithmetic might still be used to count thoughts!) applies mean that it is false? Above, Descartes has said that geometry and arithmetic can be true whether their objects "really exist in nature or not" (7:20). Hence, IH, when used to countenance the possibility that the material world does not exist, does not explicitly impugn the transparent truths of mathematics but merely their applicability to, and so their informativeness about, the material world.

Mathematics dubitable

This brings us to the second passage, which immediately follows the first:

> What is more, since I sometimes believe that others go astray in cases where they think they have the most perfect knowledge, how do I know that God has not brought it about that I similarly go wrong every time I add two and three, or count the sides of a square, or in some even simpler matter, if that is imaginable? [7:21*]

Here the transparent truths of mathematics are called directly into question through the deceiving-God hypothesis. But in what form? Presumably in the form of DDH, since Descartes has just previously mentioned that God "made me the kind of creature that I am" (7:21). Still, our origin is not mentioned here; rather, Descartes compares the situation to those in which others go wrong, even when they think they have perfect knowledge (a scenario mentioned in the *Discourse* [6:32] and described from a first-person perspective in the Fifth Meditation [7:70]).

As the passage continues, DDH becomes explicit. Descartes has the meditator reason that "perhaps God would not have allowed me to be deceived in this way, since he is said to be supremely good." This suggestion is easily put aside with the thought that "if it were inconsistent with his goodness to have created me such that I am deceived all the time, it would seem equally foreign to his goodness to allow me to be deceived even occasionally; yet this last assertion cannot be made" (7:21). The consistency of God's goodness with the possibility of deception is taken up again in Meditations 3–5. For the present, the important point is that Descartes here explicitly links the deceiving-God hypothesis to our creation by God in saying that God might have created us so as to be deceived "all the time." DDH is expressed as the hypothesis that we have a defect of reason that makes us always go wrong in simple addition or counting. Although this is not an explicit indictment of all reasoning whatsoever, it is a direct challenge to the transparent truths of mathematics.

I have described the second argument as a challenge to our "reasoning," even though Descartes did not use the term there. Moreover, earlier in the Meditation he had the meditator focus on the principle that knowledge comes through the senses. Shouldn't, then, the mathematical knowledge called into question here be limited to mere sense-based counting of objects? Is Descartes challenging reason or the intellect at all? Apparently he is. Whatever theory of mathematics the meditator might have (be she innocent of philosophy, an Aristotelian, or a philosopher of another stripe), it is hard to suppose that adding 2 and 3 to make 5 is supposed to be an act of the senses. In the course of the painter's analogy, Descartes has pulled back from the senses as a source of knowledge to consider "the simplest and most general things." He has allowed that mathematics studies these things without caring about their existence. And he has focused on acts of adding or counting, which would fit an ordinary notion of reasoning or reckoning. Descartes calls into question our ability to reason correctly about even very simple problems in mathematics.

Other origins besides divine creation

In connection with the deceiving-God hypothesis, Descartes has the meditator consider another possible origin for human beings and their cognitive faculties. The meditator considers the position of those "who would prefer to deny the existence of so powerful a God rather than believe that everything else is uncertain" (7:21). What other origin might human beings have besides divine creation? Descartes lists two alternatives. The first is "fate or chance"; humans would arise by chance, presumably from material origins. The second is "a continuous chain of events"; humans would be the product of a presumably infinitely long chain of natural events (perhaps an infinitely long sequence of parents and children). On either of these hypotheses, the meditator reasons, we would be the product of a "less powerful" original cause than if we were made by an omnipotent God. Consequently, since "deception and error seem to be imperfections," the less powerful our cause the more likely we are to be so imperfect as "to be deceived all the time" (7:21). Descartes suggests that natural causes or chance events, because less perfect than an omnipotent creator, would be more likely to produce a defective cognitive structure that might always go wrong.

The ultimate conclusion, on either the deceiving-God or defective-origins hypothesis, is that we might "be deceived all the time." Consequently, the meditator finds herself "compelled to admit that there is not one of my former beliefs about which a doubt may not properly be raised" (7:21). And since her aim is to achieve certainty, she resolves to withhold assent from her former beliefs as if they were all falsehoods (7:22).

Using doubt to correct theoretical knowledge (7:22)

Three arguments have been allowed to stand in the give and take of the First Meditation: the dream argument, which calls all sensory experience of particular kinds of body into question, and the deceiving-God and defective-origins hypotheses. Of the latter two hypotheses, the first challenges the existence of the material world, and both undermine the truths of mathematics and perhaps ultimately all our thoughts and conclusions – or at least all the meditator's former beliefs.

The meditator does not regard these reasons for doubt as arbitrary or weak. Rather, she describes them as "powerful and well thought-out" (7:21–2). Descartes' aim was not to introduce doubt simply for the sake of doubting. He would not be satisfied if the meditator simply were to *agree* at the outset that she will doubt all her beliefs; he wants her to have reasons for doubting. Why so?

In the First Meditation, he explains that reasons for doubting are needed because of the strength of the meditator's (and his) former opinions. Now he in fact knew that many of the meditator's former opinions were true. Prior to meditating, the meditator surely believed that Paris was in France, Rome in Italy, that plants die back in the winter and grow in the spring, and many other truths. Yet now Descartes wants the meditator to rid herself of even these beliefs. Why? We have seen that, as the philosophical author of the work, he thought that the metaphysical beliefs in his time were incorrectly based in sense perception, and that he knew how to tap a new (non-sensory) source of metaphysical cognition. This aim, of revealing a non-sensory source of cognition, might provide a reason for attacking the senses and sense-based beliefs. But why doubt mathematics? Here we can appeal to the Synopsis: Descartes wants to establish that the new knowledge found in the *Meditations* is absolutely beyond doubt (7:12). So if he can show that his findings are immune to the doubts raised against mathematics (the paradigm of certainty in his day), he will have provided a very firm foundation for them indeed. (We will have to wait and see how firm we judge this foundation to be.)

As Descartes made clear in the first paragraph of the Meditation, the doubt has been undertaken to achieve systematic and stable knowledge "in the sciences" (especially the "science" of metaphysics). This aim distinguishes Descartes' skepticism from classical skepticism as described by Sextus Empiricus and other ancient authors. The classical skeptics doubted in order to purge themselves of the desire to achieve theoretical knowledge. They were seeking a kind of inner peace that comes from suspending judgment. These classical forms of skepticism had been revived in Descartes' time, and he was aware of them. As Descartes makes clear to Hobbes and others (7:171–2, 476–7), he adopted and used this skepticism for very specific aims: to get rid of old, bad opinions, to "withdraw the mind from the senses," and ultimately to achieve indubitable truths. He was not a skeptic himself and was not particularly alarmed by skepticism. For the purposes of ordinary life, he considered the skeptical doubts he raised to be laughable – so much so that anyone taking them to heart in ordinary life would thereby raise questions about their own sanity (7:16, 350–1). But he found skepticism to be a useful tool in his philosophical project, of acquiring knowledge that would lead to a reform of the sciences.

Posit malicious demon as aid to will (7:22–3)

The final two paragraphs of the First Meditation reveal the importance that Descartes placed on clearing the meditator's mind of her old opinions. In the penultimate paragraph, he acknowledges the problem that the meditator's old beliefs keep coming back because they are (on the whole, but not every one of them) "highly probable," such that it is "more reasonable" to believe them than to deny them. (The reader may have suspected this all along!) This being the case, Descartes expects the meditator to have trouble avoiding her usual beliefs and staying focused on the project at hand. Even if (as he later explains) suspending our judgment is "an act of will" and so is "something in our power," we cannot simply "will" our former beliefs away (Appendix to Fifth Replies, 9A:204). Our habits of judgment are ingrained by long practice. To influence the will, we must provide "reasons for doubt" (9A:204). But even having done so, strength of habit will keep us affirming our usual beliefs. Consequently, Descartes adopts a common practice from the spiritual exercises upon which his metaphysical meditations are modeled, devising a program for training the will to keep the old beliefs at bay.

He adopts the strategy of having the meditator regard her previous beliefs not merely as dubitable (which is what his arguments were designed to show) but as "utterly false and imaginary" (7:22). He has already proposed that, given the goal of finding certain and stable knowledge in the sciences, for the time being dubitable opinions should be classed together with false ones (7:18, 22). Now he goes a step further; he enjoins the meditator to assert positively that her merely dubitable opinions actually are false. In this way, he can counterbalance the "weight of preconceived opinion" and thereby nullify the "distorting influence of habit" so that the meditator can finally "perceive things correctly" (in metaphysics). There is no danger in purposefully training oneself to regard the probable as false in these circumstances, since the aim set for the meditator is not "action" but "the acquisition of knowledge" (7:22; also 9A:204–5, 7:460–1). The aim is to reform (metaphysical) knowledge; in the meantime, the meditator's skeptical conclusions will be confined to her meditating and not applied to everyday life.

As a dramatic device for firmly fixing the notion that all her previous beliefs are false, Descartes instructs the meditator to consider that not God but "some malicious deceiver" is out to deceive her. The apparently unmotivated shift from deceiving God to evil deceiver has frequently been noted. When asked about it a few years later, Descartes granted that the demon hypothesis might seem super-fluous (given the deceiving-God hypothesis) but explained that he simply wanted to reinforce the doubt (Burman, 5:147). In fact, in the six Meditations Descartes brings up the malicious deceiver only once again, in the Second Meditation (7:26), where he treats it as equivalent to the hypothesis of a "supremely powerful" deceiver. It seems likely that he chose to call his hypothetical deceiver a "malicious demon" in order to avoid having the meditator concentrate extensively on the thought that God could be a deceiver, a proposition he considered false and one he intended to refute later (see 5:7–9). Once refuted, he did not do anything further to remove the malicious-demon hypoth-esis, presumably because he was treating that hypothesis as equivalent to the thought that an all-powerful being (God) could deceive (see 4:64). (Bourdin, however, assumed that Descartes intended the proof of God's goodness to entail that God would protect our clear and distinct perceptions from the malicious demon [7:455–6].)

In listing the things the evil-deceiver hypothesis calls into doubt, Descartes includes only external objects and one's own body (7:22–3). He does not repeat the challenge to mathematics. Does this mean that he did not really call mathematics into doubt? Hardly. More likely, here at the end of the First Meditation he is fixing those doubts in mind that are addressed in the Second Meditation. There, the doubts about mathematics do not recur; they are taken up again only in the Third Meditation (7:35–6).

On what is not called into doubt

The First Meditation was devoted to "demolishing" all the medi-tator's opinions. The exercise is deemed successful, for in the end the meditator concludes that she may be "deceived all the time" and that all of her "former beliefs" may properly be doubted (7:21).

Readers of the *Meditations* have wondered from the very start whether Descartes really did subject all the meditator's beliefs (or his own) to the doubt (7:466–72), and if not, whether that impugns his subsequent arguments. If the doubt was sufficiently radical to call all his or the meditator's beliefs into question, shouldn't they be left with nothing? And from nothing, how could he (or she) ever come to know anything? But, if the process of doubting hasn't completely emptied the meditator's mind and challenged all of Descartes' own beliefs, doesn't that reveal a failure in carrying the method through?

As we have seen, Descartes, as author of the work, constructed the First Meditation to call into question the "preconceived opinions" of the meditator (7:12, 348, 465), not his own previously acquired metaphysical beliefs. As he later explained to Burman, the Meditation presents the point of view of one who "is only just beginning to philosophize" (5:146). Its doubts are specially constructed for such a person. They serve a didactic function, as part of the meditative process.

Nonetheless, Descartes also wanted to use the doubt as a sieve for arriving at unshakeable foundations for metaphysics. If he were to presuppose those foundations without subjecting them to doubt, he could be accused of "begging the question." (To beg the question is to presuppose the truth of the very thing that is in question.) Hence, even taking Descartes' purposes into account, we must consider both the position of the beginner in philosophy (whom Descartes wishes to teach) and the ultimate goal of establishing a new metaphysics on good cognitive grounds.

A beginner in philosophy

In the first sentence of the Meditation, the meditator acknowledges the "large number of falsehoods that I had accepted as true in childhood" (7:17). In the *Principles*, Descartes explains the origin of the "preconceived opinions of childhood" (8A:32–7). They arise from the fact that the child's mind is immersed in the body and senses. The child accepts uncritically whatever the senses seem to show it – for example, that there is something in bodies "resembling" our sensations of heat, cold, light, color, and other sensory qualities (sensations of secondary qualities), and that the stars are very small (see also 7:82). As we grow to adults, we do not reconsider these prejudices and hence come to believe that all substances can be perceived by the senses and hence are corporeal (8A:37). As Descartes explains in the Second Replies, "all our ideas of what belongs to the mind have up till now been very confused and mixed up with the ideas of the things that can be perceived by the senses" (7:130–1). The procedure of doubting is intended to neutralize such prejudices.

Although Descartes described the meditator as a beginner who must overcome the prejudices of childhood, he knew full well that such "prejudices" included many tenets of Aristotelian metaphysics and epistemology. As previously mentioned, Aristotelians held that all knowledge is based in the senses. The "resemblance thesis" of sensory qualities (introduced in Meditations 3 and 6) evokes the Aristotelian theory of real qualities. Furthermore, although Aristotelians believed that God is an immaterial substance (and so incorporeal), they also held that he can be known only by analogy with, and from the evidence of, bodily things – that is, things that can be sensed. The beginner who confuses mind with sensory or bodily things also fits the Aristotelian doctrine that all thought requires a phantasm, or sense-based image in the faculty of imagination. Although many Aristotelians held that the intellect itself does not require a bodily organ, they nonetheless taught that it can operate only in conjunction with the imagination, which does require an organ; furthermore, they conceived the intellect as a power of the form of a human being, a form that is itself naturally and essentially conjoined to matter.

The First Meditation, then, is aimed at the prejudices of childhood themselves, as incorporated into Aristotelian philosophy. Descartes acknowledges this double audience in the *Search for Truth* (written at the time of the *Meditations*), in which his mouthpiece Eudoxus debates with Epistemon, a "schoolman" or Aristotelian philosopher, and Polyander, a man of good sense who is untutored in philosophy.

In weaning the mind from its sensory focus, the First Meditation attacks the reliability of sensory experience and even the existence of the material world. It also raises a radical doubt about mathematical judgments. Does it, and should it, aim to challenge all reasoning and to empty the mind totally?

Things not doubted

The Synopsis says that in the First Meditation "reasons are provided which give us possible grounds for doubt about all things, especially material things, so long as we have no foundations for the sciences other than those which we have had up till now" (7:12). This last turn of phrase suggests that the effectiveness of the arguments for doubt is conditional on the state of knowledge of the meditator; the doubt can arise only for those (including beginners and Aristotelians) who have not already found the true foundations of science (see also 7:474).

At various places, Descartes suggests that some ideas, notions, and even metaphysical principles, once they are properly considered, are immune from doubt. When Bourdin (Seventh Objections) asks why the general doubt of the First Meditation was not applied to the "clear and distinct idea of God" (4:472), Descartes answers that at that point the meditator had not yet had a clear and distinct perception of God (7:476). This suggests the reasonable principle that you can't directly call into question an idea you haven't had. But Descartes goes on to contend that the clear and distinct idea of God is in fact immune from skepticism, and he explains that if skeptics "had perceived something clearly" they would have "ceased to doubt it, and so ceased to be skeptics" (7:477). This suggests that only those who haven't yet had sufficiently clear perceptions will be drawn in by the First Meditation arguments.

In this response, Descartes suggests that Bourdin may in fact be having trouble with the arguments because he is incapable of clear and distinct perception himself (7:477). But Descartes is being a little quick here. The fact that the meditator had had few or no clear and distinct perceptions up to now does not by itself relieve Descartes of any obligation to extend his method of doubt beyond the preconceived opinions of his intended audience and apply it to his own beliefs. Moreover, even if Descartes was already convinced, prior to the *Meditations*, of some metaphysical results that he now considers indubitable, the meditator (and everyone else) is in a different situation. For her, the alleged indubitability of the Cartesian metaphysics has not been established. She may wish to be shown, in the course of the work, that both Descartes' principles and his method for proving them are truly immune from doubt.

Leaving aside his own metaphysical principles, Descartes more generally held that the procedure of doubt could not – and should not be expected to – call absolutely all thoughts into question. In the Letter to Clerselier, he acknowledges that the First Meditation doubt could never empty the mind totally (9A:204); that would be to abandon thinking altogether. In effect, he contends that the basic structure of thought itself, and the principles of reasoning, cannot be negated through a process of doubt. Not only are they called upon in evaluating the reasons for doubt but they also form the indelible structure of the mind as a mind.

Although there is something right about this point, one may still ask whether the particular structures Descartes held to be basic to the mind really are, and whether they actually do afford knowledge of things as they are in themselves. Among such structures, he includes not only "common notions," such as "What is done cannot be undone" (7:145), but innate ideas of what thought is, or what existence is (7:422). If he is right about these innate elements, the meditator should, upon further investigation, be able to recognize their indelible presence to mind. (As Descartes implies in responding to Bourdin, the proof of the pudding is in the eating [7:542].)

In addition to the common notions just mentioned, Descartes also (at least tacitly) relies on the notion of causation in the First Meditation. Instances of such reliance may be found in the deceiving-God and evil-deceiver argument, which posits a powerful being who might be causing our sensory experiences even though there are no external objects. Furthermore, in the deceiving-God and defective-origins arguments, he considers alternative causal origins for human beings and their cognitive faculties. However, such arguments do not require the causal principles to be true (as do the Third Meditation [7:40] and Geometrical Arguments [7:164–6]); they merely use such principles to provide plausible (but not certain) grounds for doubt. It is enough if the meditator understands the arguments and finds them sufficient to cast doubt. In this context, Descartes is using a commonly accepted notion of causality to undermine other commonly held beliefs. The arguments do not presuppose the truth of his metaphysical principles of causation, but they do not question those principles either.

Transparent truths and the deceiving God

In the Second Replies, Descartes explicitly addresses the question of how, and whether, various simple notions and apparently evident truths can be brought into doubt. He argues that some perceptions are "so transparently clear that we cannot ever think of them without believing them to be true"; but, since "we cannot doubt them unless we think of them," for that reason, "we can never doubt them" (7:145–6). If this argument is correct, it would seem to imply that simple mathematical propositions such as $2 + 3 = 5$ could never be doubted (see also 7:36). And yet Descartes claims to have brought such propositions under doubt in the First Meditation. Does he then believe that "transparent truths" (7:20), such as those of mathematics, can be doubted, or not?

He addresses this puzzle in the Second Replies as well, by distinguishing two cognitive relations we may have toward evident truths. First, when we think directly of such truths, they seem so evident that we cannot doubt them. But, second, if we do not think of such truths directly but merely remember having thought of them, then the hypothesis of a deceiving God is sufficient to cast doubt on them (7:146; see also 7:246, 460, and 9A:205). This subtle distinction between merely remembering evident truths and considering them directly is not raised explicitly until the Third Meditation, and it is discussed at length only in the Fifth.

This example again raises the question of how much could, and should, have been subjected to the Cartesian doubt. The answer to this question depends on a larger question, concerning the larger aim of the method of doubt. The next two sections examine two conceptions of the overall purpose of Descartes' project, with implications for the role of the doubt therein. The first conception sees him as aiming, in the *Meditations*, at a general vindication of reason. In that case, he introduces the doubt as a stringent test of reason's claim to achieve knowledge. The doubt must therefore be as radical as possible in order to test reason as stringently as can be. According to the second conception, Descartes was not trying to vindicate reason but to reform metaphysics. A key step in his reform of metaphysics was to introduce his seventeenth-century readers to a new metaphysical epistemology, one that appeals to the pure intellect independently of the senses. The doubt serves to uncover this hitherto unappreciated cognitive resource (as in the "cognitive and metaphysical" reading of Chapter 2).

The vindication of reason

Suppose that Descartes' project in the *Meditations* was to vindicate human reason (or pure intellect) generally. Accordingly, his aim in the First Meditation (or perhaps the First and Third) would be to bring forward the strongest grounds for doubt in order to see if they can be met. There are two versions that such vindication might take. The first, weak vindication, would occur if reason investigated all reasonable grounds for doubt and found them internally inconsistent or otherwise logically flawed. Reason would be vindicated by ascertaining that there are no good grounds for doubting its validity. The second version, which we will call strong validation, would undertake to prove that reason is sufficient for establishing metaphysical truths about the way things really are. It must show not merely that there are no good challenges to reason but also that it can be trusted to reveal deep truths about the structure of reality. Under both strategies, reason itself would be called upon to evaluate skeptical challenges and other arguments, since there is no other candidate for evaluating "reasons for doubt."

The strategy of strong validation may appear hopeless on the face of it. If reason's trustworthiness were to be successfully challenged, how could it hope to recover? Since it would stand alone in its own defense, the burden of proof would be insurmountable. But more importantly, even if reason should survive a skeptical challenge, that would not be enough. To achieve strong validation, reason must *prove* its own reliability as a source of knowledge about the basic structure of reality. How could it ever do so when that reliability is the very matter in question? We have granted reason's ability to check for contradictions and assess the relation between premises and conclusions. (This supposition might be challenged, but let us grant it for now.) Even so, if it checked all available grounds for doubting its reliability and found them wanting, that would not prove its reliability in establishing metaphysical truths. It would merely show that its reliability had not been disproved. On the strong validation approach, the burden of proof remains with reason, not the skeptic.

The weak vindication approach tries to make a virtue of this situation. It seeks to show that all known grounds for doubting reason, when investigated, are found wanting. Once all challenges are found wanting, reason is vindicated in the sense of having survived the strongest available attack. Weak vindication seems on the face of it more likely to succeed than strong validation, but it has the disadvantage of simply leaving reason on the field unchallenged, but unsupported by positive argument.

We must await the later Meditations to examine more fully these two strategies (and their kin). For now, let us consider an alternative reading of Descartes' project.

Discovery of the intellect

A second way of conceiving Descartes' use of skepticism in the *Meditations* focuses on its methodological function in reforming the metaphysical epistemology of the meditator. On this way of seeing things, Descartes knows from the outset that certain results can be attained by the pure intellect because he has attained them himself (see 7:542). He believes that everyone has a pure intellect, and that everyone will be convinced of his metaphysical principles if they use their intellects. But he also believes that immersion in the senses has obscured the pure intellect. Hence his problem is not to validate reason or the intellect (its results will be accepted once they are seen) but to bring his readers to the realization that purely intellectual cognition is possible. Doubting the senses in the First Meditation is a means of getting the reader to discount sensory experience for the time being. (The reason for calling mathematics into question is less immediately apparent.)

From this perspective, we can easily see why in the Preface Descartes would invite only those "who are willing and able to meditate seriously with me and to draw their minds away from the senses" to read his book (7:9*). We can also understand why, in the Second Replies, he suggests that although the skeptical arguments of the First Meditation are "precooked material," reheated leftovers from the ancients, the reader should still spend "several months, or at least weeks," doubting especially corporeal things (7:130–1). He concedes in the Seventh Replies that the radical doubt of the First Meditation "applies only to those who have not yet perceived anything clearly and distinctly"; but he further maintains that "until making such a renunciation there is virtually no one who ever perceives anything clearly" (7:476). Even if his readers have been using their intellects to varying extents throughout their lives, they have not attained the kind of intellectual clarity that comes from fully turning away from the senses. And it is that sort of pure intellectual clarity (untainted by sensory images of any kind) that is needed for metaphysics.

Accordingly, the first two Meditations are constructed to enable the meditator to discover the pure use of her intellect, in part by ignoring material things. She is to discover that thought without an image, thought that is not sense-based, is possible. That is something Descartes expected his readers either not to know (in the case of the beginner), or vigorously to deny (in the case of the Aristotelian).

On this reading, Descartes would not be begging the question if he constructed his *Meditations* on the assumption that the pure intellect exists. He would only be begging the question if he expected the reader to accept what he said about pure intellect without experiencing it for themselves. The first aim of his work would be to bring the reader to intellectual experiences that they haven't had, or haven't reflected upon, heretofore. If it succeeds in doing that, the reader will come away convinced by the arguments, and – if Descartes is right about the intellect's actual power – in possession of the one true metaphysics. If the reader doesn't find these intellectual experiences, then either they have not been attentive enough or Descartes' theory of pure intellect is wrong and his metaphysics is not grounded as he thinks it is. (An attentive but unconvinced reader will eventually lose patience with a defense that appeals to the reader's inattention.)

Such a reading makes clear why Descartes would call the senses and corporeal things into doubt in this Meditation but not why he would call mathematics, and perhaps reasoning more generally, into question. If his purpose is to discover the pure intellect, why raise any doubts about the reliability of the intellectual faculty at all? Why not simply follow the meditative procedures of sensory doubt that result in discovery of the pure intellect? Perhaps the challenge to mathematics was indeed meant to set a high standard for the intellectual perceptions that eventually turn back the doubt. Descartes claims to show that the primary notions of metaphysics "are by their nature as evident as, or even more evident than, the primary notions which the geometers study" (7:157). If he could show that intellectual perceptions supporting metaphysics equal or excel those of mathematics, that would be a strong result indeed in an age when Euclid's geometry served as a paradigm of good reasoning.

These differing conceptions of Descartes' aims raise interesting and difficult questions, which will receive further elaboration in Chapter 5. For now, in proceeding through subsequent Meditations we should keep in mind the "vindication" and "discovery" strategies as just outlined. In doing so, we should attempt to discover both what the arguments were that Descartes intended to offer and what further arguments or presuppositions (if any) may have been required actually to establish his metaphysical conclusions.

References and further reading

The First Meditation has received the most extensive analysis of any. Frankfurt devotes nearly half of *Demons, Dreamers, and Madmen* (Indianapolis: Bobbs-Merrill, 1970) to this one Meditation, viewed as preparing for a vindication of reason. B. Williams, *Descartes*, ch. 2, portrays the method of doubt as abetting "pure rational enquiry," also with the flavor of vindication. Flage and Bonnen, *Descartes and Method*, ch. 4, examine the Meditation in relation to Descartes' use of the analytic method. Any general work on the *Meditations*, such as those by Curley or Wilson, has a chapter on the First Meditation.

On skepticism in Descartes' time (and an alternative to the interpretation presented here), see R.H. Popkin, *History of Scepticism from Erasmus to Spinoza*, revised edition (Berkeley: University of California Press, 1979). On the history of skepticism more generally, see M. Burnyeat (ed.), *The Skeptical Tradition* (Berkeley: University of California Press, 1983).

On Aristotelian theories of cognition as a background to Descartes, see Hatfield "The Cognitive Faculties," in Ayers and Garber (eds.), *Cambridge History of Seventeenth Century Philosophy*, pp. 953–1002. On the role of the faculties in early modern philosophy generally, see the preface and first two essays in P. Easton (ed.), *Logic and the Workings of the Mind: The Logic of Ideas and Faculty Psychology in Early Modern Philosophy* (Atascadero, Calif.: Ridgeview Publishing, 1997), and D. Owen, *Hume's Reason* (Oxford: Oxford University Press, 1999).

Chapter 4

Discovering the nature of mind

Meditation 2: The nature of the human mind, and how it is better known than body

The Second Meditation contains the famous *cogito* reasoning. This result, in which the meditator recognizes her own existence, occurs early on. The real work then begins. The main topic of the Meditation is not the meditator's existence but her nature.

Although the Meditation's title promises a discovery about the nature of the human mind, the Synopsis warns that full knowledge of the mind's essence, as an immaterial substance, distinct from body, must await the Sixth Meditation. Whatever is learned about mind's nature in this Meditation will fall short of proving its immateriality. Through contemplating what she knows in knowing her own existence, the meditator will come to regard herself as a thing whose nature is to think, and she will examine the nature of thought itself. Prior to launching these investigations, however, she reviews the larger project underway.

The Archimedean point (7:23–4)

The opening paragraph finds the meditator mired in the doubts of "yesterday's meditation" (7:23). (Descartes here reflects a common practice in spiritual exercises, of offering several meditations to be read on successive days.) Despite the dizzying effects of this deep doubt, she resolves to "make an effort and once more attempt the same path which I started on yesterday" (7:24). She recalls the strategy that has been in play:

> Anything which admits of the slightest doubt I will set aside just as if I had found it to be wholly false; and I will proceed in this way until I recognize something certain, or, if nothing else, until I at least recognize for certain that there is no certainty. [7:24]

The meditator's immediate goal is to use doubt as a tool to achieve certainty, even if only to discover "for certain" that certainty cannot be attained.

This passage leaves the meditator momentarily in suspense about the expected outcome. But the next sentence foreshadows great consequences if even one certainty can be achieved:

> Archimedes used to demand just one firm and immovable point in order to shift the entire earth; so I too can hope for great things if I manage to find just one thing, however slight, that is certain and unshakeable. [7:24]

The ancient mathematician Archimedes observed that with a sufficiently long lever and a fixed point off the Earth, he could move the entire globe. Similarly, Descartes promises, just one unshakeable truth would also produce great things – presumably, a large body of certain knowledge.

It is not immediately evident why a single certainty should lead beyond itself. Suppose that you know just one thing with certainty, say, that your sister is now at home (and you there with her), or that $2 + 3 = 5$ (to use some neutral examples, already under doubt). Why should one such piece of knowledge lead to more knowledge? Three possibilities come to mind. First, a given piece of knowledge might provide a single first principle, from which much additional knowledge can be derived. That is, a first item of knowledge might act like an axiom or postulate, from which other items of knowledge could be derived in accordance with the synthetic method (discussed in Chapter 2). This first principle would yield, through its own fecundity, a large body of knowledge. (Call this the "foundationalist answer.") Second, perhaps some knowledge comes with connections to other knowledge "built in." That is, some knowledge, such as that $2 + 3 = 5$, might come only as part of a system of knowledge, such that it is impossible to know one thing without implicitly knowing other, coordinate, things. It is, for instance, plausible that one couldn't really *know* that $2 + 3 = 5$ without also knowing that $1 + 1 + 3 = 5$. In that case, discovering any single truth would be the tip of the iceberg. In tracing out implicit connections with the first "Archimedean" bit of knowledge, one would find a whole system of knowledge. (Call this the "systematicity answer.")

Alternatively, the meditator might hope that in finding just one piece of certain knowledge, she will discover *how* to find certainty. That is, the first item of knowledge will reveal the proper *method* of knowing. Discovering one certainty would show the way to finding other certainties by using the method over and over again. (Call this the "methodological answer"; it coheres with the cognitive reading of the *Meditations* from Chapter 2.) Let us keep these three possibilities in mind as we examine Descartes' "Archimedean point" and its subsequent use to achieve "great things."

Review of doubt (7:24); *Cogito* reasoning (7:24–5)

Descartes has the meditator review the state of doubt. Consonant with the strategy of treating as false what is merely dubitable, she maintains that "my memory tells me lies," that is, "that none of the things that it reports ever happened" (7:24). In doubting her memory, presumably she means to deny her previous beliefs about things in the world (which she now treats as mere memories) and not her memory that she is engaged in meditation, that she has been convinced by some arguments for doubting, and so on (see also Burman, 5:148). The objects of the senses are also in doubt: "Body, shape, extension, movement and place are chimeras" (7:24). A few lines later, the meditator sums up with the conclusion that "there is absolutely nothing in the world, no sky, no earth, no minds, no bodies" (7:25). At this point, she is willing to discount even the existence of minds, although not, it soon turns out, the existence of her own thoughts. Whether those thoughts entail the existence of a mind is taken up a few pages later.

In reviewing the doubt, the meditator asks whether it follows, from the fact that she has thoughts, that she exists. If she is the "author" of her own thoughts (7:24), "am not I, at least, something?" But she is doubting the existence of bodies and minds. Does that mean that she herself does not exist? No. "If I convinced myself of something then I certainly existed" (7:25). Even if a deceiver is constantly deceiving her, "in that case I too undoubtedly exist, if he is deceiving me." Indeed,

> let him deceive me as much as he can, he will never bring it about that I am nothing so long as I think that I am something. So after considering everything very thoroughly, I must finally conclude that this proposition, *I am, I exist*, is necessarily true whenever it is put forward by me or conceived in my mind. [7:25]

This conclusion was expressed in the *Discourse* through the celebrated proposition "I think, therefore I am" (6:32*). This statement is called the *cogito* because in Latin it runs *cogito, ergo sum* – although this exact wording does not appear in the Second Meditation. (It does occur in Descartes' paraphrase of the Meditation [7:140].)

Much energy has been spent interpreting the *cogito* and its significance. Differing positions have been taken on what precisely its conclusion is, how that conclusion is established, and what it means philosophically. Our investigation will be guided by three types of question: (1) What is the content of the conclusion? That is, precisely what is established? That a mind exists? That an immaterial substance exists? (2) How is the conclusion as stated in the Meditation, "I am, I exist" (in Latin, *sum, existo*), established? Is it established through deductive argument (perhaps using some suppressed premises) or in some other way? (3) What is the function of this conclusion in Descartes' philosophy? Is it supposed to provide a premise, or a set of given "data," from which other knowledge can be deduced? Is it also, or instead, supposed to exemplify a method by which knowledge can be attained? In seeking answers to these questions, we will consider not only passages from the Second Meditation but also restatements of the *cogito* reasoning in the Objections and Replies and *Principles*.

What is the conclusion?

The initial conclusion as drawn in the *Meditations* is simply "I exist." In this conclusion, the "I" remains unanalyzed; the conclusion is limited simply to the meditator's existence, which has been established by reflecting on the fact that she has doubted, or been deceived, or had various thoughts. Having reached this conclusion, Descartes launches the meditator into an investigation of "what this 'I' is, that now necessarily exists" (7:25), which takes the remainder of the Meditation. The first result of this ensuing investigation is an extended conclusion, I exist as "a thinking thing" (7:27). This new conclusion characterizes the thing whose existence is affirmed in the phrase "I exist" as a certain sort of thing – a thinking thing.

The initial and extended conclusions provoked immediate queries from the objectors and have been discussed ever since. However, they do not end the *cogito* reasoning. Descartes pursues the investigation of the "I" throughout the entire Meditation, and he reaches further conclusions about its nature.

Even the limited conclusion "I exist" has been challenged. The most famous challenge came from the eighteenth-century German thinker Georg Lichtenberg. He contended that from the fact that the meditator has thoughts (is doubting, has been deceived into false thoughts, or has any thoughts you like), she is not entitled to conclude "I exist" but only "there is thinking going on" or "there are thoughts." To posit an "I" is to move without justification beyond the mere presence of thoughts. The meditator should affirm the thoughts, Lichtenberg held, without affirming an "I" that has the thoughts.

This is an intricate matter, which we will discuss throughout this chapter. To begin with, we may ask what are the candidate interpretations of the "I" in "I exist," and are all of them subject to Lichtenberg's complaint? One possibility is that the "I" refers to René Descartes (as author and meditator), a man born in France in 1596, educated at La Flèche, living in the Netherlands, and author of the *Discourse* and *Meditations*. This historical personage lives in the world, has had various interactions with it, and so on. Given where we are in the *Meditations*, Descartes is not supposing that he has proved that such a person, subject of various geo-historical facts, exists. He is now operating under the assumption that there is no material world, or indeed anything beyond the bare "I" itself, whose existence has just been affirmed.

Lichtenberg's objection is better suited to the extended conclusion, offered a page or two after the initial result. As a result of her investigation of the bare "I," the meditator concludes that she is "a thinking thing" (7:27). One way to understand Lichtenberg's complaint is that he doesn't believe an awareness of thoughts is adequate to establish that a "thing" exists, conceived as a substance, or persisting subject, of the thoughts. (A "persisting subject" means a thing that exists over time and has now this thought, now another thought, now another, etc.) Or it may even be that Lichtenberg (as some other readers, despite Descartes' warnings) believed that Descartes wanted to prove, here in the Second Meditation, the existence of the "I" as an immaterial substance, distinct from body. In that case, Lichtenberg's objection would be misplaced.

Even once the "I" has been identified as a thinking thing, it is unclear how much Descartes intended to claim for it and therefore how far Lichtenberg's objection applies. The original *cogito* passage concludes "that this proposition, *I am, I exist*, is necessarily true whenever it is put forward by me or conceived in my mind" (7:25). This makes it seem as if the "I" does not extend beyond the current thoughts. One might then propose a "thin reading" according to which the thinking thing is wholly constituted by those thoughts that are present to the meditator. That is, in affirming her existence as a thinking thing the meditator does no more than affirm the set of thoughts that are successively present to her in the course of the *cogito* investigation. Lichtenberg allowed affirmation of such thoughts. If any version of his objection applies to the thin reading of the "I," it would be why a mere sequence of thoughts should be called an "I" at all.

The thin reading of the thinking thing posits only the existence of some consciously available thoughts. These thoughts are connected together simply in virtue of being found in a single consciousness. This fact might appear to yield a problem for the thin reading – by not positing an underlying thing to serve as a vessel for the thoughts, it fails to provide any explanation for their linkage and so can't explain in what sense the thoughts all belong to a single "I." But given the epistemic modesty of the Second Meditation, nothing more may be required to sustain the sameness of the "I" than the availability of thoughts experienced in succession. Perhaps the minimum notion of an "I" or ego is just the experiencing of successive thoughts. This minimal notion leaves aside questions of the long-term persistence of the "I" and its memories, but those questions have been set aside in the Meditation as well, which considers only the knowledge of self available in a concentrated and continuous period of time.

The thin reading is attractive because it avoids Lichtenberg's objection that the meditator's extended conclusion goes beyond present thoughts. As an interpretation of the thinking thing, however, it seems to be contradicted in the Third and Fifth Replies. In reply to Hobbes, Descartes glosses the "thinking thing" as a "thing or substance" (7:174), he allows that "we cannot conceive of thought without a thinking thing" (7:175), and says further that "it is certain that a thought cannot exist without a thing that is thinking, and in general no act or accident can exist without a substance for it to belong to" (7:175–6). In other words, individual thoughts must be regarded as the individual acts of a persisting thing, which is capable of having one thought, then another, and so on. In reply to Gassendi, he restates his conclusion from the Second Meditation as "I am a thinking substance," again treating this as equivalent to "I am a thinking thing" (7:355). These statements admittedly appear in the Replies, where Descartes speaks with full knowledge of all the results of the *Meditations*. Still, we must take seriously the fact that he effectively glosses "thing with properties" as "substance," which suggests that in speaking of a thinking thing, he intends to posit a substance (see also 8A:24–5).

If the meditator has already concluded that the thinking thing is a substance, as the Third and Fifth Replies suggest, does she fully know what kind? All she now knows are her thoughts, and she concludes only that she is a thinking thing or substance. Does this mean she knows that she is not a body, or is immaterial? Descartes claims, several times (7:13, 131, 175), to reserve that conclusion for the Sixth Meditation. Therefore, even if the Second Meditation does conclude that the thinking thing is a substance whose nature is to think, it leaves open whether this thinking thing is an immaterial substance (see 7:27). We need therefore to distinguish a thinking substance, viewed as an immaterial being, from the less determinate notion of a thinking substance whose further properties remain unknown – such as whether it is identical with bodily states, is immaterial, or perhaps is a conglomerate substance of spatio-temporally disjoint things.

Our reflections thus far offer three interpretations of the "thinking thing" in the Second Meditation (7:27):

1   *Thin reading*: "thinking thing" refers only to the stream of thoughts.
2   *Thinking substance*: no claim about its identity or non-identity with body.
3   *Thinking substance*: an immaterial substance, distinct from body.

Interpretations 1 and 2 are permitted by the initial and extended conclusions that we've reviewed thus far in the Meditation itself. Interpretation 2 is supported in the Third and Fifth Replies. Interpretation 3 is rejected in several places, although Descartes believed that the Second Meditation helped to prepare for the conclusion it expresses.

How is the conclusion established?

Consider first the initial conclusion, "I am, I exist." The meditator claims that "this proposition…is necessarily true whenever it is put forward by me or conceived in my mind" (7:25). And indeed the conclusion appears forceful. That is, it seems quite compelling that, when thinking (whether doubting, or having any other thought), we are unable to deny our own existence. (If you don't believe this, try to convince yourself that you – as a thinker, and leaving aside the existence of your body – do not exist.) But where does the conclusion get its force? Does it follow from a logical argument, that is, by deductive inference from the premise "I think," perhaps with other premises? Or is it somehow known immediately, through the mere awareness of some thoughts?

If it follows from a logical argument, then we need at least one additional premise. But at this point in the *Meditations*, besides the awareness of thoughts themselves, the conclusion "I exist" is the only positive assertion that has been made. It is not apparent where other premises would come from. So let us examine the other possibility first, that the conclusion is known immediately, without an argument.

Perhaps the conclusion is established, without argument, on the simple grounds that denying one's own existence is paradoxical. Compare this situation with the case of answering "absent" when the roll is called in a class. It is futile to give that answer, because the act of giving it undermines it. It is apparent to everyone else, and should be apparent to you, that you are present when you say "absent." The act you perform in answering the roll call allows everyone not so much to infer as directly to observe that you are present, which undermines the claim that you are absent.

It is true that in saying you are absent, or attempting to doubt or deny that you exist, you produce evidence to the contrary. Does this show that you don't need an argument to appraise that evidence? Not by itself. Perhaps to know with certainty that you are present, your classmates need to rule out the possibility that someone placed a dummy likeness of you in the back row and played a tape recording of your saying "absent." They might point to aspects of the evidence at hand to argue the adequacy of that evidence. Similarly, perhaps in the case of "I exist" some evidence must be considered, and perhaps further cognitive presuppositions are needed in conjunction with that evidence.

The decision about whether an argument is needed turns partly on what counts as an inferential argument and what as non-inferential knowledge. For the moment, put aside the Cartesian doubt and consider an ordinary case, in which you are seated at your kitchen table having a glass of water. Do you need an argument to establish that you are seated at a table, or that you have a glass in front of you? Usually, it seems that such things are known without argument, just by looking. Of course, you need to know what a table is and what a glass is in order to see that those things are there just by looking. But an argument doesn't seem to be required. Moreover, if you needed premises and arguments to conclude that a table is there, how would you support those premises if not by perceptual evidence of the same sort you have for the table and glass? Re-entering the *Meditations*, perhaps the *cogito* conclusion is established in a similar, non-inferential manner, simply through the contemplation of one's thoughts (represented in the phrase "I think"). Hence, one would simply move from the awareness of thoughts to "I exist."

For help on this topic, let us consider some passages in which Descartes speaks directly on the question of whether an inference is needed. These passages occur in the Replies, *Principles*, and conversation with Burman. However, they offer apparently contradictory answers. Some seem to affirm that the *cogito* is a logical argument that requires an added premise beyond "I think," others to deny it. Although it is possible that he changed his mind over time, or indeed contradicted himself, the fundamental position occupied by the *cogito* reasoning in his philosophy requires that we compare these passages with care.

The various passages agree on one thing: that in order to use the awareness of one's thoughts to know that one exists, one must know "what thought is" and "what existence is" (7:422; also 8A:8). Descartes repeatedly insisted that he was permitted such concepts (even in the midst of radical doubt). As he explained in the Letter to Clerselier, "I have denied only preconceived opinions – not notions like these, which are known without any affirmation or denial" (9A:206). Such concepts or notions are like elements of thought, without which no thought (not even grounds for doubt) could be framed. Accordingly, use of concepts such as *thought* and *existence* requires no justification, just as the concepts of table or glass might be presupposed in perceptual knowledge. (Both sorts of presupposition can be challenged; see Chapters 7 and 10.) These concepts are not thus far premises expressed as judgments, involving affirmation or denial (and so truth or falsity). Hence, they don't yet require that we render the *cogito* reasoning as a logical argument. To decide that question, we need to examine the various passages further.

Consider first the Second Replies, which apparently says that no inference is involved:

> When someone says "I am thinking, therefore I am, or I exist," he does not deduce existence from thought by means of a syllogism, but recognizes it as something self-evident by a simple intuition of the mind. This is clear from the fact that if he were deducing it by means of a syllogism, he would have to have had previous knowledge of the major premise "Everything which thinks is, or exists"; yet in fact he learns it from experiencing in his own case that it is impossible that he should think without existing. [7:140]

Here Descartes observes that if the conclusion "I exist" were to be deduced using "I think" as a premise, then an additional premise would be needed, that "Everything which thinks exists." But he denies that any such premise is required and asserts that the conclusion of existence is established by awareness of thoughts through "a simple intuition of the mind." We know from the *Rules* and other discussions that a "simple intuition" is something that can be seen "all at once," or encompassed in a single act of thought (10:407; also 5:136–8).

If this is Descartes' position, we might wonder how an intuitive awareness of thoughts is supposed to establish the existence of an "I" or a "thinking thing." The thin reading would help us here. If all that is meant by the "I" or the "thinking thing" is the very thoughts themselves, then intuitive awareness of them, in a single act of thought, already *is* awareness of the existence of a thinking thing. Nothing more is claimed in identifying such a thing beyond awareness of a succession of thoughts. No inference is needed.

However, if Descartes is not following the "thin reading" but takes the "I" to be a persisting thing or substance (as in position 2, above), then trouble arises for the view that non-inferential intuition can suffice. To establish the existence of a thing underlying thoughts, he would have two options. He might claim that in being aware of his thoughts he is directly aware of the substance in which they inhere. Or he might claim to know that thoughts – or indeed any attribute or activity – can exist only in a substance. He rejects the first option, that we directly intuit the substance underlying our thoughts, on the grounds that we never know substances directly but only through their acts or attributes (7:176, 222). The second option amounts to adding a premise, that thoughts, as instances of an activity or attribute, must inhere in a substance. Descartes did in fact endorse such a position (7:175–6, 222–3), but to invoke it here as an added premise at least appears to be inconsistent with the point of our first passage, that a syllogistic major premise is not needed. So let us move on to the passages in which Descartes endorses the need for this added premise.

The Letter to Clerselier (in responding to Gassendi's objections) allows that a major premise is presupposed:

> The author…claims that when I say "I am thinking, therefore I exist" I presuppose the major premise "Whatever thinks exists," and hence I have already adopted a preconceived opinion. Here he once again misuses the term "preconceived opinion." For although we can apply the term to the proposition in question when it is put forward without attention and believed to be true only because we remember that we judged it to be true previously, we cannot say that it is always a preconceived opinion. For when we examine it, it appears so evident to the understanding that we cannot but believe it, even though this may be the first time in our life that we have thought of it. [9A:205]

Descartes does not question the need for the major premise, only that it should count as a preconceived opinion. Moreover, in the restatement of the *Meditations* in the *Principles*, he explicitly affirms the need for such a premise (or, as he put it, "simple notion"):

> when I said that the proposition *I am thinking, therefore I exist* is the first and most certain of all to occur to anyone who philosophizes in an orderly way, I did not in saying that deny that one must first know what thought, existence, and certainty are, and that it is impossible that that which thinks should not exist, and so forth. [8A:8]

The addition of the premise "Whatever thinks exists" to the premise "I think" would allow a logically valid inference yielding "I exist." If we consider further that Descartes also affirms the conclusion "I exist as a thinking thing," then we might propose that he needs another added premise concerning thinghood or substance. And in fact he supplies such a premise in the Third Replies, that "no act or accident can exist without a substance for it to belong to" (7:175–6). (In this context, an "act" is an act of thought, and an "accident" is a property or attribute that something has but need not have had, such as having a particular thought at a particular time.) Using this further premise, we have the following argument:

1   I think.
2   Whatever thinks exists.
3   No act or accident can exist without belonging to a substance.

Therefore, I exist as a thinking thing, or a substance that thinks.

Premises 2 and 3 would be regarded as tacitly held, in accordance with the *Principles* and Replies. (We could also add (4), thinking is an act or accident, if we wanted to make the argument fully explicit.) Premise 2 supports the initial conclusion about existence, and 3 underwrites the extended conclusion about a thinking thing.

The proposed addition of such premises to the *cogito* reasoning invites the objection that the meditator is not in a position to assert them, since she has convinced herself that she knows nothing (9A:205). Indeed, "I exist" is supposed to be her first item of knowledge. If she really has cleared her mind of all other judgments, where do these premises come from? In the second passage quoted above, Descartes asserts that the premise "whatever thinks exists" "appears so evident to the understanding that we cannot but believe it, even though this may be the first time in our life we have thought of it." But in the Second Meditation he doesn't justify the premise or even express it, and he hasn't given any argument that the meditator should believe what appears evident to her. In fact, he has had her call even the very evident truths of mathematics into question. So if he needs this premise for the *cogito* inference, the inference seems doomed.

Nonetheless, we do believe the initial *cogito* result. So either it isn't an inference, or it must rely on yet other premises that can be legitimately presupposed, or there must be some way for the premises already listed to enter the argument legitimately.

Some readers charged Descartes with inconsistently holding both that the *cogito* is not a syllogistic inference and that it requires tacitly assumed premises (9A:205; Burman, 5:147). In response, he offered a distinction between the (tacit) inferential structure of thought and the methodological order in which such structure is discovered and presented. In essence, he argued that the judgment "I think, therefore I am" is inferentially complex and contains an implicit major premise, but that everything needed is grasped in a single intuitive act of thought. (Recall that in the *Rules* Descartes allowed that intuitive acts of thought can contain inferential structure [10:408].) The conclusion "I exist" is first known in this intuitive way; subsequently, in reflecting on how it is known, we realize that our judgment implicitly contains premise 2. Further reflection leads us to the extended conclusion, and we find that premise 3 has been implicitly assumed in achieving that conclusion.

Descartes explained these points with varying degrees of clarity. Perhaps the most concise explanation was recorded by Burman (5:147), who noted the apparent contradiction between the Second Replies (the *cogito* conclusion "is not derived by means of any syllogism") and the *Principles* passage quoted above (8A:8). Descartes replied:

> Before this inference, "I am thinking, therefore I exist," the major, "whatever thinks exists," can be known; for it is in reality prior to my inference, and my inference depends on it. That is why the author says in the *Principles* that the major premise comes first, namely because implicitly it is always presupposed and prior. But it does not follow that I am always expressly and explicitly aware of its priority, or that I know it before my inference. This is because I am attending only to what I experience within myself – for example "I am thinking, therefore I exist." I do not pay attention in the same way to the general notion "whatever thinks exists." As I have explained before, we do not separate out these

general propositions from the particular instances; rather, it is in the particular instances that we think of them. [5:147]

The major premise, whatever thinks exists, "comes first" logically, but it does not come first in the order of awareness or of legitimate argumentation (since Descartes does not require of legitimate argument that its logical structure be made explicit). It is implicitly contained in the inference. Upon analyzing our conclusion, we come to see that this major premise is presupposed, and upon considering the premise directly we accept it. Indeed, if we see that it is presupposed by the *cogito* reasoning, we have every reason to accept it, since that reasoning is itself compelling and indubitable. Descartes considered the bare reasoning from "I think" to "I am" to have adequate force on its own, prior to our explicitly remarking that the general premise is presupposed.

We can now consider again the passage from the Second Replies, denying that a syllogism is required. It says that someone who accepts the *cogito* conclusion does not deduce it from a syllogism, because "he would have to have had previous knowledge of the major premise." But, it goes on to explain, "in fact he learns [the major premise] from experiencing in his own case that it is impossible that he should think without existing" (7:140). The point about "previous knowledge" of the major premise is ambiguous. It may be questioning how the meditator could have previous knowledge of a major universal premise without considering a variety of cases, or it may be a point about the order of learning (the analytic versus the synthetic method, as in Chapter 2).

Let us consider first how the major premise "whatever thinks exists" might be learned from our own case. One possibility is that our own case serves as a single piece of evidence that supports the premise by inductive enumeration, in the way that an observer might try to form a generalization about all rabbits (e.g., that they always twitch their noses before eating) by observing many rabbits, one at a time. That would be the normal Aristotelian way of forming the major premise of a universal syllogism (the intellect grasps the universal major premise from many cases without, in their view, having to enumerate all instances).

It is unlikely that Descartes thought we can learn the general proposition from the particular by using our own case as a one-instance enumerative sample (especially given that he compared this case to the way mathematical principles are learned). It is much more likely that his major premise should be conceived not as a generalization over instances but as a conceptual point about the (only possible) relation between thinking and existence. It would say that if anything thinks, or performs any act whatever, it must exist, and that this is true whether anything actually thinks or acts at all. (On the difference between this premise and a syllogistic major premise, see the Appendix.) Indeed, in all of our passages affirming this premise, he calls it a "general" (or "simple") "notion," and he adds in one case that such notions by themselves "provide us with no knowledge of what exists" (8A:8). The meditator would learn this premise from her own case by recognizing it as a conceptual truth implicit in the *cogito* reasoning itself.

The Letter to Clerselier suggests that Descartes would affirm both the point about the order of learning or exposition and the point about the major premise being a conceptual truth. The Letter denies that in the case of the *cogito*, "knowledge of particular propositions must always be deduced from universal ones, following the same order as that of a syllogism in Dialectic" (9A:205). The use of syllogism is here equated with an order of discovery or learning in which general premises are explicitly stated first, and particular cases are arrived at through deduction. As in the passage from Burman, Descartes rejects this order of learning for the *cogito* (as in fact for other types of knowledge). The Letter continues its criticism of Gassendi:

> Here he shows how little he knows of the way in which we should search for the truth. It is certain that if we are to discover the truth we must always begin with particular notions in order to arrive at general ones later on (though we may also reverse the order and deduce other particular truths once we have discovered general ones). Thus when we teach a child the elements of geometry we will not be able to get him to understand the general proposition "When equal quantities are taken from equal

amounts the remaining amounts will be equal," or "The whole is greater than its parts," unless we show him examples in particular cases. [9A:206]

We know that Descartes held that such axioms as these – which were found in Euclid's geometry and accepted by all – can be known without appeal to sensory experience. He is not suggesting that the child learns them inductively from examining many cases. Rather, by considering examples that serve as instances of these general propositions, the child comes to see them as instantiated in the particular cases. We also know (from the Fifth Meditation) that Descartes believed general statements in mathematics can be known as conceptual truths, independently of the existence of any individual cases. Accordingly, once the child sees the general proposition, he would be able to recognize it as self-evidently true without appealing to particular cases for inductive support. And that is how Descartes has explained that the general premise "whatever thinks exists" is known: "it appears so evident to the understanding that we cannot but believe it, even though this may be the first time in our life that we have thought of it" (9A:205).

The rationalist claim that the mind can know certain kinds of general proposition without relying on inductive evidence (and even independently of existing cases) may be questioned, but that is not at stake here. For now, we are simply trying to understand the difference between using individual cases for evidence and using them as the means by which to become aware of general principles that are accepted as self-evident. Descartes believes that such general premises are at work in the logic of the *cogito* reasoning (as reconstructed above), but that they come to awareness only through reflection on particular cases of intuitively evident knowledge. They are not first seen on their own and then used to arrive at the *cogito* inference by way of formal syllogism. Rather, the inference is (rightly) accepted in a single intuition and subsequently analyzed to discover its logical structure, including the tacit general premises. In his view, the *cogito* reasoning is an argument whose conclusion can legitimately be accepted without all the premises being explicitly noted and set out in a logical schema.

What is the purpose of the cogito?

The initial conclusion of the *cogito* provides the meditator with her first certainty about anything, namely, her own existence (at least as long as she is thinking). The attainment of that certainty is of little moment in itself. Its function is not to convince the meditator that she really exists, as if that had been in serious question. Rather, it is supposed to lead to other truths, to "great things."

Some of these great things were foretold in the Meditation's title: "The nature of the human mind, and how it is better known than body" (7:23*). One purpose of the *cogito* reasoning is to aid in achieving the knowledge here promised. The Synopsis promised that the "exercise" of employing the radical doubt and discovering the existence of oneself as a thinking thing is "of the greatest benefit, since it enables the mind to distinguish without difficulty what belongs to itself, i.e. to an intellectual nature, from what belongs to body" (7:12*). Spurred by the *cogito*, investigation of the nature of mind unfolds throughout the remainder of the Meditation.

However, the Archimedean point of the *cogito* was supposed to yield even more. Elsewhere, Descartes characterized it as the first principle of his philosophy (6:32, 8A:6–7), from which all other knowledge flows (10:526). His interpreters have frequently wondered how a whole system of knowledge could arise from such a modest beginning. But that depends on how the *cogito* relates to Descartes' subsequent conclusions. Three ways of conceiving this relation were sketched above: foundationalist, systematic, and methodological.

On the foundationalist picture, the *cogito* would act as a first principle from which the rest of Descartes' metaphysics is deduced. In its simplest form, this position holds that the *cogito* conclusion, that I exist as a thinking thing, can serve as the single premise from which all further knowledge is derived. It is difficult to see how the *cogito* could play this role without requiring other, independent principles, whether implicit or explicit. Another version of the foundationalist answer would downplay the claim of self-existence in the *cogito* reasoning in favor of the meditator's immediate awareness of her own thoughts. The entire set of such thoughts would serve as the foundation for all other knowledge. Descartes would have the meditator move from incorrigible knowledge of her own mental states to knowledge of the rest of the world. This picture is similar to the sense-data foundationalism of the early twentieth century, which held that the current content of conscious sensory experience (independent of anything beyond that experience) provides the foundation for all knowledge. For it to work as a reading of Descartes, we would need to discover how awareness of one's own thoughts was supposed to yield additional knowledge without relying on further principles to move beyond one's own thoughts.

On the systematicity view, the *cogito* conclusion would come already implicitly linked to other knowledge. On one interpretation of the *cogito* reasoning presented above, implicit premises were drawn out of the intuitive certainty of one's own existence, as presuppositions needed to infer that conclusion. Perhaps other conclusions, not required for the *cogito* conclusion itself, might be reached simply by considering what is presupposed in thinking of one's mind. One of the arguments for the existence of God in the Third Meditation, which starts from the awareness of a finite mind (as in the *Discourse*), may fit this scenario.

Finally, in line with the methodological answer, we might find that the *cogito* result, by offering an instance of certain knowledge, makes the meditator aware of the proper method for attaining knowledge. With this answer, there is (in principle) no difficulty in explaining how "great things" could arise from the *cogito* finding. Other knowledge would not have to be deduced from the *cogito* or found in connection with its specific content. Rather, once the general method of knowing was derived from the *cogito*, this method could be applied to other subject matter to yield a variety of metaphysical principles. Early in the Third Meditation, we will find Descartes using the *cogito* to extract such a method.

Nature of "I" as thinking thing (7:25–7)

Immediately after achieving the initial conclusion of the *cogito*, "I exist," Descartes has the meditator remark:

I do not yet have a sufficient understanding of what this "I" is, that now necessarily exists. So I must be on my guard against carelessly taking something else to be this "I," and so making a mistake in the very item of knowledge that I maintain is the most certain and evident of all. [7:25]

The meditator decides to "go back and meditate on what I originally believed myself to be." She formerly believed herself to be a human being, or, as expressed in Descartes' text, "a man." The Aristotelian definition of a human being as a "rational animal" is briefly considered and rejected on the grounds that it requires "rational" and "animal" to be understood, necessitating further investigations and "subtleties" (the notion of "animal" surely would involve the meditator in thoughts about the now abandoned material world). The meditator then describes the "natural" and "spontaneous" conception of a human being, which is of someone with a body who is nourished, moves about, and has sense perceptions and thoughts. In this natural or ordinary conception, the soul is conceived as a material thing, a "wind or fire or æther" (7:26; recall Descartes' early conception of soul, 10:217). Under the force of radical doubt, body, nourishment, motion of limbs, and sensory activity – all associated with the body – have been rejected.

What remains? Thought alone. It alone is "inseparable from me" (7:27). Descartes leads the meditator beyond her initial conclusion of bare existence to the extended conclusion of the *cogito*:

At present I am not admitting anything except what is necessarily true. I am, then, in the strict sense only a thing that thinks; that is, I am a mind, or intelligence, or intellect, or reason – words whose meaning I have been ignorant of until now. But for all that I am a thing which is real and which truly exists. But what kind of a thing? As I have just said – a thinking thing. [7:27]

The "I" is a thinking thing, here equated with "a mind, or intelligence, or intellect, or reason."

The extended conclusion yields the first insight into the nature of mind. In wending her way to this conclusion, the meditator has accomplished two things. First, she has separated any considerations of body or bodily processes from her conception of herself. The First Meditation doubt about all things bodily has allowed her to discount such activities as nutrition, stimulation of the sense organs, and muscle-driven motions of the body from her notion of herself as a certainly existing thing. But this allows her to discover, second, that the things she can't doubt, her own present thoughts, are in some way unified. She discovers that her thoughts, as isolated through the process of doubt, can be unified under the title of thinking (or the mental).

This discovery was of no small moment in Descartes' intellectual context. It in effect marks the transition between the Aristotelian conception of soul – which included vegetative, sensory, and intellectual powers – and the Cartesian conception of mind. In the Aristotelian conception of soul, mental functions constituted only part of the nature of soul. Even the human soul, which was defined and named through its rational power, had attributed to it the powers of nutrition, reproduction, muscular movement, and nervous transmission of sensory stimulation. Descartes now purports to find a coherent notion or concept of mind that excludes those bodily activities and focuses only on thoughts. (As we shall see, it includes sensations insofar as they are experiences but excludes the neural activity of sense organs.) For this reason, as he explained to Gassendi, he equated soul with mind, but he preferred to use the latter word to avoid ambiguity (7:356).

We must be careful to note exactly what Descartes does and does not claim for this finding about the nature of mind. He claims that what the meditator can know of herself at this point is restricted to thoughts, and that the thoughts can be conceived without any reference to body. As we shall see in the next section, he does not claim that she can know whether human thoughts or a human mind actually could exist separately from a body. Correspondingly, she presumably could not claim to know at this point whether mind actually directs the processes of digestion, or provides the active power that drives the muscles. Such questions are beyond the state of knowledge in the Second Meditation.

Descartes further indicates that the very act of focusing on her own thoughts, stripped of all bodily reference, allows the meditator a new insight into what mind or intellect is, for she says that these are "words whose meaning I have been ignorant of until now" (7:27). In part, this must surely mean that she was ignorant of mind because she always thought of it as including reference to body. But now she has learned that she can at least contemplate thoughts without knowingly invoking the body. Further questions can now be posed, about how the mind is known and what is known about its relation to body.

Mind's relation to body unknown (7:27); Mind itself not imagable (7:27–8)

In the continuing investigation of the "I," Descartes has the meditator explore the cognitive faculty by which the "I" is known. First he has her try to imagine the "I" as a thinking thing. She begins by ruling out images of those things that she formerly considered a thinking thing to be: "wind, fire, air, breath" (7:27). She is now supposing that no bodies at all exist, not even air or fine matter, yet she still knows herself as a thinking thing. This fact suggests that she cannot be known to herself by means of imagination, which is literally a faculty of images; as Descartes has her recall, "imagining is simply contemplating the shape or image of a corporeal thing" (7:28). She cannot use the faculty of imagination to "picture" the "I," for picturable things are by definition bodies, or things that have "a determinable shape and a definable location" (7:26). She concludes:

> I thus realize none of the things that the imagination enables me to grasp is at all relevant to this knowledge of myself which I possess, and that the mind must therefore be most carefully diverted from such things if it is to perceive its own nature as distinctly as possible. [7:28]

The mind can become aware of itself or its states, but the imagination is irrelevant for doing so.

Descartes is not saying that individual acts of imagination, inasmuch as they are experiences, are irrelevant to grasping the nature of mind. Imagistic experiences, as in a dream, or in actually imagining one's sleeping cat, count as instances of thinking and hence as activities of the mind as a "thinking thing." But in the present case, the meditator is trying to discover what the "I" is (7:25, 27) by representing the thinking thing in itself (as opposed to experiencing its thoughts from the inside, as it were). She is attempting to take a third-person or observer's perspective on the thinking thing, which she knows thus far only from her first-person experience of thinking (i.e., having thoughts). And this attempt to imagine or picture the "I" from a third-person perspective fails. (Try the thought experiment yourself by trying to picture what your conscious experience "looks like" from the outside, without picturing your brain or any bodily part, the existence of which is now supposed to be in doubt.) In this context, the imagination (and senses) are deemed irrelevant to knowing the nature of the thinking thing.

As previously noted, Descartes did not think that the meditator could know at this point whether or not mind is identical with body. The presumed fact that she can *think of* mind without thinking of body is not itself enough to reveal how mind *is* actually related to body. Descartes has her ask: "may it not perhaps be the case that these very things which I am supposing to be nothing, because they are unknown to me, are in reality not different from the 'I' that I know?" To which she answers: "I do not know, and for the moment I shall not argue the point, since I can make judgments only about things which are known to me" (7:27*).

Variety and unity of thoughts (7:28–9)

Having determined that the "I" is a thinking thing, the meditator now asks what this "thing that thinks" is (7:28). The answer comes as a list of the thing's activities: it is "a thing that doubts, understands, affirms, denies, is willing, is unwilling, and also imagines and has sensory perceptions" (7:28). Thinking comprises a variety of activities, which include understanding, willing, imagining, and having sense perceptions. (Descartes applied the terms "thought" and "thinking" broadly, to refer to any sort of mental state or activity.)

We may wonder whether anything unifies this list. Is there something that all instances of thought share? Famously, Descartes held that all thoughts are accessible to consciousness, and he has been interpreted as equating the essence of thought with consciousness. Thus far, however, he has not invoked consciousness in describing the nature of thought, and he did not use that term anywhere in the Second Meditation. Indeed, among the six Meditations it occurs only in the Third (7:49), and then not to define thought.

Nonetheless, accessibility to consciousness provides a means for delimiting the domain of thought in connection with the list given above. Consider the fact that the list now includes sense perception, which had previously been excluded from what is known by the meditator (7:27). Sense perception, as also imagining, is here considered without respect to bodily aspects or nervous activity; it is considered merely as a type of experience that the meditator finds in her awareness. Even though the meditator is now supposing that she has no body or sense organs, and that none of the objects of imagination exist, she nonetheless has the conscious experiences known as sensing and imagining, which she counts among her thoughts.

Availability in consciousness also provides the grounds for considering all the various types of thought to be activities of one and the same thinking thing:

> Is it not one and the same "I" who is now doubting almost everything, who nonetheless understands some things, who affirms that this one thing is true, denies everything else, desires to know more, is unwilling to be deceived, imagines many things even involuntarily, and notices many things as apparently coming from the senses? Are not all these things just as true as the fact that I exist, even if I am asleep all the time, and even if he who created me is doing all he can to deceive me? Which of all these activities is distinct from my thinking? Which of them can be said to be separate from myself? The fact that it is I who am doubting and understanding and willing is so evident that I see no way of making it any clearer. [7:28–9*]

The meditator claims that it cannot be "any clearer" that these various types of activity belong to one domain of thought, and to one thinker, so that all of them are hers. What makes them all hers?

Apparently, the fact that she is directly aware of the various types of thought.

The unity of various types of thought in a single mind is a new, enlarged result of the *cogito* investigation. It addresses a point raised earlier, in connection with the thin reading. There we wondered how, on the thin reading, we could move beyond separate instances of "thinking going on" to talk about an "I." It was proposed that awareness of thoughts as connected together, or as occurring sequentially in the same consciousness, could support the minimal claim that all the thoughts are the meditator's and could underwrite the "I" in "I exist." Now we have seen the claim of unity explicitly advanced.

Let us grant that the meditator recognizes various instances of thought as belonging to her in one consciousness. Do we have reason to believe that she has access to all her thoughts? It seems not. That is, at best she now has access only to those thoughts found in consciousness. That may include all thoughts, but it may not. More generally, we have no reason (as yet) to believe that the meditator's list of types of thought is complete. That is, we don't know whether the list is simply experientially based and merely enumerates the types of thought the meditator has thus far discovered in herself, or whether it anticipates a theoretical taxonomy based on a further insight into the nature of thought. These questions await further progress. At the same time, we know from elsewhere that Descartes did not adopt the implausible position that we are reflectively aware of every thought (5:220–1); acts of thinking that are fast and habitual may go unnoticed (7:438).

Although the meditator finds it immediately obvious that the various types of thinking, and instances of thought, are all hers, this finding need not show what makes all these activities types of *thought*, and hence all *mental*. And, indeed, we may ask whether all thought has some common feature besides belonging to one consciousness.

In the Geometrical Arguments, Descartes provides a definition of the term "thought" by appealing to consciousness:

> *Thought.* I use this term to include everything that is within us in such a way that we are immediately conscious of it. Thus all the operations of the will, the intellect, the imagination and the senses are thoughts. [7:160*]

If we take Descartes to be defining the essence of thought here, then it appears that we have discovered that essence – and hence the essence of the thinking thing – tacitly invoked in the Second Meditation to frame the list of kinds of thinking. But we must be careful. This quotation says merely that he is *defining the term* "thought," not that he is describing the essence of the thinking thing. And there is a well-known sense of "definition" that means setting boundaries, or setting the domain of application of a word (we might say its "extension"), rather than describing the essence of what is so defined. This "definition" may be doing no more than has so far been achieved by the epistemic isolation of thoughts in the Second Meditation; that is, it may simply be circumscribing the domain of characteristic mental activities (will, intellect, etc.) by appealing to the fact that we are "immediately conscious" of all of them.

Granted that consciously available thoughts are all the meditator now knows, we may still ask what makes them all instances of thought. Is it simply a bare fact that they are all thoughts? Does consciousness provide a unifying essence? Or is there some further property or properties that constitute the essence of thinking?

One way to think about these questions is by considering the charge (leveled by later philosophers) that Descartes simply lumped together a hodge-podge of activities under the title of "thought" or "the mental," using consciousness as an arbitrary criterion. According to this criticism, sensing, imagining, understanding, and willing don't really share a common nature. They are simply four activities of which human beings have immediate awareness.

Yet Descartes has promised to reveal "the nature" of the human mind, or thinking thing. Earlier in the Meditation, he equated a "thing that thinks" with a "mind, or intelligence, or intellect, or reason" (7:27). This suggests a new answer to our question. Intellect (or reason) is the essential feature of the thinking thing; it provides us with the nature of thought. And, indeed, in reply to Hobbes, Descartes apparently suggests this very answer. There he says that the various "acts of thought, such as understanding, willing, imagining, having sense perceptions...all fall under the common concept of thought or perception or consciousness" (7:176). Perhaps, then, the various acts are all thoughts inasmuch as they are perceptions (hence acts of the intellect [see 7:78; also 8A:17]). Under this conception, Descartes did not single out consciousness as the essence of thought but rather considered consciousness to be intrinsic to thoughts inasmuch as they are acts of the intellect. At any rate, we should keep this possibility in mind as we continue through the *Meditations*.

Wax argument – knowledge of body (7:29–33)

Having arrived at an enlarged conception of the thinking thing, Descartes has the meditator pause and change scenes. Up to this point she has accepted that states of mind can be known, while the existence of body remains in doubt. She has accepted that the *existence* of a thinking thing is better known than that of body, but Descartes has promised to show that the *nature* of mind is better known than that of body.

To focus the meditator on the natures of mind and body, Descartes frames for her a supposedly nagging question:

> But it still appears – and I cannot stop thinking this – that the corporeal things of which images are formed in my thought, and which the senses investigate, are known with much more distinctness than this puzzling "I" which cannot be pictured in the imagination. [7:29]

In fact, in the course of the Meditation, the meditator has not made any protests on behalf of bodies but has dutifully doubted their existence. This newly framed worry, which acknowledges a reservation that readers might actually have, serves two functions. First, it raises a question about the comparative knowledge of the natures of mind and body. Second, it frames this question in relation to the cognitive faculties by which mind and body are known.

Earlier in the Meditation, Descartes presented considerations to convince the meditator that mind is not known through images or the imagination. He now raises a small protest against this point (by characterizing the unimaginable "I" as "puzzling"). Recall that the meditator, whether an Aristotelian or an untutored person of good sense, previously thought of both mind and body using the imagination. More generally, she supposedly had considered the senses and imagination to be essential in all knowledge. Descartes now intends to lay this preconceived opinion to rest.

Descartes returns to a topic from the First Meditation, our knowledge of "the bodies we touch and see." The meditator is not asked to reconsider whether such bodies exist; rather, she is now to consider how, or whether, she "understands" them. In this context, to understand a body is to know what it is – that is, to understand its nature. Descartes presents individual bodies as "the things which people commonly think they understand most distinctly of all" (7:30). True, as a result of the First Meditation the meditator now considers bodies to be "doubtful, unknown and foreign to me" (7:29). But, for the purposes of this new investigation, she is permitted her old belief that bodies are distinctly known and is allowed to assume that she sees and touches actual bodies.

There is no harm or inconsistency in allowing the meditator to suppose that she can see and touch bodies. The matter in question does not concern the existence of bodies. Rather, the meditator is undertaking a thought experiment concerning the nature of body.

The argument to show that the nature of mind is better understood than that of body is an indirect proof. Descartes has the meditator grant an opposing assumption – that bodies are understood better ("more distinctly") than mind because we have images of them. He then attempts to show two things. First, that even the nature of body is not known through images. Second, that this finding shows that the nature of mind is better known than that of body.

Perceiving the wax

The investigation to determine what is distinctly understood in body focuses on a particular body, a piece of beeswax just taken from a honeycomb. (Although Descartes focuses the meditator on a piece of wax, we should keep in mind that his aim is for her to investigate what is known in bodies more generally; the wax is just an example.) The wax retains the flavor of honey and the scent of flowers, is cold and hard, makes a sound when tapped, and has a particular color, shape, and size (7:30). When placed by the fire, however, all these properties change: it loses its flavor and scent, changes color, becomes liquid and hot, and alters its shape and size as it melts into a small puddle.

Through all these changes, we consider ourselves to be perceiving the same wax.

> Does the same wax remain? It must be admitted that it does; no one denies it, no one thinks otherwise. So what was it in the wax that I understood with such distinctness? Evidently none of the features which I arrived at by means of the senses; for whatever came under taste, smell, sight, touch or hearing has now altered – yet the wax remains. [7:30]

The meditator adopts the position that whatever it is that we understand in the piece of wax, it must be something found in it both before and after it melts. The wax has a particular color, odor, and shape before it melts and a different color, odor, and shape afterwards, yet we perceive and understand it to be the same stuff throughout its transformation. Therefore, what we understand in the wax (as the body that persisted through these changes) cannot be the particular instances of those properties. So the meditator sets out to determine what is known in the piece of wax despite such changes.

Finding what is understood in the wax

The meditator is investigating the nature of bodies, or what is understood in them, by contemplating some changes in a piece of wax. She carefully examines what remained in the wax throughout the changes:

> Perhaps the answer lies in the thought which now comes to my mind; namely, the wax was not after all the sweetness of the honey, or the fragrance of the flowers, or the whiteness, or the shape, or the sound, but was rather a body which presented itself to me in these various forms a little while ago, but which now exhibits different ones. But what exactly is it that I am now imagining? Let us concentrate, take away everything which does not belong to the wax, and see what is left: merely something extended, flexible, and changeable. [7:30–1]

The nature of the wax will be something it always has, not something it loses if heated or reshaped. And, indeed, although its sensory properties changed it remained an instance of "body" throughout. So perhaps what is understood in a body is more basic than any of those sensory properties. The meditator seeks to isolate what was understood throughout the changes and concludes that the wax remained something "extended, flexible, and changeable." "Extension" just means that it has spatial extent. "Flexible" and "changeable" mean that it has the capacity to change shape, size, and perhaps other properties (although Descartes focuses on only shape and size, where size means the apparent size of its outer boundary). The wax retained these capacities even as its particular properties changed.

Careful contemplation of the wax has purportedly shown that its determinable spatial properties – its extension, its capacity to have a size and shape – remain, even when other properties, including the way in which it is extended (e.g., its determinate shape, or its degree of rigidity) change. (The word "determinable" is used to refer to the fact that a property can have many instances without referring to any one of them; the word "determinate" indicates that some particular instance, such as a specific size or shape, is referred to.)

The wax certainly does have, as we would now say, spatio-temporal continuity. It has spatial extension, which changes in location, size, and shape over time. When Descartes says it is "extended, flexible, and changeable," the latter two words suggest that it, the wax, is capable of many changes of shape, across which it remains the same. However, an Aristotelian or an untutored person of good sense might observe that the wax is also capable of taking on various colors, odors, and temperatures. When it melts, it doesn't completely lose all color and odor; rather, it becomes a translucent, whitish material with a waxy odor. So why doesn't Descartes find that it is "changeable" as regards color, odor, temperature, etc.? Why focus on the bare spatial properties as what is understood in bodies?

Consider Descartes' thought experiment for yourself. In doing so, you must ignore scientific knowledge subsequent to the time of Descartes: knowledge that mass is a fundamental property of matter, that different kinds of matter differ in specific gravity and in chemical composition, that beeswax is a complex hydrocarbon in which some other compounds are suspended, etc. Now think about the transformation of the wax as it melts. It seems right that we clearly grasp the wax, through its changes, as a bounded region that alters shape and size. That part of his positive result is sustained. But do we not also see that it remains determinable as regards color and temperature? That is not ruled out. But are these properties understood with great "distinctness" (7:30)? Do we understand the property of the wax that renders it determinable as regards color with the same clarity as we understand its mutability as regards its overall shape?

It is difficult to answer this question through the thought experiment alone. It must therefore remain open. But we should recall that Descartes' audience – whether an Aristotelian, or a person of good sense tutored in geometry without reaching the philosophy curriculum – would be familiar with Euclid's geometry. Euclid's geometry was the basis of mathematical education and was regarded as the very paradigm of intelligibility. Perhaps Descartes was relying on an intuitive clarity in the notion of "capable of changes of shape" that he expected not to be found in "capable of changes of color." That might draw in his opponent for a moment. But, in fact, he moves on to a potentially more devastating argument, according to which the sensory images of the wax – which were *supposed* to allow it to be known with such distinctness – do not permit us to grasp its nature at all.

Discovering how the wax is understood

In contemplating the wax the meditator has thus far concluded that its nature consists in a determinable extension that can alter its determinate spatial properties over time. How is this property, the wax's mutable extension, perceived? Is it perceived by sight or touch? Is it grasped through the imagination, by picturing the various changes in shape that are possible? Descartes answers "no" in both cases, and in so doing he purports to arrive at a new insight into how the wax is known and also into the mind that knows the wax.

He offers the meditator an argument from elimination, which seeks to rule out the imagination as the faculty that grasps the mutability of the wax's extension. The argument involves a further examination of the wax's mutable shape:

> But what is meant here by "flexible" and "changeable"? Is it what I picture in my imagination: that this piece of wax is capable of changing from a round shape to a square shape, or from a square shape to a triangular shape? Not at all: for I can grasp that the wax is capable of countless changes of this kind, yet I am unable to run through this immeasurable number of changes in my imagination, from which it follows that it is not the faculty of imagination that gives me my grasp of the wax as flexible and changeable. [7:31]

One key premise is the claim that "I can grasp that the wax is capable of countless changes of this kind." This points to something that the meditator is supposed to discover about her own understanding of the wax – that a flexible extended thing can take on indefinitely many shapes. A second key premise is that the imagination is unable to "run through," that is, separately to imagine, each member in the full series of shapes. A further implicit premise is that the only way the imagination, the faculty of images, could allow us to grasp this series would be for it to picture each member individually. But it is unable to. Hence the imagination cannot be the faculty by which we grasp the nature of the wax (now considered simply as a mutable body).

Thus far, the argument rules out the imagination as the faculty by which the wax is grasped. What is left? Here is where the argument from elimination comes in. The imagination is unable to represent the changes. The senses represent even fewer shapes (only the ones the wax actually takes on). But we nonetheless grasp its ability to undergo countless changes. How? The answer comes: it is done "by the mind alone" (7:31).

This answer requires some explanation. In preparation, let us consider the argument as it might be evaluated by an Aristotelian. The argument can be formulated as follows:

1   I can grasp that this melted wax is flexible and changeable so as to be capable of innumerable changes of shape.
2   Imagination could allow me to grasp this fact only by representing these changes by an image of each possible shape.

3   My imagination cannot represent the innumerable shapes required.
4   It is not the imagination that allows me to grasp this capability of the wax.
5   But I do grasp this capability, so it must be by a faculty other than (sense or) imagination: call it the mind itself.

Although the meditator is supposed to accept premise 1 as a result of the melting episode, that episode as perceived by sense cannot be its sole support. The Second Meditation does not make clear whether premise 1 might be based on many observations of wax and other bodies or must itself arise through a purely intellectual perception of bodies as extended. An Aristotelian would claim that premise 1 is grounded in previous experience, which permits the intellect to grasp the mutability of the wax. He might further grant premises 2 to 4 but observe that in his view a finite sequence of images would provide the intellect with sufficient basis on which to abstract the intelligible extension of the wax. He might then add a few premises of his own (about all thoughts requiring images) and rephrase the conclusion (5) to say: "I grasp this capability through the intellect, which must use the images in the imagination."

An Aristotelian would find other aspects of the argument misdirected. According to an Aristotelian account, to grasp the nature of the wax, one would need to grasp its substantial form, which wouldn't even include extension, flexibility, and mutability (since the Aristotelians considered extension to be a universally present accident in bodies but not any part of their essence), but would include the qualities of the wax (the hot, cold, wet, and dry of the elements, and perhaps others). Moreover, he would expect to grasp one nature in wax and another in any other body. However, Descartes has explicitly characterized the piece of wax as a representative example of how any sort of body is known or understood (7:30). To the extent that the wax argument supports the claim that what is distinctly known in the wax is simply extended body, it provides a beginning for Descartes' argument that extension is the essence of all material substance and hence of all bodies. But it is not adequate by itself to establish that conclusion, and Descartes avoids claiming that it has (7:175).

Returning to the conclusion of the argument, the claim that "the mind alone" grasps the nature of the wax is at first enigmatic. Descartes immediately elaborates on it. He says that our perception of the nature of the wax "is a case not of vision or touch or imagination – nor has it ever been, despite previous appearances – but of purely mental inspection" (7:31*). Such inspection can be "imperfect and confused, as it was before" – presumably, when the mind was using the senses and imagination to try to understand the nature of the wax – "or clear and distinct as it is now, depending on how carefully I concentrate on what the wax consists in" (7:31). To the Aristotelian and the untutored person of good sense, each of whom believed that the senses and imagination are always involved in thoughts about bodies, this would truly be a revelation. As Descartes has it, even when we use the senses to see the wax, we grasp "what the wax consists in" through the mind alone.

Near the end of this Meditation, Descartes provides the meditator with a name for the faculty by which this mental scrutiny takes place – it is the intellect (7:34), which is what he means by "the mind alone." In the meantime, however, he considers an objection that arises from considering how we speak about the relation between sense perception and acts of judgment (involving intellect).

Analysis of perceptual judgment (cloaked men) (7:32)

We usually think of philosophy as something that exists through words, whether written or spoken. In recent times, some philosophers and other thinkers have held that thought (or at least theoretical thought as found in science and metaphysics) can occur only through language. Whether one accepts this position or not, Descartes did not hold it. He agreed that language is used to express thoughts, but he conceived of the thoughts as having their own mental standing, independent of language. Acts of contemplation or meditation go on, as he puts it, "within myself, silently and without a word" (7:31–2*).

Nonetheless, in considering how the topic of sense perception is normally discussed in words, Descartes sees a problem: "the words themselves bring me up short, and I am almost tricked by the use of speech" (7:32*). The problem arises because, although the meditator has concluded that seeing the wax and grasping its nature are accomplished not by the eyes but by "the mind alone," that does not accord with what we say:

> We say that we see the wax itself, if it is there before us, not that we judge it to be there from its color or shape; and this might lead me to conclude without more ado that knowledge of the wax comes from what the eye sees, and not from the scrutiny of the mind alone. [7:32]

That is, ordinarily we think that, through vision (or other senses), we are immediately aware of various objects in our surroundings, whether wax, a table, or a friend who has just called us away from our meditation. And we experience them as being wax, a table, or a friend. Isn't this a purely sensory matter?

Descartes says that it is not. To recognize something as being wax, a table, or a friend, we need an additional mental act beyond experiencing the mere images of the senses. Here is his argument:

> If I look out of the window and see men crossing the square, as I just happen to have done, I normally say that I see the men themselves, just as I say that I see the wax. Yet do I see any more than hats and coats which could conceal automatons? I *judge* that they are men. And so something which I thought I was seeing with my eyes is in fact grasped solely by the faculty of judgment which is in my mind. [7:32]

It may happen, when we observe people walking away from us in chilly weather, that we only see their clothing: hats and coats. Yet we say that we "see" the people themselves. The perceptual image that we have is consistent with our seeing mechanical constructions, now called robots, that have been clothed and made to walk like people. Given that the sensory image could be the same in the two cases, what counts for our taking the content of our current experience (rightly or wrongly) to be people? Descartes locates the added content, going beyond the bare image, in a judgment. We (tacitly, it seems) judge that human beings are before us. Indeed, as we shall see in Chapter 9, Descartes believed that much of the content we ordinarily ascribe to bare sense perception actually results from tacitly made judgments.

In this example, as with the wax, Descartes speaks of grasping an object of perception "solely by the faculty of judgment" as opposed to seeing it with the eyes. It might therefore seem as if he is saying, even in the case of seeing a particular piece of wax, or people in the square, that the eyes (or visual experience, considered simply as an experienced image) play no role in these perceptions. That would be an odd position, for it would assert that we can perceive a particular piece of wax, or people in the square, without any sensory input! That is not Descartes' point. He is saying that the purely sensory component of perception, which he equates here with the experienced "pictures" of things (the spatially organized array of colors we experience in a scene), cannot constitute our perception of the nature of the piece of wax or of the fact that "men" (as he puts it) are present. For these richer perceptual achievements, a judging mind or intellect is required, beyond the bare image. (As we will see in Chapter 6, the will is also required for judgment to occur, but that doesn't affect the present point about the necessary role of intellect. Furthermore, in the Sixth Replies Descartes refined his account of purely sensory images, which he assigned to the "second grade of sense" or sense perception proper, as distinguished from our fully formed sensory experience, produced through unnoticed or habitual judgments [7:437–8].)

Moreover, Descartes tells us, it is this intellectual capacity that separates human beings from animals. He places mere sensory and imaginal representation on the level of non-human animals; the perception of the nature of the wax, of the wax "without its outward forms," requires a human mind (7:32). This contrast would not have been lost on his audience. The standard view was that humans differ from animals precisely in the possession of intellect or reason. We will see later, in Chapter 9, that Descartes denied sensory awareness to animals. According to his theory, sensory awareness occurs only in beings possessing an intellect. The relation between sensation and intellection is further examined in Meditation 6.

Mind better known than body (7:33–4)

Descartes now returns to applying these considerations to the project of knowing the "I." The analysis of the perception of wax reveals that mind is better known than body in at least two ways. First, its existence is more firmly known. As he puts it, "if I judge that the wax exists from the fact that I see it, clearly this same fact entails much more evidently that I myself also exist" (7:33). Any act of perceiving a body provides evidence for the existence of mind, since a mind is required for perception. (At this point, we still don't know whether mind differs from body; but it remains that a mind is required for knowing wax, and hence that that mind's existence is known.) However, it is difficult to see why the wax argument would be needed to make this point, since he had already established earlier that instances of putative seeing provide evidence for the existence of mind (7:28–9). (See also Gassendi's Objections, 7:274–6.)

However, there is a second, deeper, point to be found in the wax discussion, which moves beyond the mind's existence to reveal a special and defining aspect of mind. The new finding arrives in two consecutive passages that conclude both the wax example and the entire investigation of the "I" in the Second Meditation. The first passage continues the argument that the existence of mind is proved by any act of perception, including touching the wax or imagining it. In each case, it follows "that I who am now thinking" exist. Descartes proposes that such results also reveal the nature of mind:

> Moreover, if my perception of the wax seemed more distinct after it was established not just by sight or touch but by many other considerations, it must be admitted that I now know myself even more distinctly. This is because every consideration whatsoever which contributes to my perception of the wax, or of any other body, cannot but establish even more effectively the nature of my own mind. But besides this, there is so much else in the mind itself which can serve to make my knowledge of it more distinct, that it scarcely seems worth going through the contributions made by considering bodily things. [7:33]

Two claims of great moment are made here. First, Descartes says that every case of perceiving the wax, in any manner, establishes "even more effectively the nature of my own mind." How each case does so is not immediately apparent. Presumably, the nature of the mind is revealed through the various instances of perceiving the wax, because these instances share something in common. What is common to the various cases of perceiving the wax, whether by sight, touch, imagination, or the "mind alone"? Consciousness would be one candidate, but Descartes does not mention it. But he has just mentioned that a judgment of the intellect must be ascribed to each of these acts. Indeed, he has argued at some length that an essential property of mind present in any act of perceiving the wax is (intellectual) judgment.

The passage makes a second important claim, that there is "much else in the mind itself," beyond sense perceptions and imaginings, that would allow it to be known distinctly. Sense perception and imagination take bodies as their object. The things "in the mind itself" presumably do not have bodies for their object or involve the perception of bodies in any way. The point that mind is not known through images has been made twice before in the Meditation, when Descartes argues that mind cannot be directly imagined (7:27–8), and that even though the mind cannot be pictured, it is better known than body (7:29–30). Mind must be able to be known independently of picture-like experiences. Hence, the primary things that have come to be known "in the mind itself" are the judgments of the intellect involved in every act of perception of any sort. Our knowledge of such judgments, and hence of the judging mind, is something over and above, or outside, images.

The second passage sums up the results of the investigation of the "I":

> I see that without any effort I have now finally got back to where I wanted. I now know that even bodies are not strictly perceived by the senses or the faculty of imagination but by the intellect alone, and that this perception derives not from their being touched or seen but from their being understood; and in view of this I know plainly that I can achieve an easier and more evident perception of my own mind than of anything else. [7:34]

The fact that any genuine perception of bodies depends on "the intellect alone" permits a "perception" of his own mind. What sort of perception? *That* it exists? This has long been established in the Meditation, and in any event the title has promised us an insight into "the nature of the human mind." Although Descartes is not completely clear about what this perception of the mind reveals, our investigation suggests that it reveals that judgment and intellect are essential properties of the mind or are required for a human mind. Indeed, we have seen that in the Synopsis (7:12) he promised that the Second Meditation would enable the mind to discriminate its own "intellectual nature" from things that belong to bodies (even without establishing whether an intellectual nature can also be material). As the *Meditations* continues, we will see that in becoming aware of the pervasive function of the intellect in human cognition, Descartes believed he had discovered the essential feature of the human mind, the common element in its nature.

The *cogito* investigation

The Second Meditation may be seen as one long investigation into the nature of the "I." This investigation begins just after the conclusion, "I exist," has been reached. It examines both the "I" and the means by which the "I" is known. Initially, it is found that the "I" can be known independently of any thought of bodily processes (such as digestion, locomotion, or the activity of sense organs). The inquiry then turns to the faculties by which both mental and bodily things are known. This second line of inquiry unites with the primary investigation at the end of the Meditation, when it is discovered that the intellect, by which the "I" is grasped, and which is implicated in every act of sense perception, is a fundamental feature of the "I" as known thus far.

The *cogito* investigation can be summed up through four conclusions, from the initial to the final result. Each conclusion starts from and expands a previous result. The initial conclusion begins from an awareness of the meditator's own thoughts:

Initial conclusion: I exist.
Extended conclusion: I exist as a thinking thing.

Enlarged conclusion: A thinking thing is a thing that doubts, understands, affirms, denies, is willing or unwilling, imagines, and has
sensory perceptions.

Final result: The intellect is an essential feature of myself as a mind,
and of all mental activities.

The *cogito* reasoning is completed only with the final result.

Descartes believed that the final result, awareness of an intellectual
faculty that can know things independently of images, would be difficult for his readers to grasp. As he explained in the Second Replies,
"protracted and repeated study is required to eradicate the lifelong
habit of confusing things related to the intellect with corporeal things,
and to replace it with the opposite habit of distinguishing the two."
The effort to do so, which should take at least "a few days to acquire,"
was worthwhile because it was required for distinguishing in thought
"the properties or qualities of mind" from "the qualities of body"
(7:131). The latter distinction – which arises in the Second Meditation
through the exercise of doubting body while affirming mind, and the
further exercise of seeing how the natures of both mind and body are
understood – subsequently serves as a basis for the real distinction
between mind and body. The Second Meditation does not reach that
far. It is devoted to teaching the meditator to achieve awareness of the
mind as something that can be known without thinking of bodily
attributes or processes, and of intellect as the faculty that cognizes
"intellectual things" without contemplating images. In the Third
Meditation, Descartes will contend that not only the mind or soul but
also God is cognized through the pure intellect. And in the Sixth
Meditation, he will argue that extension, or the essence of matter, can
also be cognized in this way, as well as through the images of sense
perception and imagination.

References and further reading

The *cogito* reasoning, usually restricted to the initial and extended
results above, has been extensively analyzed, as have the "thinking
thing" and the wax argument; see the commentaries of Curley,
Dicker, and Wilson. Recent work on the *cogito* is reviewed in P.

Markie, "The Cogito and Its Importance," in Cottingham (ed.), *Cambridge Companion to Descartes*, pp. 140–73.

B. Williams examines Lichtenberg's challenge in his *Descartes: The Project of Pure Enquiry*, ch. 3; he also distinguishes Descartes' general premise from a syllogistic major premise. For translation and discussion of Lichtenberg's aphorism on the *cogito*, see J.P. Stern, *Lichtenberg: A Doctrine of Scattered Opinions* (Bloomington: Indiana University Press, 1960), pp. 270, 314. J. Carriero reads the Second Meditation against the background of Aristotelian accounts of self-knowledge in "The Second Meditation and the Essence of the Mind," in Rorty (ed.), *Essays on Descartes' Meditations*, pp. 199–221.

On the sense of the term "definition" as delimiting a domain of application (among other senses), see the glossary by J.J.E. Garcia appended to his translation of F. Suarez, *On Individuation* (Milwaukee: Marquette University Press, 1982), pp. 175–279, at pp. 200–1. This glossary explains much of the vocabulary of scholastic Aristotelianism, which Descartes knew and adapted to his needs. For instance, in Aristotelian philosophy the term "nature" might mean a principle of motion or activity, and in other contexts it might mean essence or common nature. Descartes may well have been trading on both meanings in revealing the "nature" of mind (its characteristic activities) in the present Meditation, although he only fully arrived at its essence as a substance in the Sixth Meditation. (Although often, as in the Fifth Meditation, he uses "essence" and "nature" interchangeably.)

Study of the place of consciousness in Descartes' philosophy has been rendered difficult for readers of English translations. E. Anscombe and P. Geach, in their *Descartes: Philosophical Writings* (Indianapolis: Bobbs-Merrill, 1971), translated the Latin *cogitatio* (thinking, a thought) and related words as "consciousness" or "experience." CSM doesn't offer "consciousness," even for the Latin *conscius*, but instead uses "aware" (7:49), which it also uses for other words found more often in the text, such as *animadvertere* (to notice, to attend to) or *cognoscere* (to cognize, to know). I have emended passages from CSM to be closer to the Latin. In any case, study of local word usage won't settle questions about consciousness and the essence of thought in Descartes; the reader should consider the issue in light of Descartes' systematic presentation of his metaphysics and should avoid putting great weight on single words without consulting the original language editions.

M. Williams, "Descartes and the Metaphysics of Doubt," in Rorty (ed.), *Essays on Descartes' Meditations*, pp. 117–39, reads Descartes as treating the incorrigibly known contents of (sensory) consciousness as building blocks for subsequent knowledge, like the sense data of earlier twentieth-century philosophy. R. Rorty, *Philosophy and the Mirror of Nature* (Princeton, NJ: Princeton University Press, 1979), ch. 1, draws on earlier versions of that reading and also claims that Descartes "invented the mind" through a mistaken equation of thought with the contents of consciousness.

Chapter 5

Truth, God, and the circle

Meditation 3: The existence of God

The Third Meditation promises to establish a meta-physical result, "the existence of God." Descartes offers two proofs of that result, both from effects. Each proof argues that a known effect can be explained only if a supreme being exists. The effects he uses are the meditator's idea of God and her existence as a finite being.

However, the Third Meditation is by no means limited to God's existence. It begins by re-examining the *cogito* reasoning, hoping to extract from that first success a method for coming to know other truths with equal certainty. It then reconsiders the deceiving-God hypothesis, which is ultimately rejected on the ground that God's perfection rules out such deception. In preparation for the proofs from effects, it analyzes the notion of an idea and offers a theory of ideas and their content, and the mind's relations to that content. It also draws an important distinction between the "teachings of nature" and "natural light." This distinction is used in evaluating the origins of the meditator's ideas and is later invoked (in the Sixth Meditation) in reframing the place of the senses in human cognition.

In connection with the proofs about God, Descartes introduces a variety of metaphysical terms and concepts that later serve as foundations for his physics (discussed in Chapter 9). The present chapter focuses on the methodological extraction of a rule for recognizing truth, the relation of the rule to the natural light, and the use of the natural light in the proofs for the existence of God.

Review: doubts body, knows mind (7:34–5)

The reviews at the beginning of each meditation serve to refocus the investigation in light of preceding results. The beginning of the Third Meditation reiterates the meditator's knowledge of her own thoughts and existence and reaffirms her intent to "withdraw" from the senses and "eliminate from my thoughts all images of bodily things" (7:34). Since such an elimination is "hardly possible" (the images of the senses keep arising, despite what we will), she will simply consider such images as "vacuous, false and worthless." She repeats the conclusion that "I am a thing that thinks" and reprises the list of kinds of thinking she finds in herself (7:34–5). For the meditator, her existence as a thinking thing, and the list of acts of thinking, comprise "everything I truly know, or at least everything I have so far discovered that I know" (7:35). She will now look for knowledge of "other things" within herself that she may not yet have noticed. The first such "thing" turns out to be a method for acquiring knowledge.

Extraction of truth rule, clear and distinct perception (7:35)

The meditator considers the question of "what is required for my being certain about anything" (7:35). She asks whether the *cogito* conclusion, and the cognitive acts supporting it, might offer a general model of what is required for "being certain," or achieving certain knowledge, about anything. This often neglected passage is in fact quite important, for if Descartes could extract a method (or *the* method) for achieving certain knowledge here at the beginning of the Third Meditation, he would have found an Archimedean point from which "great things" – that is, more knowledge – might be achieved. He would perhaps have discovered the key to the "stable" and "lasting" knowledge foreseen in the opening paragraph of the First Meditation.

It will, therefore, be worthwhile to examine this passage carefully. It starts by reasserting the extended *cogito* conclusion and continues by extracting a rule for recognizing truth:

> I am certain that I am a thinking thing. Do I not therefore also know what is required for my being certain about anything? In this first item of knowledge there is simply a clear and distinct perception of what I am asserting; this would not be enough to make me certain of the truth of the matter if it could ever turn out that something which I perceived with such clarity and distinctness was false. So I now seem to be able to lay it down as a general rule that whatever I perceive very clearly and distinctly is true. [7:35]

Here the meditator restates a piece of knowledge and asks how it is known. The question does not concern the particular premises or evidence supporting the extended *cogito* conclusion; rather, it seeks a criterion or rule of truth implicit in this first result. The rule here proposed, "that whatever I perceive very clearly and distinctly is true," will come to guide the meditator's subsequent metaphysical investigations. But here she concludes only that she "seems" to be able to lay down this rule. We therefore need first to examine the argument and then (in the next section) to consider what reason the meditator has for pause.

The argument may be summarized in three premises. This summary assumes that when Descartes wrote of "certainty" about the conclusion of the *cogito* reasoning, he implied a claim to *know* the truth of that conclusion (as the wording in the quotation indicates):

1   I know with certainty that I am a thinking thing.
2   This knowledge is based solely on a clear and distinct perception of its truth.
3   Clear and distinct perception would not be sufficient to yield such knowledge if it were in any way fallible.
4   Therefore, clear and distinct perception provides a sufficient ground for knowledge; whatever I so perceive is true.

Some of the premises are more straightforward than others. If the meditator has accepted the *cogito* reasoning, then premise 1 is already allowed. Premise 3 reports the standard of infallible knowledge as accepted in the First Meditation (and frequently accepted throughout the history of philosophy), so it is not problematic in this context. One might wonder whether it can be used to establish the general reliability of clear and distinct perception as a method of knowing, using only a single instance of knowledge (as reported in premise 1). In principle, there is nothing wrong with this procedure, as long as other appropriate conditions are met, such as that the paradigmatic instance really is acquired solely through the method in question. This condition is asserted by premise 2, which does the real work in the argument and so requires further examination.

Premise 2 addresses the cognitive basis for the claim in premise 1. It does not address the specific premises that support the conclusion of premise 1 – such as "I am having such and such thought" – but concerns the method by which such premises were seen to yield the truth of this conclusion. The method is alleged to be "clear and distinct perception." Premise 2 claims that the *cogito* result relies only on clear and distinct perception. The meditator can evaluate this claim only by examining the contents of her own mind to find the salient feature of the *cogito* reasoning, the one that establishes its certainty and thereby (presumably) its truth.

The argument given above is logically valid. For it to be sound, premise 2 must report the actual method used by the meditator to establish the extended *cogito*. If the meditator is deceived about the basis of the *cogito* reasoning, and it does not depend on clear and distinct perception, or if it does not depend on that alone, then the argument is unsound (because this premise is false). But if premise 2 accurately reports the method that establishes the truth of premise 1, then, given premise 3, the conclusion (4) has been established.

The conclusion of the argument is that clear and distinct perception yields *truth*. Yet the quotation above says only that the *cogito* conclusion is *certain*. Is there a distinction between certainty and truth? Ordinarily there is. We can be certain of something (say, that our friend will win the chess tournament) and yet be wrong. Certainty of belief is ordinarily considered to be consistent with the belief's falsehood. In interpreting Descartes, however, we will assume that he used the term "certainty" to mean "certain knowledge of the truth," so that his writings do not permit a terminological distinction between mere certainty and truth. (He must still show that his arguments for certainty are arguments for certain knowledge of the truth, not merely for certainty in the ordinary sense.)

Even if we accept that the above argument establishes a method for finding truth, a problem remains. How are we to recognize when our perceptions are clear and distinct? We have, presumably, all been convinced by the *cogito*. But do we find a quality of mind attending this conviction that we can recognize and therefore use as a sign of truth in other cases? Gassendi raised this question in the Fifth Objections (7:318), and it has been raised many times since. If we can't recognize clear and distinct perceptions and distinguish them from other perceptions that are not clear and distinct, the proposed truth rule is useless.

Descartes offers no definition of or criterion for clear and distinct perception in the *Meditations* proper. One might expect to find a definition in the Geometrical Arguments, which seek to demonstrate the main metaphysical conclusions of the *Meditations* directly and briefly. But in that exposition, the exact phrase "clear and distinct perception" appears relatively late, and it remains undefined (7:164). Descartes introduces the correlative methodological notion through a series of instructions to his readers for noticing and reflecting on things that can (allegedly) be clearly and distinctly perceived. He first directs his readers to shun the senses and reflect on their own mind until they are "in the habit of perceiving it clearly" (7:162); he then asks them to consider "self-evident propositions" (Latin *per se nota*) so as to exercise their "intellectual vision" or "perspicuity" (7:163*); he asks them to consider ideas of the natures or essences of various things, including God, and then to reflect on the examples of clear and distinct perception, as well as of obscure and confused perception, from the various Meditations (7:164). In effect, he relies on his readers to recognize clear and distinct perceptions through examples. (In the *Principles*, he defines "clear" and "distinct" [8A:21–2], although not in a way that avoids appeal to his readers' own abilities to recognize instances.)

In the remaining Meditations, new examples of clear and distinct ideas or perceptions are offered at regular intervals, including, further on in the Third, the "utterly clear and distinct" idea of God (7:46). In that way, the Geometrical Arguments mimic the actual procedure of the main work. However, beyond appealing to instances, in the Fourth Meditation Descartes offers an additional factor useful for recognizing clear and distinct perceptions, to be examined in Chapter 6.

Dialectic of doubt (7:35–6)

The meditator immediately considers some reasons for pause concerning the proposed rule of truth. She observes that she previously accepted many things "as wholly certain and evident" (7:35) that she now doubts. These include all the objects she thought she apprehended through the senses. She now questions her earlier, habitual belief "that there were things outside me which were the sources of my ideas and which resembled them in all respects" (7:35). This "resemblance thesis" will undergo further scrutiny in the Sixth Meditation and there be rejected. At present, that thesis is one of the "preconceived opinions" that the meditator used to think she perceived clearly but now (by comparison with the clarity and distinctness of the *cogito*) finds she did not. The fact that she once firmly held such preconceived opinions does not really challenge the new criterion; rather, comparison with the new standard of clarity allows her to reaffirm the doubtful status of her previous beliefs.

The most serious challenge to the truth rule is the unresolved deceiving-God hypothesis. This hypothesis was used in the First Meditation to cast doubt even on the transparent truths of mathematics, such as that $2 + 3 = 5$. Yet those truths, now described as "simple and straightforward" (7:35), must surely meet the newly proposed standard of clear and distinct perception. The meditator reflects on just this point:

> Did I not at least see these things clearly enough to affirm their truth? Indeed, the only reason for my later judgment that they were open to doubt was that it occurred to me that perhaps some God could have given me a nature such that I was deceived even in matters which seemed most evident. And whenever my preconceived belief in the supreme power of God comes to mind, I cannot but admit that it would be easy for him, if he so desired, to bring it about that I go wrong even in those matters which I think I see utterly clearly with my mind's eye. [7:36]

This passage sets up an opposition between the "simple," "clear," and "most evident" truths of mathematics and a "later judgment" that they were open to doubt. But, interestingly, the ground for doubting them is now itself described as a "preconceived belief" in an all-powerful God. The passage pits clear perceptions, for which the meditator has a newly found appreciation, against grounds for doubt that are based on mere preconceived opinion.

Descartes now has the meditator engage in a kind of dialectical interplay between doubt and certainty. As previously noted, the truths of mathematics can be doubted "whenever my preconceived belief in the supreme power of God comes to mind." But there is another side:

> Yet when I turn to the things themselves which I think I perceive very clearly, I am so convinced by them that I spontaneously declare: let whoever can do so deceive me, he will never bring it about that I am nothing, so long as I continue to think I am something; or make it true at some future time that I have never existed, since it is now true that I exist; or bring it about that two and three added together are more or less than five, or anything of this kind in which I see a manifest contradiction. [7:36]

In this passage, the mathematical equation $2 + 3 = 5$ is placed on a par with the *cogito* conclusion. Furthermore, the wording suggests that doubt about such truths cannot arise when one is directly contemplating them; it can arise only when one turns to the deceiving-God hypothesis. (Descartes reaffirms this contrast in the Second Replies [7:144–6].) And this suggests that the deceiving-God hypothesis can have its effect only when one is not directly considering the clear and distinct perception of some particular truth. Moreover – and this implication is somewhat astonishing – it would seem that when one is considering that hypothesis, it is able to cast aspersion on all clear and distinct perceptions considered in general (and so including the *cogito* conclusion). Thus the meditator is caught: while thinking of some beliefs, she cannot but affirm their truth. But when considering the deceiving-God hypothesis, she can apparently doubt anything. (However, we may note that since this very act of doubting provides grounds for subsequently reaffirming the *cogito*, a blanket doubt covering the *cogito* conclusion provides grounds for undermining itself, in a way that a blanket doubt covering mathematical truths does not; hence the *cogito* retains its special status [see 7:145–6].)

Nonetheless, the deceiving-God hypothesis cannot be shaken simply by staying focused on clear and distinct perceptions. There are two reasons for this, one practical, one theoretical. As Descartes explains elsewhere, it would actually be impossible to stay focused on a clear and distinct perception all the time, for we are psychologically incapable of doing so (7:62; see also 4:116). Second, the meditator is involved in a search for stable truth. As long as the deceiving-God hypothesis remains alive, the meditator has a standing objection that impugns her clear and distinct perceptions. The fact that she may not be thinking of that objection while having clear and distinct perceptions, or that the hypothesis has no effect on her assent to such perceptions during that particular time, is irrelevant if her aim is some "stable" and "lasting" truth. Presumably, she doesn't want merely to be momentarily free from doubt; she wants to remove the doubts she has raised once and for all.

In fact, Descartes presents the situation in just this manner. In continuing the passage quoted above, he explains why the deceiving-God hypothesis must be investigated and, if possible, laid to rest:

And since I have no cause to think that there is a deceiving God, and I do not yet even know for sure whether there is a God at all, any reason for doubt which depends simply on this supposition is a very slight and, so to speak, metaphysical one. But in order to remove even this slight reason for doubt, as soon as the opportunity arises I must examine whether there is a God, and, if there is, whether he can be a deceiver. For if I do not know this, it seems that I can never be quite certain about anything else. [7:36]

He here presents the deceiving-God hypothesis as "slight" and "metaphysical." (In calling it "metaphysical," he presumably means to emphasize its removal from everyday concerns, and from an everyday standard of what is *certain enough* – a standard then known as "moral," by contrast with "metaphysical," certainty [see 6:37–8].) Even so, the hypothesis remains sufficient to undermine the sort of knowledge the meditator seeks, which must meet the high standard of being immune from doubt – not from willful or arbitrary doubt, but from reasoned doubt. Hence, the reason for doubt provided by the deceiving-God hypothesis, however slight, must be examined thoroughly. That examination occupies the remainder of the Third Meditation.

Review of sources of ideas (7:36–40)

In preparation for considering the deceiving-God hypothesis, Descartes has the meditator investigate the structure of thought as it pertains to ideas and judgments. The aim is to find out which kinds of thought "can properly be said to be the bearers of truth and falsity" (7:37). This investigation presumably forms part of the larger inquiry into the truth or falsity of any hypothesis, including the deceiving-God hypothesis. The meditator's basis for this inquiry is restricted to the content and activity of her own mind, where Descartes must expect her to find adequate grounds for his theory of ideas and their role in thought, and subsequently for proving the existence of God.

Ideas, volitions, judgments

Descartes proposes that ideas, properly speaking, "are as it were the images of things." Examples of such "images" include the thoughts of "a man, or a chimera, or the sky, or an angel, or God" (7:37), which the meditator is supposed to find among her own thoughts. From the Second Meditation, she has the example of human beings crossing the square fresh in her mind. The *idea* of those human beings would have as its content, at the least, the visual experience of certain shapes and colors moving in a certain way. To say that ideas are "as it were the images of things" is (in part) to say that our experiences present to us various individual things, which, in the case of vision, are presented as spatially structured and chromatically variegated.

But not all the ideas listed can be literally imagistic, and hence not all ideas are genuine images. Descartes, like his Aristotelian predecessors, maintained that there can be no sensory images of immaterial beings such as God (7:136–8, 181). By including God and other immaterial beings (angels) in the list of ideas that are "like images," he implies that even ideas that do not possess spatial structure (hence are not literally imagistic) are still comparable to images in some way. Two points of comparison meet this condition with respect to the list. Ideas, like images, *represent* things (see 7:373); and the ideas in the list, like images, represent *individuals*. Ideas represent individuals as having various properties, as an image of a man might show him as having a head, two arms, and two legs, as sitting or standing, etc. The idea of God, although not literally imagistic, nonetheless represents him as having various properties (as we will soon see). In the Sixth Meditation, Descartes will explain that even the ideas of material things need not always be genuine images (7:72–3).

Descartes now explains that "other thoughts have various additional forms: thus, when I will, or am afraid, there is always a particular thing which I take as the object of my thought, but my thought includes something more than the likeness of that thing" (7:37). This passage again suggests that all thoughts are like images inasmuch as they are representational, or present an object of representation; but it adds that some thoughts include something else besides the bare representation of something. Thoughts with this added factor include volitions, emotions, and judgments. Emotions attach a feeling to the idea, whereas volitions and judgments involve an action taken by the mind in relation to an idea. For example, if one desires an apple (an emotion), the feeling of desire (the added "form") is felt together with the idea of an apple, which provides the content or object of the desire. If one now decides to eat that apple, that is an act of will, or a volition.

The objects of our desires or volitions need not exist. An idea can represent something as present even if it is not. One may decide to eat an apple that exists in plain sight, but one might also decide to eat an apple from the cupboard when there are none left. In that case, an apple, as represented in our idea, is the object of the volition, but there is no such apple in the cupboard.

Descartes recognizes cases of desiring the non-existent but does not classify them as, in themselves, "the bearers of truth and falsity" for which the meditator is now searching. As he explains, "even if the things which I may desire are wicked or even non-existent, that does not make it any less true that I desire them" (7:37). So merely having a certain desire, even for a non-existent thing, doesn't yield falsity. Falsity (and truth), he says, arise through judgment alone (7:37, 43). My desiring, or deciding to eat, an apple from the cupboard (when there aren't any in there) would yield falsity only if I also *judged* that the apple was in fact in the cupboard. (It might be that we would only decide to eat an apple if we judged or believed one to be present; Descartes' discussion simply locates the falsehood in such cases in the judgment or belief, not in the decision to eat.)

Judgments affirm or deny something. As with volition and desire, ideas provide the content of judgments. But in the act of judging we take a stand on whether the content of the idea holds true of something. In judging, either we affirm that what the idea represents is the case (affirmation), or we assert that it is not the case (denial). Suppose the idea is that there is an apple on the table. The act of judging simply affirms or denies its content. An affirmative judgment asserts that there is an apple on the table. If the apple is there, the judgment is true; if not, it is false. The opposite judgment denies that there is an apple on the table and is false if in fact an apple is there.

Judgments and ideas

The *Meditations* is intended to show the way to true judgments, so it is reasonable for us to dwell a moment on the theory of the content of judgments. A problem seems to arise if we suppose that (in some cases, at least) genuinely imagistic ideas are supposed to provide, by themselves, all the content for a judgment. We usually think of judgments as expressed through a sentence, as in "there is an apple on the table." Such a sentence seems in some ways more abstract than imagistic ideas and in other ways more specific. A visual image of an apple on a table ordinarily shows the apple as red, yellow, or green, the table as covered by a cloth or not, the cloth as checkered or not, and so on. The image includes more information than is found in a typical judgment expressed by a sentence (such judgments "abstract" from these details). Furthermore, faced with a bare image, say an image of a boy that exhibits various details about him (he is in the yard, has black hair, etc.), and given the instruction to affirm "what the image represents," we would be hard pressed to know exactly what to assert. Do we simply say "this is how things are," mentally pointing to the whole image and so asserting that the boy is in the yard, wearing these clothes, running toward the rear, etc.? What if the boy is our cousin? Does the image represent that? It would seem not (in any explicit manner). Yet we can certainly judge that the boy in the yard is our cousin – an ability that would be difficult to explain if the content of judgments was restricted to bare images.

However, Descartes did not believe that he could or should reduce the content of judgments to pictures or images. Far from it. As mentioned, he held that not all ideas are genuine images, and an example of this sort (the idea of God) will become the subsequent focus of this Meditation. Furthermore, as in the case of the cloaked men from the Second Meditation, some ideas act as concepts of things, which serve in the recognition of a thing as being of a specific kind, such as a human being. (Descartes used the terms "concept" or "notion" to refer to general ideas, although without formally explaining his terminology; as we saw in Chapter 4, examples of such concepts or notions include those of "thought" or "thing," which serve as elements of thought. He did not specify how many such elements there are.) The content of such ideas is not restricted to individual, concrete things (although they may be used to classify such things). Moreover, ideas can be complex, containing simpler ideas as components. Presumably, non-imagistic ideas can be combined in thought with the content of imagistic ideas. And within imagistic ideas, Descartes allowed a role for attention. When contemplating an imagistic idea, say of a particular shape, we can focus on aspects or dimensions of it (7:72).

All these aspects come together in the example of our cousin in the backyard. From seeing the boy in the yard and knowing he is our cousin we might judge that our cousin has black hair. The non-imagistic idea of "cousinhood" would be added to the visual image we have of the boy; we would attend to the hair (presumably also invoking ideas of "hair" and of the color "black") and affirm the resulting complex idea, that our cousin has black hair.

Although Descartes did not work out a detailed theory of judgments and their contents, the discussion thus far should meet our interpretive needs. One important question not addressed by the Third Meditation search for the location of falsity in ideas and judgments concerns reflexive judgments about the contents of our own mind, such as the judgment that we are now having the idea of an apple, or that we do or do not desire an apple (see 5:220–1). Such judgments do not go beyond the content of our own mind, but, being judgments, they permit of truth and falsity. (The standard of truth is the fact of the matter about whether we in fact are now having the idea of an apple!)

Sources for ideas

The meditator now finds that ideas seem to fall into three categories, according to their source. Some are "innate," some "adventitious," and some "invented" (7:38). Innate ideas include "my understanding of what a thing is, what truth is, and what thought is." Here Descartes affirms what we found to be presupposed in the *cogito* reasoning, namely, that the mind is innately stocked with a variety of ideas, including those just mentioned. Adventitious ideas are those that arise unbidden, and that the meditator hitherto believed to come from external causes; examples would include a noise, or the warmth felt from a fire. Invented ideas are like those of a "siren" (a mythical sea nymph) or a "hippogryph" (a mythical monster with the head and wings of an eagle and the body of a horse).

Although the official topic of inquiry concerns the existence and possible deceptiveness of God, Descartes adopts the strategy of having the meditator more generally examine the contents of her ideas. She allows that at this point the classification of particular ideas into the above categories is uncertain; as far as she knows all her ideas might be innate, or adventitious, or invented (7:38). But she begins her examination with those ideas that seem to arise unbidden (adventitious sensory ideas). This strategy is reasonable, since she had previously considered her sensory ideas to provide grounds for believing that something exists outside herself, and Descartes will soon want her to consider whether any ideas at all provide evidence for an external existent. Focusing for the moment on sensory ideas considered as representations of external things, she reconsiders her earlier reasons (as an Aristotelian or an untutored person of good sense) for believing that such ideas "resemble" external objects that cause them in her (7:38).

External objects and the resemblance thesis

As previously stated, the resemblance thesis holds that "there were things outside me which were the sources of my ideas and which resembled them in all respects" (7:35). It holds that external objects exist and that our ideas reveal their basic physical properties. This belief provided an example of something the meditator thought she "perceived clearly" but in fact did not. The meditator now examines three reasons, offered as the original grounds for the belief: that nature "taught me to think this," that sensory ideas "do not depend on my will, and hence that they do not depend simply on me," and that the most obvious thing to believe was that "the thing in question transmits to me its own likeness rather than something else" (7:38). She now finds that they are not enough to support the resemblance thesis.

The first reason, that nature teaches the belief, means that "a spontaneous impulse leads me to believe it" (7:38). We experience objects as having various properties, among which is color. We "naturally" believe that the objects are colored in a very specific sense: that the color in them "resembles" our experience of it. What you see is exactly what is there (as opposed to some other theory of object color, e.g., that it is a physical microstructure that affects the reflection of light). Descartes explains this natural impulse in the Sixth Meditation, where the meditator recalls that when she formed the resemblance thesis, her only source of knowledge about external objects was the sensory ideas themselves, so that "the supposition that the things resembled the ideas was bound to occur to me" (7:75). She naively affirmed that her sensory ideas present the qualities of objects just as they are. This "natural impulse" is laid aside here by an argument from fallibility. The meditator recalls that her natural impulses have led her astray previously, so she sees no reason to trust them now (7:39).

The second reason attributes sensory ideas to an external cause because they come to mind unbidden. Descartes offered two examples to show that even though these ideas are not under the control of the meditator's will, they might still be caused by an unknown faculty in her rather than have an external cause. First, natural impulses, whether concerning sensory objects or our own choices and desires, can seem "opposed" to our wills, and yet these impulses arise within us. Second, in dreams ideas are produced in us "without any assistance from external things" (7:39). Hence, sensory ideas might be produced in us like dreams are. Therefore the possibility that they arise from within the meditator cannot be ruled out, so the presence of sensory ideas does not now serve as a proof for the existence of something beyond the meditator's own mind. (Even if the meditator might later conclude that the brain is in fact involved in dreaming.)

As to the "obvious judgment" that the contents of our ideas fully resemble external objects, the meditator asserts: "even if these ideas did come from things other than myself, it would not follow that they must resemble those things" (7:39). In support of this assertion, she considers two ideas of the Sun. Our sensory idea of the Sun makes it appear small in the sky. The other idea is based on astronomical reasoning, which teaches that the Sun is much larger than the Earth. She concludes: "Obviously both these ideas cannot resemble the sun which exists outside me; and reason persuades me that the idea which seems to have emanated most directly from the sun is highly dissimilar to it" (7:39*). So even if our sensory ideas are caused by external objects, those ideas may not directly reveal the objects' true properties.

Natural light (7:38–9)

In discussing the resemblance thesis, Descartes distinguishes a "spontaneous impulse" to believe something from what is revealed "by some natural light." He explains:

> There is a big difference here. Whatever is revealed to me by the natural light – for example that from the fact that I am doubting it follows that I exist, and so on – cannot in any way be open to doubt. This is because there cannot be another faculty both as trustworthy as the natural light and also capable of showing me that such things are not true. [7:38–9]

In the seventeenth century, the "natural light" was contrasted with the light of grace, or supernatural illumination directly from God (7:148). The natural light is the natural or intrinsic cognitive power found in all human minds. This passage, parenthetically inserted into the discussion of natural impulses, makes two important claims about this light. First, it ascribes the *cogito* conclusion to the natural light. Second, it asserts that this light cannot "in any way" be doubted. Does this mean that the natural light by itself dissolves any remaining doubt, without any need to defeat the deceiving-God hypothesis?

If we assume that the meditator is seeking stable knowledge, then the deceiving-God hypothesis must actually be defeated; it is not enough simply to remark that the natural light cannot be doubted. That same quality has just earlier been asserted about clear and distinct perceptions (while we are having them).

One function of the above passage may be to introduce the "natural light" as a name for the faculty that will continue the investigation of the deceiving-God hypothesis. This reading is plausible, because Descartes frequently invokes the natural light in the remainder of the Meditation (7:40, 42, 44, 47, 49, 52). But it raises the question of the relation between the natural light and the proposed truth rule, that clear and distinct intellectual perceptions are true. The quoted passage says that the *cogito* reasoning is seen by the natural light. Earlier, the same conclusion was attributed to clear and distinct perception. It therefore seems that the natural light and clear and distinct perception are the same thing described in two different ways. (The Geometrical exposition supports this interpretation, for it effectively equates "intellectual perspicuity" and "clear and distinct perception" (7:163*, 164), while not mentioning the natural light.)

Nonetheless, the above passage introduces something new into the mix, for it says that the natural light "cannot in any way be open to doubt," and this because "there cannot be another faculty both as trustworthy as the natural light and also capable of showing me that such things are not true" (7:38–9). This wording takes us beyond the indubitability of clear and distinct perception when we have them; it suggests that the fact that the natural light is all we have somehow makes it unimpeachable as a source of truth. We will return to this suggestion in the final part of the present chapter.

The meditator now continues her evaluation of the deceiving-God hypothesis by sifting through her ideas, seeking grounds for inferring the existence of something beyond her own thoughts. This takes us further into the metaphysics of ideas and their causal origin.

Degrees of reality in ideas (objective and formal being) (7:40)

Descartes has the meditator consider her ideas from two perspectives: first, simply as individual states of her own mind, without paying attention to their content; and, second, as states of her mind that represent (or at least seem to represent) things to her. As states of mind pure and simple (leaving aside content), all her ideas seem to be equivalent. But they differ among themselves in what they represent or seem to represent. Some ideas present her with horses, some with houses, others with trees, human beings, God, or angels. Since her present aim is to determine whether anything, including God, exists outside her (7:40), she now asks whether any of her ideas have a content that could not exist unless produced by the thing represented through that content. In other words, do horses have to exist for me to have the idea of a horse? Does God have to exist for me to have an idea of God? Or could I make up or produce such ideas myself?

Descartes introduces this question as something that would occur to the meditator through reflection on her own states of mind:

> Insofar as the ideas are simply modes of thought, there is no recognizable inequality among them: they all appear to come from within me in the same fashion. But insofar as different ideas represent different things, it is clear that they differ widely. Undoubtedly, the ideas which represent substances to me amount to something more and, so to speak, contain within themselves more objective reality than the ideas which merely represent modes or accidents. Again, the idea that gives me my understanding of a supreme God, eternal, infinite, omniscient, omnipotent and the creator of all things that exist apart from him, certainly has in it more objective reality than the ideas that represent finite substances. [7:40]

This quotation may or may not make defensible distinctions among the degrees of reality found in the contents of ideas – we will examine that in a moment. But first we need to penetrate the technical language that Descartes has put into the mouth of the meditator. The technical notions of substance and mode first appear here in the text of the six Meditations (but see 7:13), although without much explanation. A few pages hence (7:44), almost as an aside, he glosses a substance as something "capable of existing independently" or on its own (save for divine preservation, introduced below). Examples might be a stone, a horse, or a mind or thinking thing. The definition in the Geometrical Arguments recounts that all properties must reside in substances, as their subject (7:161). The term "mode," found in the above passage and environs, is otherwise used sparingly in the *Meditations* (e.g., 7:78, 165), without being explicitly distinguished from various related terms, including property, attribute, and accident (7:161, 176) – terms that are distinguished and defined more closely in the *Principles* (8A:25–8). For our purposes, we can consider a mode to be a "modification" of a substance (the shape or size of the horse, the various thoughts or ideas in a mind).

The above passage also introduces the notion of "objective reality," which Descartes adapted from scholastic authors, where it was contrasted with "formal reality." Putting aside for a moment talk of greater or lesser objective reality, let us focus on the objective–formal distinction itself. According to Descartes, formal reality is what something has simply in virtue of existing (7:41, 161). All the ideas in a mind have formal reality, merely as states or modes of mind. By contrast, the objective reality of an idea is the "reality" of the "object" presented in the idea, considered merely insofar as it is represented in the idea. It is not the horse in the field but the image or representation of the horse as presented in the meditator's thought (independently of whether the horse in fact is in the field). (The terminology is confusing, because today we think of an "object" as an externally existing physical object. But think of an "object" of desire – a championship for your favorite sports team, say. It may not now exist, and it need never have existed. In Descartes' terminology, what has "objective reality" is something contained in the subject's mental state and so may even be called "subjective" in present-day terms.)

To bring back the image or picture analogy for ideas, the formal reality of the idea is like the reality of canvas and paint. The objective reality is like the organization of the paint so that it represents a house, or a tree, or whatever. Assume for the moment (contrary to fact) that all Cartesian ideas could be represented on canvas using paint. In this comparison, assume that just as all one's ideas are in the same mind, all images are painted on one kind of canvas, using the same oils. They would then all have the same formal reality, since they are all made of the same stuff. But depending on whether the image is of a house or a tree, the paint is organized differently on the canvas. These different patterns are like the differing objective realities of ideas.

Now let us add the notion of degrees of reality, or degrees of being. Descartes held that all human ideas have the same degree of formal reality – they are simply states of a human mind. The idea of a shape, the idea of a finite substance such as a tree, and the idea of an infinite being (God) each has the same degree of formal reality, because each is simply an idea or state of a finite mind. But they differ in degree of objective reality according to whether the object represented has more or less "reality." Descartes appeals to a three-level hierarchy of reality or being that depends on his substance–mode ontology. According to the hierarchy, a mode has less reality than a finite substance (modes, as modifications of substance, depend on substances for their existence), and a finite substance has less reality than an infinite substance. Consequently, the idea of a mode, such as an idea of shape, has less objective reality (less reality in its represented content) than an idea of a finite substance, and the idea of a finite substance has less objective reality than the idea of an infinite one.

The metaphysics of degrees of objective reality is a heady result for the meditator to gain from contemplating her own ideas. At the same time, the metaphysics is thus far only applied to ideas and their contents; it does not presuppose that there is an infinite substance, or any finite thing or substance other than the meditator herself, and any other modes or states of that substance than ideas. We can better examine the claim about degrees of objective reality in connection with another metaphysical thesis accepted by the meditator, concerning causes and effects.

Causal principle (7:40–2)

The meditator now considers a causal principle, allegedly revealed by the natural light: "It is manifest by the natural light that there must be at least as much in the efficient and total cause as in the effect of that cause" (7:40). The term "efficient cause" means what actually produces an effect. A "total cause" must include everything needed to produce its effect. The causal principle here enunciated says that the degree of being, or reality, of the cause must be equal to or greater than the degree of being of the effect. In a rough sense, this says that you can't get something from nothing. In terms of the notion of a hierarchy of being, something with lesser being cannot cause something with greater being; the cause must equal or exceed the effect in degree of being.

While we might have questions about its application in particular cases, the principle that you can't get something from nothing does not seem particularly objectionable (as metaphysical principles go).

And indeed it was widely accepted by philosophers. (Only one of the objectors took exception to the causal principle in its general form [7:123] – although two others objected to Descartes' specific application [7:92–4, 288–9].) In the Geometrical Arguments, Descartes presents several causal theses as axioms or common notions (7:165), that is, as something he expects his readers to grant, presumably on the basis of "the natural light." (We will consider later whether the meditator should be permitted to draw on the natural light before the deceiving-God hypothesis, and other grounds for doubt, have been removed.)

Descartes applied the causal principle not only to the formal reality of ideas but also to their objective reality:

> In order for a given idea to contain such and such objective reality, it must surely derive it from some cause which contains at least as much formal reality as there is objective reality in the idea. For if we suppose that an idea contains something which was not in its cause, it must have got this from nothing; yet the mode of being by which a thing exists objectively in the intellect by way of idea, imperfect though it may be, is certainly not nothing, and so it cannot come from nothing. [7:41]

For a "thing" to exist in the intellect is, in Descartes' terms, simply for us to have an idea with that thing as its content. He is saying here that the content of the idea requires a cause equal to the degree of being of the thing represented. The content needs a cause, which may be independent of the cause of the formal reality of the idea (as simply a state of mind).

Consider again the painting analogy. The formal reality of a painting is accounted for by the formal reality of the paint and canvas. But the paint must also be organized on the canvas so that it represents the house or tree. Descartes is in effect saying that the cause of the organization of the paint must possess a degree of reality equal to the degree of intricacy of the image (see also 7:14, 103–4). Presumably, it is easier to make a painting that has only one color and no pattern than it is to make one that represents (looks like) a many-colored mountainside. From the notion that the content of the painting – or, returning from the analogy, of the idea – requires a cause equal to its intricacy, Descartes constructed a proof for the existence of God.

First proof of God's existence, from the idea of God (7:42–7)

The existence of the idea of God is the basis for Descartes' first proof from effects. The proof claims that the content of the meditator's idea of God could exist only if God produced that content himself. Here is the strategy:

> If the objective reality of any of my ideas turns out to be so great that I am sure the same reality does not reside in me, either formally or eminently, and hence that I myself cannot be its cause, it will necessarily follow that I am not alone in the world, but that some other thing which is the cause of this idea also exists. But if no such idea is to be found in me, I shall have no argument to convince me of the existence of anything apart from myself. [7:42]

For a "reality" to exist "eminently" in the meditator is for her to be able to produce that reality (in this case, the content of an idea), even though she does not formally or actually possess it herself. For example, if God existed he would be able to create matter, even though he is not material; the reality of matter would be in God eminently, but not formally. The meditator examines her ideas, seeking one with a degree of objective reality that she does not contain formally or eminently, and so could not cause. She classifies them into ideas of corporeal inanimate things (and their modes), her idea of herself, ideas of animals and other human beings, of angels, and of God.

The meditator proposes that the ideas of corporeal things can be formed from the idea she has of herself, even though she is thinking of herself only as a mind. She thinks of both mind (considered for now as a thing that thinks and is not extended) and body (considered as an extended, non-thinking thing) as substances (7:43–4). In both cases, "substance" simply means something "capable of existing independently" (7:44) or (as will be explained) requiring only divine preservation to exist. (An individual substance could in principle be held in existence while the rest of the world is annihilated.) Since both mind and body are conceived as finite substances, the idea of a body contains no greater reality than that of a mind. Since the meditator can produce an idea of herself as a finite mind, she should be able to produce an idea of body, for it contains no greater objective reality than her idea of herself.

This argument, although consistent with the causal principle, is unsatisfying. It assumes that the meditator could produce the idea of body out of her own resources. But if there really were no bodies, where would she (in today's vernacular) "get the idea" for the idea of extension? At this point, she has no answer. All the same, she needs only to establish that the idea of body is not a clear case in which an external cause would be required to produce the idea. Since she is at the worst unsure at the moment of whether she could produce it, she can move on.

The argument for the existence of God does not require that the meditator prove that she is the source of her idea of body. It depends on locating an idea that demands an infinite cause. The ideas of other human beings and angels are again of finite substances and so could be modeled on the meditator's awareness of herself. But the idea of God, she comes to think, requires an infinite cause.

Descartes' argument requires that the meditator find within herself the idea of God, or of "a substance that is infinite, independent, supremely intelligent, supremely powerful, and which created both myself and everything else (if anything else there be) that exists" (7:45). Two challenges might be posed to this requirement. First, the meditator might claim that she does not possess such an idea. Second, granting that one has the idea, one might question whether it really requires an infinite cause; perhaps the idea of an infinite substance could be constructed by thinking of a finite substance and then saying that God is like that, except without any limit (7:186).

Descartes sought to answer both challenges by having the meditator consider the relation between the finite and the infinite. She now affirms that "my perception of the infinite, that is God, is in some way prior to my perception of the finite, that is myself" (7:45). Her very conception of the finite presupposes a positive idea of the infinite, for her idea of the finite arises from introducing limits to this infinity (see also 3:547, 5:355–6). Compare this problem with that of a finite or infinite spatial extent. Consider a shaped area that has a determinate boundary. To think away the boundary is to remove it in thought. And yet, one might argue, the very presence of the boundary can serve only to divide the finite area from a surrounding area. No matter how large the bounded shape, it would still presuppose a surrounding area. Generalizing, infinite or unlimited being is implicated in the thought of finite being, which is conceived by introducing limits into this prior notion.

But our two challenges have not been fully met. Even assuming that the idea of the finite presupposes the infinite, we may still ask whether it must presuppose the idea of God (i.e., of something supremely intelligent, supremely powerful, and the creator of everything else). Wouldn't the idea of any sort of infinite being do as a conceptual backdrop to the idea of a finite being? Furthermore, even granting that the idea of an infinite being does require an infinite cause, must that cause be God? If a finite mind can serve as the model for the idea of a finite body, perhaps the idea of an infinite body can provide the model for the idea of God.

Descartes' full answer to these challenges invokes a special unity among the attributes of a truly infinite being. For he now glosses the idea of God as the idea of a supremely *perfect* being (7:46). In the philosophical terminology of the time, perfection implied completeness of reality or being (see 7:165). Perhaps any truly infinite being would contain all perfections, and so would of necessity be God. This proposal is developed in the second proof for God's existence.

Second proof, from preservation (7:47–51)

At the end of the first proof, the meditator asks whether, since she has experienced a gradual increase in knowledge, she might not contain within herself, at least potentially, all the perfections of God. In that case, she might herself (unwittingly) be the infinite cause of her idea of God. But Descartes has her consider that the idea of God is not that of a being who might develop so as to become infinitely perfect, but is the idea of an eternal, supreme being. God does not grow and develop in knowledge. The fact that the meditator experiences ignorance and growth of knowledge in herself is enough to show that she is not like God (7:46–7).

The meditator now considers "whether I myself, who have this idea [of God], could exist if no [more perfect] being existed" (7:48). This question leads to the second proof, which argues that the existence of any finite being can be explained only if there exists an infinite creative power.

The proof proceeds by a process of elimination. Descartes divides the possible causes of the meditator's existence into four: she causes her own existence, her parents cause it, other beings less perfect than God, or God. He then rules out each of the first three candidates, leaving only God. The meditator could not have caused her own existence, for if she could create herself from nothing she would be God – on the assumption that it takes an infinite power to create something where nothing existed before. The meditator reasons that if she had the power of creation, she would not deny herself other (easier to create) attributes, such as infinite knowledge, in which case she would know she was God (7:48).

The thought that anything capable of creating something would be God plays a central role in the remaining cases. But first Descartes adds a new wrinkle. He has the meditator consider the hypothesis not that she created herself but that she has existed for all time just as she is now (that is, as she now considers herself to be: as a thinking thing). This argument is ruled out by a metaphysical thesis. Descartes contends that the lifespan of the meditator (even if infinitely long)

> can be divided into countless parts, each completely independent of the others, so that it does not follow from the fact that I existed a little while ago that I must exist now, unless there is some cause which as it were creates me afresh at this moment – that is, which preserves me. [7:49]

This thesis assumes that time can be divided into instants or moments and then asserts that the existence of a finite substance at any one moment does not give it the power to exist at a subsequent moment. In other words, the power of staying in existence from moment to moment is the same as the power it takes to bring something into existence in the first place. The meditator affirms that "the distinction between preservation and creation is only a conceptual one, and this is one of the things that are evident by the natural light" (7:49).

The point about preservation, if combined with the claim that only an infinite being can create, is adequate to rule out the other causes of one's existence. These include one's parents and other beings less perfect than God. Even if one's parents were to be (as the meditator previously believed) the cause of her body through procreation, God would still be needed to preserve in existence (from moment to moment) the material substance of which her and her parents' bodies are composed. Any contributing cause less powerful than God would still have to depend on the infinite power of God for its very being. God's power is left as the only explanation of the continuing existence of all finite beings.

Descartes presents one further argument to establish that the infinite being must be God. It repeats the point that any being that "has the power of existing through its own might" would give itself all the perfections that God has (7:49–50). This point was used earlier to rule out that the meditator was God (7:48). Now it provides an argument that any infinite being that could create and preserve the meditator, or create and preserve any finite being, would of necessity be God. Like the others, this argument puts a lot of weight on the meditator's own ideas of perfection, infinity, and God. So let us turn to Descartes' explanation of the origin of those ideas.

Idea of God innate (7:51–2)

The question that began the second proof asked not only about the source of the meditator's existence but also about the origin of her idea of God. The meditator considers the candidate sources listed early in the Meditation: the idea is from the senses (adventitious), is invented, or innate.

She rules out the senses by saying that the idea "has never come to me unexpectedly, as usually happens with the ideas of things that are perceivable by the senses" (7:51). The ideas of trees, houses, tables, and chairs can arise in us unbidden. The idea of God, apparently, is one we must induce ourselves to experience (or to experience clearly). But to rule out an "adventitious" source, Descartes must further show that the idea of God could not be modeled on sensory things, or cobbled together from various things found in the universe, whether material (an infinite body) or immaterial (a powerful, but evil, demon).

The first proof argued that only an infinite being could cause the idea of God. That argument does not itself show that an infinite body could not be the cause of, or provide the model for, the meditator's idea of God. In the Third Replies, Descartes contends that "nothing in God resembles what is found in external, corporeal things" (7:188), which would seem to rule out an infinite body as the model for the idea of God. But, it might be objected, if the universe was infinite, wouldn't it resemble God in that respect? Apparently, Descartes considers the infinity found in the idea of God to be a special infinity of power and perfection, and so sufficiently dissimilar from (and perhaps incomparable with) an infinity of extension. (Descartes made this very point in the First Replies, saying that since the universe is not "limitless in every respect," its unboundedness should be called "indefinite" rather than infinite [7:113].) Toward the end of the Third Meditation, he adds that the idea of God contains a special unity among its attributes (of infinity, omnipotence, omniscience, and so on); he requires a cause not only for the idea of each of the attributes but also for the meditator's "understanding" of that unity (7:50). This latter cause (which, by the first proof, must be infinite) must also give her the idea of the other infinitary attributes. Must the being that gives her the idea of a unity of infinitary attributes also possess the unity? According to the argument we reviewed above, yes. If an infinite cause, that is, one sufficient to produce the meditator's idea of God and to create the meditator herself, could be expected to give itself all other perfections, then any infinite cause would be God and would thus have that unified set of attributes that Descartes purports to find in the idea of God. (Assuming that the attributes could consistently be combined in one being.)

The meditator next rules out that the idea of God is invented, arguing that "I am plainly unable either to take away anything from it or to add anything to it" (7:51). Presumably, we are able to tinker with ideas of our own invention, adding or taking away whatever we like. Hence the idea must be innate. The content of an innate idea is presumed to be fixed, once and for all. In a later work, Descartes explains that innate ideas need not be fully preformed in the mind but can be latent in "the power of thinking" (8B:358). The power of thinking, or intellect, has a fixed structure. As explained in the Fifth Replies, this means that we are able to discover new aspects of the intellect's latent content but cannot add or take away elements (7:371). But the idea of God requires a special provision. Its content cannot arise from our natural, finite power of thinking (per the first proof); hence God must specifically enable the intellect to form the idea of an infinitely perfect being. This innate (latent) idea of God is like "the mark of a craftsman stamped on his work" (7:51).

Just as the *cogito* reasoning depended on several innate ideas, Descartes' argument for the existence of God requires innate ideas besides that of God (or perhaps extricated from the idea of God). These include the positive idea of infinity (upon which the idea of the finite allegedly depends), the ideas of unity, simplicity, perfection, substance, and immateriality, and the ideas required by the causal principle. Such ideas must be innate, because they pertain to things that cannot be represented by the senses or imagination (as with God and his attributes). Or at least so Descartes argued in contending that the infinity of God could not be modeled on any lesser being.

The existence of innate ideas has been presupposed all along in Descartes' use of the meditational approach. The procedure of turning away from the senses and imagination won't work if there is no source of cognition independent of the senses and imagination. Descartes permits no other source for the ideas of metaphysics. This restriction puts a heavy burden on arguments such as those in the Third Meditation. Not only must they be well formed logically, they must also convince each reader of their soundness by prompting them to find within themselves various innate ideas, along with metaphysical principles that are manifest to the "natural light." If one follows Descartes' work carefully but cannot find the innate idea of God as described therein, then his arguments are in trouble. Several of the objectors, including some who shared Descartes' religious belief, denied that they possessed an innate idea of God such as the meditator was expected to find within herself (7:96–7, 123–4, 186–7, 307).

God is no deceiver (7:52)

Finally, the meditator returns to the deceiving-God hypothesis. From the idea of God as an infinite, perfect being, she concludes that God "is subject to no defect whatsoever." From this, it follows "that he cannot be a deceiver, since it is manifest by the natural light that all fraud and deception depend on some defect" (7:52). God's perfection excludes deception. Perfection was typically associated with goodness; deception is obviously taken here to depart from goodness and perfection.

If God is no deceiver, then the "slight" and "metaphysical" ground for doubt from the First Meditation has been removed. The Fourth Meditation explores more fully the implication of a non-deceiving God for our knowledge, but before continuing, let us examine a problem raised by even the earliest readers of the *Meditations*.

The Cartesian circle

In the Third Meditation, Descartes appeals to the natural light, or the faculty of clear and distinct perception, to prove the existence and non-deceptiveness of God (7:40–50). The fact that God exists and is no deceiver releases the meditator from the doubt about the reliability of clear and distinct perception (7:35, 52).

This procedure has the appearance of circularity. A particular method of ascertaining the truth (clear and distinct perception) is vindicated by proving that God exists and is no deceiver, but this proof relies on that very method. (Note that a similar problem might arise no matter how Descartes attempted to validate clear and distinct perception; the Cartesian circle is an instance of a general problem concerning how one could ever know that one's method of knowing was sound.)

The charge of circularity was leveled by Arnauld in the Fourth Objections:

> I have one further worry, namely how the author avoids reasoning in a circle when he says that we are sure that what we clearly and distinctly perceive is true only because God exists. But we can be sure that God exists only because we clearly and distinctly perceive this. Hence, before we can be sure that God exists, we ought to be able to be sure that whatever we perceive clearly and distinctly is true. [7:214]

The first sentence paraphrases a line from the Fifth Meditation, where the meditator reasons explicitly from having perceived "that God exists," "that everything else depends on him," and "that he is no deceiver" to the conclusion that "everything which I clearly and distinctly perceive is of necessity true" (7:70). And it describes the order of the Third Meditation, in which the trustworthiness of clear and distinct perception was made to depend on the investigation of God's existence. The second sentence makes the assumption that the appeal to the "natural light" in the Third Meditation proofs is equivalent to an appeal to clear and distinct perception. The third sentence points out that the appeal to clear and distinct perception in the proof of God's existence has nothing to back it up, if indeed our trust in such perception depends on our having proved God's existence and goodness.

Descartes responded to this charge of circularity in the Fourth Replies (drawing also on the Second):

> I have already given an adequate explanation of this point in my reply to the Second Objections, under the headings *Thirdly* and *Fourthly*, where I made a distinction between what we in fact perceive clearly and what we remember having perceived clearly on a previous occasion. To begin with, we are sure that God exists because we attend to the arguments which prove this; but subsequently it is enough for us to remember that we perceived something clearly in order for us to be certain that it is true. This would not be sufficient if we did not know that God exists and is not a deceiver. [7:246]

This reply makes it seem as if the reliability of clear and distinct perception was never itself really placed in doubt, merely our ability to remain convinced of its reliability when we aren't having such perceptions. Descartes seems to be claiming that the charge of circularity is not a problem, because the proof of God's existence (which relies on clear and distinct perception) merely gives the meditator license to trust the remembered results of clear and distinct perceptions when she is not having them – presumably, by removing the "slight" and "metaphysical" doubt of the deceiving-God hypothesis. But, this reply presupposes, there was no need to justify clear and distinct perception itself, even as the power that investigates the grounds for doubt.

This response seems not to meet the objection. Arnauld directly questioned the grounds for believing that clear and distinct perceptions are true. The fact that we cannot doubt clear and distinct perceptions while we have them would seem to be irrelevant. His concern is not whether we are psychologically capable of doubt in the face of clear and distinct perceptions but whether in fact clear and distinct perceptions are true. Arnauld appears to be suggesting that whether or not we can doubt them, they might still be false. In that case, we should want a proof of their validity that does not rely on clear and distinct perception. It is that proof that Arnauld rightly says Descartes has not supplied.

This construal of Arnauld's objection implicitly distinguishes between mere psychological certainty and truth. Earlier, we supposed that Descartes was not interested in mere psychological certainty and that he treated certainty as equivalent to truth. But, Arnauld might object, even if Descartes believes that certainty yields truth, he must provide a reason for accepting that human certainty (of the right kind: clear and distinct perception) is a sufficient criterion for truth. Accordingly, Descartes' response did not address the demand that drove Arnauld's charge of circularity.

Assessment of the circle depends on what Descartes hoped to achieve in the *Meditations*. In previous chapters, we distinguished the aim of vindicating reason (or now, clear and distinct intellectual perception) from the more restricted aim of reforming metaphysics. And we distinguished the project of discovering the intellect from that of proving the intellect to be reliable. Depending on which aim we choose and how we read Descartes' argument, different responses to the charge of circularity arise, and different conclusions about the success of Descartes' project. We may also arrive at differing conclusions depending on whether we ask what Descartes intended to argue, as opposed to what he needed to argue to achieve his results (which is what Arnauld asked, and ultimately what we should ask as well).

Interpretations of the circle must take into account various elements that have already been mentioned. These include the extraction of the truth rule, the appeal to the natural light, and the proof that God exists and is no deceiver. As a guide for our further investigations, let us consider four distinct approaches using these and other elements.

Certainty, not truth

We have been assuming that Descartes' aim in the *Meditations* is not merely to find a metaphysics that his readers would accept but to demonstrate to them that his metaphysics is true. However, there are some passages in the Second Replies that apparently suggest that Descartes was not out to show he had the truth. These passages, on one reading, suggest that he merely sought to show that his metaphysics achieves maximal human certainty. Here is the main passage:

> As soon as we think that we correctly perceive something, we are spontaneously convinced that it is true. Now if this conviction is so firm that it is impossible for us ever to have any reason for doubting what we are convinced of, then there are no further questions for us to ask: we have everything that we could reasonably want. What is it to us that someone may make out that the perception whose truth we are so firmly convinced of may appear false to God or an angel, so that it is, absolutely speaking, false? Why should this alleged "absolute falsity" bother us, since we neither believe in it nor have even the smallest suspicion of it? For the supposition which we are making here is of a conviction so firm that it is quite incapable of being destroyed; and such a conviction is clearly the same as the most perfect certainty. [7:144–5]

Firm conviction is equated with "perfect certainty," which is (apparently) distinguished from "absolute" truth or falsity.

If we accept this distinction for the moment, Descartes' response to Arnauld can yield the following strategy for avoiding the circle. We will suppose that his aim is perfect, or unshakeable, certainty (now distinguished from truth). Clear and distinct perceptions provide such certainty while we are having them. When we are not having them, the deceiving-God hypothesis can undermine that certainty, for it raises a general doubt about whether such perceptions should be accepted. The proofs for the existence of a non-deceiving God use clear and distinct perceptions, and we are utterly convinced of those proofs; hence, we are no longer moved by the deceiving-God hypothesis. We have not shown that clear and distinct perceptions are true and so have not shown that the proofs of God are true. But we have shown that they are maximally certain, thereby reaching our goal of unshakeable belief.

On this reading, Descartes was really seeking to induce in the reader a kind of psychological equanimity regarding his new metaphysics. In this way, he was like the ancient skeptics who sought peace of mind. But in contrast to true skepticism, this peace of mind arises from inducing the reader to affirm metaphysical principles strongly (rather than suspending judgment). If disturbing doubts should arise, the remedy lies ready in the clear and distinct perceptions of the Third Meditation.

The "certainty, not truth" reading provides a way out of the circle by having Descartes abandon his avowed goal of truth (7:69–70, 577–8). Given this cost, one may ask whether the quoted passage really demands a distinction between certainty and truth. Notice that Descartes does not say we should not care if our results are "absolutely false." Rather, he asks why we should care about "alleged" absolute falsity, "since we neither believe in it nor have even the smallest suspicion of it" (7:145). A few paragraphs later, he maintains that the clarity of our perceptions "does not allow us to listen to anyone who makes up this kind of story," that is, who might "make out that such truths might appear false to God or to an angel" (7:146). And further on, in response to a presumed question about whether human concepts actually match reality, he suggests that to deny that they do would be to undermine all human knowledge "for no good reason" (7:151). Perhaps Descartes was indeed after genuine truth but dismissed unsupported warnings of allegedly possible "absolute falsity" as arbitrary and without basis.

Assuming, as seems reasonable, that Descartes was seeking metaphysical truths, the "certainty, not truth" approach neither accords with his intent nor reveals what he would need to achieve his goal. A second approach might begin from his remark that we have no reason to suspect absolute falsity. He might here be invoking the First Meditation point that an arbitrary ground of doubt is not sufficient; the alleged "absolute falsity" should receive no weight if there is no good ground for it. This suggests a second strategy for avoiding the circle.

Remove the doubt

On the "remove the doubt" strategy, Descartes was not aiming to prove that clear and distinct perception is true, only to show that the grounds for doubting such perception do not withstand scrutiny. When Descartes says above that the circle can be avoided by carefully distinguishing between having clear and distinct perceptions and merely remembering having them, he was reminding Arnauld that the deceiving-God hypothesis at first seems forceful only because we consider it in relation to remembered, as opposed to directly experienced, instances of reasoning (see also 7:473–4). In this context, which precedes a full scrutiny of the deceiving-God hypothesis, that hypothesis appears to provide a "well thought-out" reason for doubting even evident perceptions (7:21). But upon investigating the hypothesis itself, we find an internal contradiction: God, who is perfect, could not be a deceiver. The supposed reason for doubt is removed, and the circle is (allegedly) avoided. (This outcome provides "weak vindication" for reason, in the terminology of Chapter 3.)

The "remove the doubt" strategy fits Descartes' intent as stated in his reply to Arnauld. But it has its own problems. Granted, Descartes does not permit arbitrary grounds for doubt. However, it is not at all clear that once the deceiving-God hypothesis – or the other grounds for doubt, such as defective origins – has been framed, that clear and distinct perception of the idea of God (and of the other metaphysical apparatus of the Third Meditation) suffices to remove that doubt. The argument attempts to exclude the deceiving-God hypothesis on the grounds that it is logically flawed because it attributes deception to a being who, upon careful consideration, is conceived as perfect. But this "contradiction" depends on our idea of God accurately representing him as perfect. How can we be sure that our idea of God accurately represents his properties and that deception is incompatible with perfection? More generally, we may wonder whether simply finding an internal problem with the deceiving-God hypothesis would be adequate to remove other First Meditation grounds for doubt. In seeking to remove the defective-origins hypothesis, it seems we must appeal to clear and distinct perception to prove that God (who is no deceiver) created us, as opposed to our having a possibly defective natural origin. In that case, for the doubt to be removed the substantive metaphysical principles used in the proofs that God exists and is no deceiver must be affirmed as true, apparently on the basis of clear and distinct perception. It seems that the reliability of clear and distinct perception must again be presupposed, and the circle returns.

Presumption in favor of the intellect

What if Descartes believed that the meditator could reasonably begin with, or at some point adopt, a presumption in favor of the human intellect? That is, what if the burden of proof were on the doubter? In that case, a "remove the doubt" strategy might suffice, when paired with this presumption. To evaluate this possibility, we must step back for a moment and again consider Descartes' aims in the *Meditations*.

In Chapter 3, we considered the possibility that the *Meditations* did not aim for a strong validation of reason but for the discovery of pure intellect in order to reform metaphysics. Suppose for a minute that those are the aims. Descartes' intent would then not be to prove the intellect is reliable but to reveal its force in actual cases of metaphysical reasoning. To this we would now add that the reason he didn't feel the need for strong validation was his belief that we should trust the best use of our cognitive faculties to yield truth unless we have some compelling reason not to. Removing the grounds for doubt then banishes such reasons, and we are left with our presumption. (This outcome moves beyond the weak vindication of the bare remove-the-doubt strategy, via the presumption; once the doubt is removed, we are left with a faculty presumed to yield truth.)

On this reading, Descartes first brings the meditator to appreciate the existence and apparent force of clear and distinct perception through the *cogito* and the extraction argument. The extraction argument is now read not as proving the truth of clear and distinct perception but as simply establishing that method as the one responsible for the *cogito*. Having discovered the pure intellect, or the natural light, the meditator then proceeds to use this cognitive resource in evaluating the metaphysical basis of the deceiving-God hypothesis. A thorough investigation shows that the grounds for doubt are wanting. Our clear and distinct perceptions tell us that God exists and is no deceiver. Assuming that these arguments are otherwise valid, we would simply be left to assess their soundness by asking whether the "natural light" actually extends to the causal principle, and whether we actually find the needed idea of God within ourselves.

This strategy frees the Third Meditation from the charge of circularity, for it relieves the meditator of the burden of having to prove that clear and distinct perceptions are true. But it does raise the question of whether we should accept a presumption in favor of our human cognitive faculties.

In the Fourth Replies, Descartes contends that we normally do make such a (general) presumption. He is explaining to Arnauld why he could not prove the mind–body distinction in the Second Meditation but had to wait until the Sixth.

> I should have added nothing more in order to demonstrate that there is a real distinction between the mind and the body, since we commonly judge that the order in which things are mutually related in our perception of them corresponds to the order in which they are related in actual reality. But one of the exaggerated doubts I put forward in the First Meditation went so far as to make it impossible for me to be certain of this very point (namely whether things do in reality correspond to our percep-

tion of them), so long as I was supposing myself to be ignorant of the author of my being. [7:226]

Leaving aside the point about mind and body, the passage says that in general we "commonly judge" that reality corresponds to our perception of it. Here is a direct statement of a presumption in favor of the intellect.

The quotation implies that to prove the mind–body distinction, knowledge of God's existence and goodness is needed. Is Descartes saying that he had to prove God's existence in order to get a divine guarantee for clear and distinct perception? Or rather that he examined his knowledge of God so as to see that the "exaggerated doubts" of the First Meditation are in fact ridiculous, and should be dismissed? If the first, he is following a strategy other than presumption. The second reading is consistent with the presumption strategy, which can be pursued a step further.

Recall that in the natural light passage, Descartes said that what is revealed by the natural light "cannot in any way be open to doubt," because "there cannot be another faculty both as trustworthy as the natural light and also capable of showing me that such things are not true" (7:38–9). It clearly does not follow from the fact that the natural light is our most trustworthy faculty that it in fact cannot be defective. Additional premises or presuppositions must be at play.

The passage does not say that natural light cannot be defective, only that its results cannot be doubted. Why should this follow from the fact that there is no other faculty capable of showing us that the natural light is defective? It might simply be that no doubt can be posed about the natural light itself, since it is our most trusted faculty and so must be used to evaluate any ground for doubt. To put the matter loosely, this would be to say that reason cannot undermine itself. As the arbiter of doubt, it is above the fray. (But, incidentally, a version of skepticism called "Pyrrhonian" has been interpreted as saying that reason can undermine itself.)

As we granted in Chapter 3, the process of doubt must rely on a reasoning faculty to carry it out, inasmuch as it depends on the presentation of arguments. By itself, however, this merely provides us with grounds not to abandon the natural light as an adjudicator of reasons for doubt. It does not give us any reason to trust the natural light in establishing positive metaphysical results. For that we would need something further, which might be gained by reading the passage as an instance of presumption. Descartes might here be suggesting that it simply is not reasonable to doubt our best cognitive performances for no good reason. Accordingly, although the deceiving-God hypothesis at first seemed like a good reason, after improving the clarity of our thought through the *cogito* exercise we are now better able to evaluate it. Using our best cognitive abilities, we find that God exists and is no deceiver. The doubt is removed and the presumption in favor of the human intellect remains unchallenged.

This result is not circular, although it might be accused of having other defects, such as begging the question about the power and reliability of the human intellect. We will return to that question in Chapter 7.

Strong validation

A final reading of Descartes' aims is implicit in Arnauld's charge. He accused Descartes of relying on clear and distinct perception not merely to establish "certainty not truth," or to "remove the doubt" so as to leave a "presumption" in favor of the intellect, but to prove the existence of God, who then guarantees the truth of clear and distinct perception. This conforms to a "strong validation" reading.

Although Descartes did not accept this construal of his aims in replying to Arnauld, we know that he understood the question of whether the human intellect actually represents things as they are in themselves. The presumption passage itself raises this question only to put it aside, and Descartes acknowledges it elsewhere (e.g., 7:150–1). We may also find that aspects of the arguments in Meditations 4–6 tend in this direction. Moreover, whether or not Descartes intended a strong validation, we should ask whether he needed one, given his metaphysical ambitions.

There are some apparent resources for a strong validation in the Third Meditation. The extraction argument, if correct, would provide independent grounds for believing in the truth-presenting power of clear and distinct perception. The argument was put forward on the basis of the *cogito* alone. Although the resulting truth rule was held in doubt until the deceiving-God hypothesis had been removed, one might contend that the extraction argument supplies a legitimate method for investigating and removing that hypothesis as a ground for doubt. The meditator would be using the independently legitimated truth rule to prove the existence of God, but God's existence and goodness would play no validating role except to establish the emptiness of the deceiving-God hypothesis as a ground for doubt.

The natural light passage, if read literally, says that the natural light cannot be put in doubt, because there is no other faculty for checking it. Perhaps Descartes was after all suggesting that the "highest appeal" status of the natural light offers grounds for its absolute indubitability and absolute truth. But that argument is hard to swallow. The need to use a reasoning faculty in adjudicating the doubt would not seem to require that the faculty be able to deliver absolute truth, or that the faculty be able, as Descartes will ultimately claim, to sustain metaphysical conclusions about things as they are in themselves. The natural light passage as quoted above does adumbrate another argument, in the Sixth Meditation, where Descartes invokes God as the supplier of our faculties and argues that because we do not possess yet further faculties for checking their results, they can be trusted, on the grounds that God is no deceiver (7:79, 80). In that case, the passage might prefigure later grounds for a divine guarantee of clear and distinct perception. According to this strategy, the proof of God's existence and goodness would be needed to guarantee that the natural light, or clear and distinct perception, yields truth.

The strong validation argument affirms the absolute ability of the human intellect to find and certify the first principles of metaphysics. These principles include not only the existence and attributes of God but also, subsequently, the essences of things. It was Descartes' goal to achieve such results. Still, the reasoning thus far offered in support of strong validation, whether appealing to God or relying on the extraction argument, appears circular. The extraction argument, in particular, could break the traditional Cartesian circle by establishing the truth of clear and distinct perception independently of God's guarantee. And yet, how is that argument to be assessed, except through clear and distinct perception itself? This assessment does not merely examine some grounds for doubt but must establish the truth of an argument in support of the allegedly universal instrument of truth used to evaluate the argument.

Meditations 4–5 contain additional passages relevant to the circle. We should keep in mind the four readings outlined here (and especially the final three) while proceeding through them. We should also consider whether, outside those considered here, Descartes had other resources available for addressing the problem.

References and further reading

Many discussions of the Third Meditation focus on the metaphysical apparatus used in proving the existence of God – formal and objective reality of ideas, and the causal principle – along with the notorious Cartesian circle. Helpful studies are provided by Curley, Flage and Bonnen, B. Williams, and Wilson. Dicker's thorough and accessible treatment includes the extraction argument.

Descartes' proofs for the existence of God "from effects" belong generically to a type associated with Thomas Aquinas. For Aquinas, the effects include change in the world, the very existence of contingent beings, and the existence of order in the world; on his arguments, see E. Gilson, *Philosophy of St. Thomas Aquinas*, translated by E. Bullough (Cambridge: Heffer, 1929), chs. 4–5. Descartes' first proof, using the idea of God in the human mind, contrasts with Aquinas' focus on nature and its order. His second proof, using a finite being, is closer to Aquinas. Both proofs echo an Augustinian theme, of moving from the imperfection of the human mind to an infinite mind as a model through which our finiteness and imperfection are understood (see also 7:53). On Descartes' relation to Augustinian thought, see Menn, *Descartes and Augustine*. The notion of a hierarchy of being, used in the first proof, had both Platonic and Aristotelian precedents; on the Aristotelian background, see E.J. Ashworth, "Petrus Fonseca on Objective Concepts and the Analogy of Being," in Easton (ed.), *Logic and the Workings of the Mind*, pp. 47–63. For a systematic study of the relations between Cartesian and scholastic metaphysics, see J. Secada, *Cartesian Metaphysics: The Scholastic Origins of Modern Philosophy* (Cambridge: Cambridge University Press, 2000).

The literature on the Cartesian circle is large and varied. W. Doney (ed.), *Eternal Truths and the Cartesian Circle: A Collection of Studies* (New York, Garland, 1987), collects seminal papers. L. Loeb, "The Cartesian Circle," in *Cambridge Companion*, pp. 200–35, offers entry to the literature and examines the question of certainty or truth. Frankfurt, *Demons, Dreamers, and Madmen*, argues that Descartes was not seeking truth in the classical "correspondence" sense (correspondence of thought with knower-independent objects) but held a coherentist view (we give up correspondence and accept beliefs that best cohere among themselves). An older response to the circle, called the "memory defense," is unsound; see Frankfurt, "Memory and the Cartesian Circle," *Philosophical Review* 71 (1962), 504–11.

Chapter 6

Judgment, error, and freedom

Meditation 4: Truth and falsity

At the end of the Third Meditation, the meditator remarked that God's perfection is inconsistent with deception, hence he cannot be a deceiver. The Fourth Meditation pursues this conclusion more fully. In addition, the Synopsis promised that this Meditation will prove "that everything that we clearly and distinctly perceive is true" (7:15), which implies that the real argument for the truth rule occurs here. And, indeed, the Meditation does more than simply observe that deception is incompatible with God's perfection. It argues that God's role as creator, when paired with his perfection, entails that he would create us so that we can avoid error and reach the truth. Beyond simply removing the possibility that God might be a deceiver, the Meditation argues that God guarantees that our faculty of judgment is a truth-finder.

Review: immaterial things known without images (7:52–3)

The Meditation begins with the now familiar review of the meditator's cognitive situation. She proclaims her epistemic achievements: "During these past few days I have accustomed myself to leading my mind away from the senses; and I have taken careful note of the fact that there is very little about corporeal things that is truly perceived, whereas much more is known about the human mind, and still more about God" (7:52–3).

Not only does she have new knowledge about God and the human mind, she has also achieved a new cognitive procedure for achieving knowledge. She now has no difficulty "in turning my mind away from imaginable things and towards things which are objects of the intellect alone and are totally separate from matter" (7:53). Although she is not yet in a position to claim that the human mind is really distinct from matter, her idea of mind portrays it as immaterial; she claims a very clear idea of the human mind "insofar as it is a thinking thing, which is not extended in length, breadth or height and has no other bodily characteristics" (7:53).

The meditator also reports her firm conviction, gained in the Third Meditation, that God exists. She now claims that "from this contemplation of the true God," she can "see a way forward to the knowledge of other things" (7:53).

God is no deceiver (7:53)

She first repeats the brief remark from the end of the Third Meditation, that God is no deceiver:

> To begin with, I recognize that it is impossible that God should ever deceive me. For in every case of trickery or deception some imperfection is to be found; and although the ability to deceive appears to be an indication of cleverness or power, the will to deceive is undoubtedly evidence of malice or weakness, and so cannot apply to God. [7:53]

God is not a trickster; while he could if he wanted to, he does not act to deceive us. This language might simply rule out the case in which God would deceive us through positive intervention, as in the intervention hypothesis from Chapter 3 (God intervenes to give us false thoughts). But if that were so, then God's not being a deceiver provides no positive grounds for asserting that clear and distinct perceptions are true. It only says that, supposing we would naturally be able to reach the truth on our own, God will not step in to trick us.

Implications for my mental power (7:53–6)

In further considering God's perfection and the possibility of human error, the meditator returns to the issues from the First Meditation concerning the origin of her mind and its cognitive faculties. In God's purported role as the creator of the human mind, together with the incompatibility of perfection and deception, she finds a positive argument for the trustworthiness of human cognitive faculties.

Descartes invites her to reason as follows:

> Next, I know by experience that there is in me a faculty of judgment which, like everything else which is in me, I certainly received from God. And since God does not wish to deceive me, he surely did not give me the kind of faculty which would ever enable me to go wrong while using it correctly. [7:53–4]

It is a question here not of intervention but of the original constitution or design of our faculties. God made us, or so the meditator has accepted as proven in the previous Meditation. But God is incapable of deception. Hence he would not create us with a faculty that would inevitably make us go wrong. The idea seems to be that if God gave us a faculty that inevitably leads to errors, he would be responsible for the errors themselves, since he was our designer.

Thus far, the argument does not show that our faculties must yield truth. The condition laid down, that we must be able to avoid error, might be met in other ways. For instance, God might have given us very limited faculties but also given us the natural impulse to act according to probabilities without affirming anything as true. We would then be able to negotiate the necessities of survival reasonably well; but we would avoid the error of false judgment by never affirming the truth or falsehood of anything. However, the meditator persists in her analysis, presumably because she wants to understand God's relation to her mental powers as instruments of truth.

She now considers a problem analogous to the theological problem of evil. If God is perfectly good and can do anything, why is there evil in the world? If God is no deceiver and can do anything, why doesn't he make us so that we never fall into error at all? Yet there is evil, and we do fall into error.

In responding, Descartes drew upon two standard responses to the problem of evil, both stemming from Augustine's Neoplatonic theology. The first maintained that evil is not a real thing. It is the mere absence of good; it is not a positive quality but a form of "nothingness" or "non-being" (7:54). Therefore God does not, strictly speaking, create evil (since it doesn't "really exist"). Furthermore, if he is to create at all, he inevitably must produce things that partake of nothingness, since, on this view, anything that is not totally perfect partakes of non-being. Only God contains every perfection. Anything he creates must, therefore, fall short of complete perfection and goodness in various ways.

How shall an all-perfect creator organize a creation that must fall short of total perfection? Here the second response comes in. A universe with variety in it, including things that are both closer to and further from perfection, is alleged to be better than a universe in which less perfect beings are left out. As the meditator reasons near the end of the Meditation, "there may in some way be more perfection in the universe as a whole because some of its parts are not immune from error, while others are immune, than there would be if all the parts were exactly alike" (7:61). Variety is the spice of creation. It is better to have a variety of beings, including some who err. (If this argument fails, Descartes might appeal to our ignorance by claiming that God's purposes are beyond our knowledge [7:55].)

These two aspects of Descartes' responses do not completely cover his analysis of error. He now defines error as a case of failing when we shouldn't. Error in this sense is not simply a matter of being wrong; it involves being wrong when we should be able to avoid it: "error is not a pure negation, but rather a privation or lack of some knowledge which should somehow be in me" (7:55*). In the special sense of "error" defined here, it is not simply equated with false judgment. False judgment becomes a necessary but not a sufficient condition for cognitive error. By analogy with moral error, we err only when we judge falsely and should have been able to avoid it. It is not an error (in this special sense) if the false judgment is unavoidable. As finite beings, we cannot be expected to know everything. Moreover, because variety is good, we need not feel that God should have given us more knowledge than we have. The problem, as Descartes sees it, is not that we should know everything and don't. To locate the "privation" or "lack of knowledge" that yields error, we must look for a further standard (beyond mere truth and falsity) of what we "should do" in judging, violation of which will count as error.

Descartes acknowledges that God, being all-powerful, could have avoided the whole issue by making us so that we in fact never judge falsely, hence never err cognitively in any sense. (For instance, he might have preprogrammed us with all the right answers.) So why does he allow us ever to judge falsely? Descartes again offered a solution along Augustinian lines. False judgments arise from something good that God gave us: freedom of will. Inasmuch as we sometimes exercise our freedom by making judgments about matters that we do not perceive clearly and distinctly, we can judge falsely. This position allows him to assert that God gave us a perfectly good intellect that would never yield falsehood if used correctly, while leaving us responsible, through free will, for the false judgments we do make. The privation that leads to error resides in our making judgments we should not, as a result of using our free will in connection with our finite intellect.

Analysis of judgment: intellect/will (7:56–7)

The further account of error requires an explanation of how judgment occurs. Judgment depends on two faculties, the "intellect" or "faculty of cognition," and the "faculty of choice" or "freedom of will" (7:56*). The intellect is a faculty of cognition or representation; it perceives ideas (is aware of the objective reality, or content, of ideas). The will affirms or denies what is represented in such ideas. A judgment occurs only once the will has acted. Since, technically speaking, falsehood can only arise in judgments, falsehood requires that the will has affirmed or denied that the content represented by the intellect is true. The intellect by itself can make no mistakes, because it cannot assert (affirm or deny) anything.

The Fourth Meditation provides only a sketch of how intellect and will interact in judgment. The role of the intellect "is to enable me to perceive the ideas which are subjects for possible judgments; and when regarded strictly in this light, it turns out to contain no error in the proper sense of that term" (7:56). The will responds to this content presented by the intellect. It may affirm the content, deny it, or refrain from judging (7:57, 59).

Descartes' account of judgment can be filled out through comparison with its scholastic Aristotelian counterpart and by looking to other parts of the *Meditations*. On standard scholastic accounts, the intellect judges. It affirms or denies the content presented to it. It also perceives and affirms logical connections among contents, as in syllogistic reasoning. In Descartes' account, the will, not the intellect, does the affirming or denying. But perception of the relations and connections among ideas remains a job for the intellect, as when we perceive what properties flow from the essence of a triangle (7:64). Only if the will affirms the relations or connections do we have a judgment.

According to Descartes, the ideas we have of things present those things as having properties. Triangles are perceived as essentially having three sides and three angles, as being closed plane figures, and so on. Moreover, the clear and distinct ideas we have of finite objects such as triangles present them as possibly existing; our very idea of the thing allows us to perceive that it could exist (7:263). Other objects we perceive, such as chimeras (a mythical beast having a lion's head, goat's body, and serpent's tail) are perceived as unable to exist (7:383). Furthermore, the intellect perceives relations among ideas. For instance, it may perceive that God is perfect, that perfection excludes deception, and that God is therefore no deceiver.

The will's role is to affirm, deny, or refrain from judging when presented with such contents. Thus, when presented with the idea of a triangle and two right angles, the will might affirm or deny that the angles of a triangle equal two right angles. When presented with the idea of a chimera, the will might affirm or deny its actual or possible existence. When presented with the sequence of ideas allegedly leading to the conclusion that God is no deceiver, the will might affirm or deny that the sequence of ideas supports the conclusion. To say that the will is "presented" with these ideas makes it seem as if the will itself must perceive the content of the ideas and then affirm or deny. But that would be to ascribe to the will the sort of perceptual capacity that Descartes attributed to the intellect. We must consider the notions of truth and falsity before pursuing further the question of how the will interacts with the perceptions of the intellect, and how the interaction yields error.

Error involves (but is not equated with) false judgment. But what do truth and falsity consist of? Here Descartes gave the standard answer, from Aristotle to Kant. He wrote to Mersenne in 1639 that "*truth*, in the strict sense, denotes the conformity of thought with its object" (2:597). In the case of an actually existing object having certain properties, truth consists in affirming an idea that represents the object as existing when it does exist and represents it as having properties it has; falsity, in judging the existent as non-existent, or the existent as having properties it doesn't have. As we will see in Meditation 5, he held that we can make true or false judgments about the essences of things (7:64) without affirming or denying the existence of those things (leaving aside for now the case of God). Geometrical objects have essences, and a false judgment would result from affirming ideas that misrepresent an essence, or denying ideas that actually belong to the essence – as would happen if we affirmed that the sum of the two smaller angles of a triangle always equals the third, or denied the Pythagorean theorem (7:244). (Descartes held that we cannot make such mistakes when having clear and distinct perceptions of the ideas in question, but that is another matter.)

Analysis of error, consistent with God's goodness (7:56–62)

Descartes' job is to provide an analysis of human error that meets the conditions so far set out. The meditator needs to assure herself that, consonant with God's perfection and goodness, each of our human faculties is "perfect of its kind" (7:55). Both the intellect and the will, taken in themselves, must be free of defect. She must now find what it is that should occur in the interaction of intellect and will but does not in cases of error. She is looking for some knowledge "that should somehow be in me" but isn't (7:55*).

The meditator reasons that the intellect is perfect of its kind, that is, is as good as need be for us. Being finite, it does not contain ideas of everything. Some of its ideas, especially those from the senses, are confused and obscure. Indeed, in the Third Meditation, some sensory ideas were said to be "materially false," which means that they provide material for false judgment (7:43). (Such judgments occur when we affirm the resemblance thesis – that is, when we conclude that external objects have properties in them that resemble our sensations of color, sounds, and other so-called secondary qualities.) But none of this shows that the intellect is defective of its kind, merely that it is of the finite, or limited, kind (7:60). Its finitude would not result in false judgments, she reasons, if we would stick to things the intellect understands perfectly well: its clear and distinct perceptions.

The will is also perfect of its kind. That is, we are perfectly free. The meditator affirms that our will is as great as can be: "it is only the will, or freedom of choice, which I experience within me to be so great that the idea of any greater faculty is beyond my grasp; so much so that it is above all in virtue of the will that I understand myself to bear in some way the image and likeness of God" (7:57). The will consists in "our ability to do or not to do something (that is, to affirm or deny, to pursue or avoid)" (7:57). As long as we are not constrained by outside forces, we are free. Our judgments, as depending on the will, are up to us. (This does not mean that they are not determined by our nature – the specifics of Descartes' conception of freedom are taken up in the next section.)

Neither the intellect nor the will is the culprit, on Descartes' account. Rather, error originates from the relation between them. The will's freedom is so great that it overflows the boundary of the intellect's clear and distinct perceptions; we make judgments about ideas that are not perceived with sufficient clarity and distinctness.

What then is the source of my mistakes? It must be simply this: the scope of the will is wider than that of the intellect; but instead of restricting it within the same limits, I extend its use to matters which I do not understand. Since the will is indifferent in such cases, it easily turns aside from what is true and good, and this is the source of my error and sin. [7:58]

God's perfection means that he gives us faculties that, if used correctly, allow us to avoid falsehood. We go wrong when we judge outside the bounds of clear and distinct perception. In those cases, we are responsible, since it is our choice to make the judgments in question. We could avoid falsehood by withholding judgment where clear and distinct perception is lacking. Here is a condition for error that involves more than simply judging falsely: we err by making judgments in circumstances where we know falsehood can creep in.

Our errors are our responsibility because we make them freely. Even though he designed our faculties, God is not responsible for our own free use of them. Descartes addresses other details, arguing that the will would not be perfect of its kind if it were artificially limited by God so that it affirmed only clear and distinct perceptions (7:60). We are not truly free, it seems, unless we are free to err! But a difficulty remains. He still hasn't ruled out the case in which we avoid falsehood and error simply by not judging at all. So we don't yet have an explanation for why God should go beyond allowing us to avoid falsehood and design us to achieve truth.

God's culpability, in case clear and distinct perceptions are not true, arises from a further aspect of the relation between intellect and will. Descartes not only held that our free will allows us to refrain from judging when our perception is not clear and distinct; he also maintained that when we do perceive something clearly and distinctly, the will cannot refrain from affirming it.

During these past few days I have been asking whether anything in the world exists, and I have realized that from the very fact of my raising the question it follows evidently that I exist. I could not but judge that something which I understood so clearly was true; but this was not because I was compelled so to judge by any external force, but because a great light in the intellect was followed by a great inclination in the will, and thus the spontaneity and freedom of my belief was all the greater in proportion to my lack of indifference. [7:58–9]

The will is inclined toward the true (and the good), as presented to it by the intellect. (It is as if the will is drawn to the true and the good appetitively.) In the case of clear and distinct perceptions, it is ineluctably inclined to affirm their truth. If we "cannot but judge" some perceptions to be true, we would inevitably go wrong if in fact those perceptions weren't true. Since God made both the intellect and the will and placed them in relation to one another, he would bear the responsibility for a design flaw if perceptions whose truth we cannot help but affirm could ever yield falsehood.

This answer explains why God should be held responsible for the truth of clear and distinct perceptions. He made us so that we cannot help but affirm them. But this leads to another problem. How are we free in our judging if we cannot keep from affirming (sufficiently) clear and distinct perceptions? The answer lies in Descartes' theory of free will.

Freedom of will (7:57–9)

Descartes provides a characterization of will, and freedom of will, in the midst of his discussion of judgment and error:

> The will simply consists in our ability to do or not do something (that is, to affirm or deny, to pursue or avoid); or rather, it consists simply in the fact that when the intellect puts something forward for affirmation or denial or for pursuit or avoidance, our inclinations are such that we do not feel we are determined by any external force. [7:57]

Many readers of Descartes find two different conceptions of freedom implied by this passage. The first is freedom of indifference. Such freedom consists in the ability to determine ourselves to choose one way or the other, that is, to go either way in any given instance. The second conception finds our freedom in our acting in accordance with our own will, as opposed to our acts being determined by external force or constraint. This is called the freedom of spontaneity (where "spontaneous" means self-acting but not necessarily uncaused). As described by Descartes, this spontaneous choice may be completely determined by our nature. As he put it in the Second Replies, "the will of a thinking thing is drawn voluntarily and freely (for that is the essence of will), but nevertheless inevitably, towards a clearly known good" (7:166). To be drawn inevitably means that we cannot but so choose. So on this second conception, we are free even if determined, so long as we are determined internally, by the nature of our will.

Compatibilism and non-compatibilism

If we take each of these conceptions as a general account of freedom, we are forced to engage the modern problem of compatibilism. A compatibilist holds that freedom of the will is compatible with determinism. That is Descartes' position in the second conception above. A non-compatibilist holds that freedom requires the ability to do or not to do without being determined even by our own nature. To be free, we must be able to have chosen the opposite of what we did choose. Descartes seems to say both things about freedom, and thus to contradict himself by holding both compatibilist and non-compatibilist views.

However, we should note that the two conceptions of freedom we located in the above quotation are contradictory only if we treat the first as providing a general definition of, or a necessary condition for, freedom. But we need not do that. Descartes might consistently hold that freedom is compatible with inner determination but also hold that in some circumstances we choose in a way that is not internally determined (not determined by the clear perception of the intellect, or any other factor). He might have affirmed the compatibility of freedom with inner determination, while also allowing that we are not always determined in this way.

There is no doubt that Descartes believed that freedom is compatible with inner determination, for he directly affirmed this position in the continuation of the above quotation:

> In order to be free, there is no need for me to be inclined both ways; on the contrary, the more I incline in one direction – either because I clearly understand that reasons of truth and goodness point that way, or because of a divinely produced disposition of my inmost thoughts – the freer is my choice. Neither divine grace nor natural knowledge ever diminishes freedom; on the contrary, they increase and strengthen it. But the indifference I feel when there is no reason pushing me in one direction rather than another is the lowest grade of freedom; it is evidence not of any perfection of freedom, but rather of a defect in knowledge or a kind of negation. For if I always saw clearly what was true and good, I should never have to deliberate about the right judgment or choice; in that case, although I should be wholly free, it would be impossible for me ever to be in a state of indifference. [7:57–8]

On this view, we are free when we act from our own choice. That choice may be fully determined by a clear perception of the true or good. Freedom is acting according to our own will, but that will need not be unstructured. In fact, Descartes holds that it is the essence of human will to be drawn toward the true and the good. As he explains in the Sixth Replies (in distinguishing human from divine freedom), "as for man, since he finds that the nature of all goodness and truth is already determined by God, and his will cannot tend towards anything else, it is evident that he will embrace what is good and true all the more willingly, and hence more freely, in proportion as he sees it more clearly" (7:432). We are naturally determined to affirm the truth and cannot help but do so when we see it clearly and distinctly.

At the same time, Descartes also allowed that humans are free when indifferent between two options. In the above quotation, such indifference is described as "the lowest grade of freedom."

In a letter to the Jesuit Mesland in 1645, Descartes distinguished two senses of such "indifference" (4:173). The first says simply that our perceptions do not incline us in one direction or another; we are indifferent because nothing attracts the will. (This sort of indifference is not incompatible with the will being determined by other factors, such as habit, to choose one way rather than another.) He told Mesland (4:173) that he had this meaning in mind in the quotation above. In the same letter, he identified a second meaning of "indifference" as the "positive faculty of determining oneself to one or other of two contraries." This is the ability (in some circumstances) to direct the will to choose in a completely undetermined manner. In the Fifth Replies, he affirmed that in some cases the will has "the freedom to direct itself, without the determination of the intellect, towards one side or the other" (7:378). Indeed, in the letter to Mesland he allowed that we can "hold back" from a clear and distinct perception of the good or the true "provided we consider it a good thing to demonstrate the freedom of our will by so doing" (4:173). In a previous letter, Descartes had explained how this might happen through a momentary suspension of judgment. Having acknowledged that it is "impossible" for the will to refrain from affirming a current clear and distinct perception, he maintained that once such a perception has dimmed (or, in the present case, prior to achieving the perception fully) we are able to "suspend judgment" by bringing forth reasons for doing so (4:115–16). These might be reasons for doubt (as in the case of mathematical propositions), or the reason of wanting to demonstrate one's freedom.

Freedom as the power to choose

It seems, then, that Descartes has it both ways: in cases of indifference we can choose without being determined; in cases of clear and distinct perception we choose with inner necessity. Does this indicate that Descartes had two conceptions of freedom? Not at all. As he explained to Mesland, in both cases freedom is the power to determine oneself – for even an inner determination is a determination of oneself!

> And so, since you regard freedom not simply as indifference but rather as a real and positive power to determine oneself, the difference between us is a merely verbal one – for I agree that the will has such a power. However, I do not see that it makes any difference to that power whether it is accompanied by indifference, which you agree is an imperfection, or whether it is not so accompanied, when there is nothing in the intellect except light,

as in the case of the blessed, who are confirmed in grace. And so I call free in the general sense whatever is voluntary, whereas you wish to restrict the term to the power to determine oneself only if accompanied by indifference. [4:116]

It makes no difference to Descartes whether the inner determination comes from the will's response to a "great light in the intellect" (7:59) or from its own determination of choice in the face of indifference (in the second, wholly unconstrained sense from above). Both are instances of freedom. The non-compatibilist's concerns are not Descartes' concerns. But neither does he deny an undetermined power to choose (in some cases).

The central idea in Descartes' response to Mesland is interesting in its own right. He suggests that the power to choose need not imply the ability to choose in more than one way on every occasion. To see how this works, consider a phrase that may be thought to capture the notion of free will: we can choose what we want. The phrase is intriguingly ambiguous. It can mean: we are able to choose whatever and however we want. The implication here is that the will can choose anything, bounded solely by any limit on our ability to conceive what we want. But the phrase can also mean: we are able to choose that which we do in fact want (even if determined by our nature to want it). Here, the implication is that nothing prevents us from choosing the things we want, even if our will is built to want specific things. For Descartes, we want (to affirm or pursue) what is true and good. For him, freedom of will can simply mean that no external constraint prevents us from actually willing what, by the nature of our will, we are determined to will. Free choice of the former kind, choosing however we want, is limited to cases in which the will is not so determined.

Freedom and the privation that constitutes error

Assuming for now that this is a correct interpretation of Descartes' position on freedom, it may seem odd that he would choose to display both an indifferentist and a determinist side of this complicated picture in the midst of the Fourth Meditation. But he had a reason for doing so. He needed both sides to accomplish his aims. He needed to be able to hold God responsible for the truth of clear and distinct perceptions while also making us responsible for our own errors. To accomplish the first, humans must not be able to avoid error simply by suspending judgment in all cases. If we are determined (freely) to affirm the truth of a clear and distinct perception, God would be guilty of deceit-inducing design if such perceptions were not true. But to preserve this picture of God's perfection, God must be released from responsibility for our errors. The freedom of indifference accomplishes this – although one might ask whether the weaker notion of indifference, ascribed by Descartes to the passage from this Meditation, adequately supports a notion of responsibility. In any case, Descartes' position is that we must take responsibility for the false judgments that arise when we affirm or deny something, even though the will has not been ineluctably drawn to a clear and distinct perception.

Descartes classified all cases in which the will is not compelled as cases of indifference (in the first sense, above). Such indifference does not require that there be no reasons at all "drawing" the will to one side or the other; rather, it includes "every case where the intellect does not have sufficiently clear knowledge at the time when the will deliberates" (7:59). Probable conjectures may draw the will in one way, but the "mere knowledge" that such conjectures are dubitable allows one to suspend judgment (as the meditator's experience "in the last few days" exemplifies).

We are now in a position to understand the privation or lack of knowledge that constitutes error. It is not the "lack of knowledge" displayed by false judgment itself; rather, it is a failure to follow the rule that only sufficiently clear and distinct perceptions should be affirmed as true.

> If, however, I simply refrain from making a judgment in cases where I do not perceive the truth with sufficient clarity and distinctness, then it is clear that I am behaving correctly and avoiding error. But if in such cases I either affirm or deny, then I am not using my free will correctly. If I go for the alternative that is false, then obviously I shall be in error; if I take the other side,

then it is by pure chance that I arrive at the truth, and I shall still be at fault since it is clear by the natural light that the perception of the intellect should always precede the determination of the will. In this incorrect use of free will may be found the privation which constitutes the essence of error. [7:59–60]

The "privation" or "lack" in us comes from not following the rule that the will should be determined in judging by clear and distinct perceptions. Faced with uncertainty, we should withhold judgment rather than follow confused perceptions, habits, or preconceived opinions. Therefore, we should affirm only our clear and distinct perceptions (a rule we cannot always follow when everyday action is required [7:149, 248]).

This position is not without problems. Descartes acknowledges that a God who can do anything could leave us our freedom and still preserve us from error. God could have "impressed it unforgettably on my memory that I should never make a judgment about anything which I did not clearly and distinctly understand" (7:61). To respond to this potential objection, Descartes must either fall back on our ignorance of God's overall plan – that is, to the mystery of God's ways (7:55) – or affirm that since greater perfection results from variety, we should not complain about not being more perfect than we are (7:61). Nonetheless, his use of two conceptions of freedom to make God's perfection the basis for a divine guarantee of the truth rule, while leaving responsibility for our errors to us, may be admired for its subtlety and skill.

Clear and distinct perception is true (7:62)

At the conclusion of the Fourth Meditation, Descartes returns to the truth of clear and distinct perceptions and leaves no doubt that he has intended to reveal a divine guarantee for their truth:

Every clear and distinct perception is undoubtedly something, and hence cannot come from nothing, but must necessarily have God for its author. Its author, I say, is God, who is supremely perfect, and who cannot be a deceiver on pain of contradiction;

hence the perception is undoubtedly true. So today I have learned not only what precautions to take to avoid ever going wrong, but also what to do to arrive at the truth. [7:62]

The warrant for clear and distinct perception comes from God. The argument does not merely preclude God from intervening to trick us. God has responsibility for creating the human intellect with its clear and distinct perceptions, and the will that cannot help but assent to them.

The truth rule and the will

In his Objections to the Fourth Meditation, Gassendi insists that Descartes should provide a method for discovering when we have clear and distinct perceptions, since we can believe we have them when we don't (7:318) – an objection he had raised (7:277–9) in connection with the truth rule from the Third Meditation. Descartes counters that he had already provided a method "for determining whether or not we are deceived when we think we perceive something clearly" (7:361). He provided this method "in the appropriate place, where I first eliminated all preconceived opinions and afterwards listed all my principal ideas, distinguishing those which were clear from those which were obscure or confused" (7:362).

This passage suggests that the method for discerning when our perceptions are clear and distinct is provided by the method of doubt and the discovery of the thinking thing and the idea of God. What is the common factor here to suggest that there is a "method" at work? In Chapter 5, we considered the possibility that Descartes simply intends the reader to see what is common to cases of clear and distinct perception by considering examples; and that is in effect what he says to Gassendi. However, drawing on the Fourth Meditation, we can now propose a more definite way of deciding, namely, the absence of indifference or uncertainty in the will. He has said that in the case of the *cogito* reasoning, the will is compelled by the "great light" in the intellect (7:58–9). There is no indifference (7:59). In the case of the idea of God and the remaining elements of the argument in the Third Meditation, the "natural light" of the intellect shows the way (7:42,

44, 47, 49); such cases, described as involving "utterly clear and distinct" ideas (7:46), presumably do not permit indifference. But in the case of his "former beliefs," doubt is possible, a sign of indifference (7:59). Lack of dubitability is a sure sign of clear and distinct perception (the will is compelled); indifference and uncertainty, which permit dubitability, are sure signs that such perception has not been achieved.

Still, might we not mistake whether the will is compelled? Could we not confuse strong force of habit, or our own stubborn belief, with genuine compulsion? Gassendi raises a similar objection in observing that some people face death for their convictions, even though others face death for opposite convictions (7:278). Since, presumably, both parties can't be right, at least one died for a falsehood. Descartes grants the facts but responds that "it can never be proved that they clearly and distinctly perceive what they so stubbornly affirm" (7:361). On the other side, however, it cannot be proved in any given case that we have not mistaken clear and distinct perception for habit or stubbornness. And in other cases, we might possess potentially clear and distinct ideas but not pay sufficient attention for the will to be compelled. Descartes may have no further response in such cases, except to recommend caution, or repeated meditation.

The divine guarantee and the circle

In Chapter 5, we considered four responses to the problem of the Cartesian circle. These were "certainty not truth," "remove the doubt," "presumption in favor of the intellect," and "strong validation." The divine guarantee at the end of the Fourth Meditation apparently runs counter to the first three. The claim that clear and distinct perception yields truth contradicts the proposal that Descartes was after mere psychological certainty. His appeal to God's certification of clear and distinct perception does more than simply "remove the doubt" that a deceiver might be at work. While Descartes may have accepted a general presumption in favor of the intellect, in the Fourth Meditation he offers more: a strong external validation of the intellect. The Meditation supports ascribing a strong validation strategy to Descartes.

That strategy has its costs. To the extent that the actual existence of God the creator is required by the arguments of this Meditation, Arnauld's original objection of circularity arises. Having used clear and distinct perception to prove God's existence and perfection in the Third Meditation, the meditator would now be appealing to God's existence and perfection to guarantee the truth of clear and distinct perception in the Fourth.

Although the Fourth Meditation appears to aim for strong validation, we might seek instead to read it through the "remove the doubt" or "presumption" strategies. Perhaps examining the view that a non-deceiving God created our intellect and will simply provides firmer grounds for removing the deceiving-God hypothesis. Accordingly, strong validation is not intended – only thorough support for the conclusion that the deceiving-God hypothesis has internal problems. On the presumption reading, one might hold that Descartes was not really out to validate clear and distinct perception in the Meditation but to explain how the reality of human error is consistent with a clear and distinct perception from the Third Meditation: that God exists and is no deceiver. The problem with this last interpretation is that in the Synopsis Descartes says that the "clear and distinct" truth rule is first established in the Fourth Meditation. If we read the Meditation as providing the argument for this rule, it is difficult to avoid strong validation.

The *Meditations* doesn't stop here, and neither should our interpretation of Descartes' responses to the circle. His response to Arnauld relied on a distinction between having a clear and distinct perception and remembering having had one, which is discussed extensively in the Fifth Meditation. Moreover, we should be open to the possibility that Descartes had more than one argument for accepting his truth rule. In that case, perhaps some fall prey to the charge of circularity, and some don't.

References and further reading

The Fourth Meditation is sometimes omitted from standard commentaries (e.g., Dicker). Kenny, ch. 8, Wilson, ch. 4, and B. Williams, ch. 6, examine will and judgment.

Menn, *Descartes and Augustine*, ch. 7, explores the Augustinian elements of the Fourth Meditation. A. Kenny, "Descartes on the Will," in J. Cottingham (ed.), *Descartes*, Oxford Readings in Philosophy (Oxford: Oxford University Press, 1998), pp. 132–59, provides an advanced discussion of the theory of will in the Fourth Meditation and other Cartesian texts. V. Chappell, "Descartes's Compatibilism," in Cottingham (ed.), *Reason, Will, and Sensation: Studies in Descartes's Metaphysics* (Oxford: Clarendon Press, 1994), pp. 177–90, examines the indifference and spontaneity conceptions of freedom in connection with the Jesuit D. Mesland (with scholastic Aristotelian leanings) and the Oratorian G. Gibieuf (with Augustinian and hence Neoplatonic leanings). D. Rosenthal, "Will and the Theory of Judgment," in Rorty (ed.), *Essays on Descartes' Meditations*, pp. 405–34, analyzes Descartes' theory of judgment in detail.

Chapter 7

Matter, God, and the circle again

Meditation 5: The essence of material things, and the existence of God considered a second time

The Fifth Meditation opens with the meditator resolving "to try to escape from the doubts into which I fell a few days ago, and see whether any certainty can be achieved regarding material objects" (7:63). She acknowledges that she has already discovered some things concerning herself as a thinking thing or mind, and concerning God. It is now time to move on. The title of the Meditation promises that the "essence of material things" will be discovered.

Meditation on this essence occurs early and is over quickly. Its discovery leads the meditator (in accordance with the analytic method) to reflect on how that knowledge arose, and she finds that it depends on innate ideas (7:64–8). She has already found, in the Third Meditation, that she had an innate idea of God. Now she makes additional discoveries, or at least additional claims, concerning innate ideas. First, she affirms that such ideas reveal the "true and immutable natures" of things. This discovery in turn leads to a new proof for the existence of God. And the new proof leads to a final consideration of the earlier grounds for doubt, and of clear and distinct perception as a source of truth. Hence, although the Meditation achieves new positive results, it is devoted equally to continued methodological reflection. Indeed, of all the Meditations, it addresses most explicitly the question of how metaphysical knowledge arises.

Essence of matter is extension (7:63, 71)

The Third and Fourth Meditations purportedly established "clear and distinct" intellectual perception as the method for discovering truth. It makes sense, then, for the meditator now to say, concerning material objects: "before I inquire whether any such things exist outside me, I must consider the ideas of these things, insofar as they exist in my thought, and see which of them are distinct, and which confused" (7:63). That is, the meditator will seek to "escape" the earlier doubts not by considering the existence of material objects, which might require using the senses, but merely by examining her ideas of such objects. And these ideas purportedly reveal the essence of material things.

It may by now seem natural to turn to the ideas of essences first, since in the Second Meditation Descartes directed the meditator toward ideas of her nature as a thinking thing, and in the Third toward the idea of God. But for his Aristotelian readers this method as used here would seem revolutionary, since they would consider knowledge of existence to precede knowledge of essence. In their methodology, essences are known by contemplating sensory images of existent things and "abstracting" the common nature they share – whether the nature of one kind of thing, such as a rabbit, or the essence of extension, considered simply as a property that all bodies happen to have.

In fact, Descartes has prepared such readers for this procedure in meditating on self and God. An Aristotelian would believe that those meditations, too, must always involve sensory images. And yet

Descartes has directed the meditator to "withdraw the mind from the senses" in carrying them out. Assuming that the meditator has been able to follow this instruction and has found the ideas that Descartes expected (no small assumptions!), the way has been prepared for investigating even material things in this manner. (Indeed, the Sixth Meditation explicitly claims that the essence of material things can be grasped independently of any sensory or imaginal ideas [7:72–3].)

Turning to her ideas of material objects, the meditator finds:

> Quantity, for example, or "continuous" quantity as the philosophers commonly call it, is something I distinctly imagine. That is, I distinctly imagine the extension of the quantity (or rather of the thing which is quantified) in length, breadth and depth. I also enumerate various parts of the thing, and to these parts I assign various sizes, shapes, positions and local motions; and to the motions I assign various durations. [7:63]

This brief passage contains the list of properties that form or follow from the essence of matter (or that pertain to all finite substances in the cases of number and duration). "Extension," or "continuous quantity," is the essence of matter. Extension should be thought of as a three-dimensional spatial field – with the qualification, mentioned previously, that Descartes did not distinguish space from matter. Cartesian extension is a three-dimensional volume of matter. This extended matter is divided into parts, which possess sizes, shapes, positions, and local motions. The division into parts allows for enumeration, or counting of the parts, and the motions of the parts, as the parts themselves, exist through a duration of time.

Without calling attention to the fact, Descartes here outlines his metaphysics of material substance. In the *Principles*, he explains that each substance has a "principal attribute" or "property" that "constitutes its nature and essence, and to which all its other properties are referred" (8A:25), including all its modes. He discusses the list of properties found in the passage above, identifying extension as the principal attribute of material substance (and thought as the principal attribute of mental substance), and describing size, shape, position, and local motion as modes or modifications of that principal attribute. These modes must be understood "through" the principal attribute (8A:25–6; see also 7:120–1). To understand a mode "through" an attribute is to grasp the mode as a limitation or modification of that attribute. Although one can understand an attribute without thinking of a particular mode, one cannot think of a particular mode without thinking of the attribute. Thus, while we might be able to think of extension without motion, we cannot think of motion without there being an extended area for it to traverse. Similarly, we are to conceive size, shape, and position as modifications of extension that arise by creating boundaries (hence creating parts) in the field of extension. But we can also understand an indefinitely large field of extension without thinking of particular sizes, shapes, and positions. (Because the field of extension is conceived as indefinitely large, Descartes avoids assigning it a boundary, hence a size and shape; and since he posited no space "outside" the field of extension, that field has no position – rather, position is defined within the field of extension, by relations among parts.)

In his proposal that the essence of material substance is extension, Descartes not only violated Aristotelian epistemology by claiming to know this essence independently of existence, but he also contradicted the basic conception of corporeal or bodily substance in Aristotelian physics. All Aristotelian corporeal substances possess active natures that direct their motion – where "motion" is broadly defined to include qualitative changes (e.g., from cold to hot), mineral processes (magnetic attraction), and biological and psychological processes (bodily growth and the acquisition of knowledge). The bare property of extension, which contains no notion of activity, or any principle of growth or change, was not considered a possible candidate for the essence (or substantial form) of a substance. Extension was regarded as a "universal accident" of all bodily things. All bodies take up space, or have extension, but no corporeal thing could exist having extension as its sole property (i.e., without having a substantial form or active principle of change).

The phrase "the essence of material things" occurs only in the title of the Fifth Meditation but not in the text, where the essence is described. Indeed, the meditator explicitly first ascribes her idea of extension to a possibly existent "corporeal nature" at the end of the

Fifth and beginning of the Sixth Meditations (7:71). Why such indirectness? Perhaps we have here an instance of the strategy that Descartes confided to Mersenne, of hoping that readers "will unwittingly become accustomed to my principles, and will recognize the truth, before they notice that my principles destroy those of Aristotle" (3:298*). He wanted to replace the Aristotelian conception of corporeal substance without initially drawing special attention to that fact.

Innate ideas of essences (7:63–5)

Having achieved a clear idea of extension, the meditator reflects on the character of this knowledge:

> Not only are all these things very well known and transparent to me when regarded in this general way, but in addition there are countless particular features regarding shape, number, motion and so on, which I perceive when I give them my attention. And the truth of these matters is so open and so much in harmony with my nature, that on first discovering them it seems that I am not so much learning something new as remembering what I knew before; or it seems like noticing for the first time things which were long present within me although I had never turned my mental gaze on them before. [7:63–4]

Descartes makes four points here concerning the recent contemplation of her "distinct" ideas of extended things, which in turn reveal his model of how the basic truths of metaphysics are known. He first has the meditator notice that the ideas (of extension, shape, size, etc.) she has been contemplating are "very well known and transparent." Second, he has her consider that other knowledge of "shape, number, and motion" – all instances of geometrical or arithmetical properties – arises when she attends to her very distinct ideas of extension, its parts and modes. Her ideas are epistemically complex and support a wider system of knowledge; they are cognitively fecund. Third, in comparing such knowledge to something remembered, he alludes to the Platonic doctrine of reminiscence, according to which all knowledge is innate. (In the *Phaedo*, Plato suggested that such knowledge is innate because revealed directly to the soul prior to birth. Descartes, by contrast, held that innate ideas are placed in the mind by God and so did not hold that the mind directly perceives Platonic Forms or eternal essences independently of God.) And, fourth, he further describes the knowledge not only as transparent or "open" but also as "in harmony" with the meditator's nature, although newly discovered to be so. Furthermore, in characterizing the ideas as both "clear" (7:64–5) and "distinct" (7:63), he indicates their strong epistemic credentials. In effect, here he describes for the meditator the experience she should have in becoming reflectively aware of the intellectual ideas that form the basis of metaphysical and physical knowledge.

These four properties of the ideas of extended things – transparency, fecundity, innateness, and discovered harmony – tell the meditator what it is like to become aware of her innate ideas. As Descartes explained elsewhere, these innate ideas should not be thought of as static entities sprinkled into the mind like raisins in a cake; rather, they are ideas that we have the power to form in virtue of our natural or innate power of thinking (8B:357–8). They are the latent structure of our intellect, which becomes manifest through thinking. The Fifth Meditation describes and explores this "transparent" and innately accessible knowledge to reveal its implications for metaphysics.

The next three paragraphs contain a three-step process, which moves from recognizing the inherent integrity and cognitive unity of various ideas, to finding grounds for the reality and truth of the ideas, to asserting a correspondence between such ideas and possible or actual things in the world. Descartes wants the meditator to discover that her ideas reveal the natures of things and the inherent necessity of God's existence. These passages are at the heart of his rationalist epistemology of metaphysical knowledge.

The meditator now concludes that the ideas of extension reveal the "true and immutable natures" of things, whether these things exist outside her or not (7:64). Her initial evidence that the ideas reveal "true and immutable natures" is that they don't depend on her own will. Or rather, since the ideas can be "thought of at will" (7:64), it is their content that is not invented by her. Proof for this point arises from contemplating the "nature, essence, or form of the triangle":

various properties can be demonstrated of the triangle, for example that its three angles equal two right angles, that its greatest side subtends its greatest angle, and the like; and since these properties are ones which I now clearly recognize whether I want to or not, even if I never thought of them at all when I previously imagined the triangle, it follows that they cannot have been invented by me. [7:64]

Various properties can be "read from" the idea of a triangle. These properties are *discoveries* of what is contained in or follows from the idea of the triangle and are not *inventions* of the meditator's own mind.

Descartes' point becomes clearer if we compare sensory ideas with the innate idea of a triangle. Descartes has earlier allowed that sensory ideas do not depend on the meditator's will but come to her whether she wants them to or not. Thus the meditator feels the heat of the fire whether she chooses to or not (7:38). In that case, both the arrival of the idea and its content (whether, near the fire, she feels heat or cold) are beyond the control of the meditator. With the idea of a triangle, its arrival is under the control of the meditator. She can choose to think of something else, such as a circle or a horse, or she can choose to focus on present sensory experience (say, of a room with a fire). But in thinking of the triangle, its properties, including hitherto unimagined ones, come to her whether she wills or not. And they do not simply fill her experience, as the heat of the fire might, but they compel recognition, or cognitive acknowledgment. As she says, there are properties of the triangle "which I now clearly recognize whether I want to or not, even if I never thought of them at all when I previously imagined the triangle" (7:64). The idea of the triangle has an ineluctable internal structure that reveals connections among various properties to which the meditator "cannot but assent" (7:65). (Here we have a kind of phenomenology or "what it's like" for clear and distinct perception.)

In the second of the three paragraphs, Descartes considers the possibility that the idea of a triangle has been gleaned from sensory experience of triangular bodies (as in the Aristotelian process of abstracting an essence or common nature). The meditator rejects this possibility. The evidence is again her ability to discover various properties pertaining to any number of shapes, including many "other shapes which there can be no suspicion of my ever having encountered through the senses" (7:64). However, although she takes this ability as evidence that these ideas of shape are innate, an Aristotelian might instead appeal to the power of abstraction and contend that we generalize from instances of sensory shapes to the idealized shapes in geometry, and to new shapes. Throughout the history of philosophy, there has been a more general debate between abstractionist and innatist accounts of geometrical knowledge, which recurs in the Objections and Replies. Gassendi (as a new empiricist) formulates an abstractionist position (7:320–1), to which Descartes responds (7:381–2). In the Sixth Meditation, Descartes will offer introspective evidence for non-sensory ideas of geometrical figures (7:72–3).

From her mental perception of these various geometrical properties of shapes, the meditator draws a strong conclusion:

> All these properties are certainly true, since they are clearly cognized by me, and therefore they are something, and not merely nothing; for it is obvious that whatever is true is something; and I have already amply demonstrated that everything which I cognize clearly is true. And even if I had not demonstrated this, the nature of my mind is such that I cannot but assent to these things, at least so long as I clearly perceive them. [7:65*]

In the first sentence, Descartes argues from the meditator's "cognizing clearly" some properties, to their being true, to their being something and not nothing. The second sentence apparently offers a fall-back position, that even if it had not been demonstrated that "everything which I cognize clearly is true," the meditator cannot help but assent to her perceptions of the properties of the triangles. (Again raising a question about the relation between unavoidable assent and truth.)

But what has been assented to? In what does the truth and "something-thinghood" of properties (as opposed to things) consist? We should remember that at this stage in the *Meditations* the existence of material things is still in doubt. So the truth here concerns the essences of triangles and other geometrical figures, whether they exist in bodies or not. These essences are themselves taken to be "something," inasmuch as they are represented in and understood by the human mind. Furthermore, these clearly perceived truths concern material things; the title of the Meditation says that we are to learn the "essence of material things" (7:63), and the final sentence of the Meditation speaks of knowledge of "the whole of that corporeal nature which is the subject-matter of pure mathematics" (7:71). These truths define the essence of a matter that is now (in the meditator's epistemic situation) considered as merely possible. But they inform the meditator of properties that matter *must* have (in the case of extension itself) and *can* have (in the case of various shapes and so on) if it exists. Matter can have the shapes that extension or pure quantity can have, and geometry provides knowledge of those shapes. Thus, in any truly spherical bit of matter, all the radii will be equal; but if some bits are not quite regular spheres, their radii will be somewhat unequal, and so on.

Descartes' claim to know the essence of matter prior to its existence is, then, a claim to know the possible properties of things (see 7:71). The metaphysics of such a possibility is complex. Descartes, like many of his contemporaries, made such a possibility depend on the creative power of God. However, his theory of such possibility is complicated by his special claim that the eternal truths of geometry are God's free creations (7:380, 432, 435–6; discussed in Chapter 9). For now, let us suppose that the knowledge of geometrical essences found in the Fifth Meditation concerns the actual eternal truths as laid down by God, which determine the real possibilities of the world of created matter, if that world exists.

In the third of the three paragraphs, Descartes offers his first statement of what was later called the "ontological argument" for the existence of God. In introducing the argument, he states the core principle of his metaphysical epistemology. The meditator asks:

> But if the mere fact that I can produce from my thought the idea of something entails that everything which I clearly and distinctly perceive to belong to that thing really does belong to it, is not this a possible basis for another argument to prove the existence of God? [7:65]

The ontological argument will be taken up shortly. For now, consider the strong claim that Descartes makes about the relation between ideas in the human mind and the properties of things. The meditator claims that the fact that she has a clear and distinct idea of a thing's properties *entails* that the thing has those properties. If she clearly and distinctly perceives that the radii of a circle are equal to one another, or that the squares constructed on the sides of a right-angled triangle follow the Pythagorean theorem, then these properties are true of all circles and all right-angled triangles. What the human mind clearly and distinctly perceives as in a thing does truly belong to it.

If Descartes were speaking of sensory perception, we could understand how human thought might correspond to the properties of things. That is, on the assumption that sensory perception is reliable (an assumption that Descartes has called into question), our ideas derived through sensory contact with things could be expected to correspond to those things. But Descartes is here speaking of innate ideas, which the human mind has independently of the existence of the things in question (such as circles or triangles). Descartes' claim is very strong, because in general there is no reason to assume that just because an idea is innate it is true. There is nothing incoherent about a mind coming equipped with innate ideas that are false or inaccurate, or at least that yield "material for error" (as in the Third Meditation discussion of sensory ideas, 7:43–4). So Descartes must explain why he takes his innate ideas as true. Thus far, he has relied on their clarity and distinctness as the mark of their truth. But we can again raise the question of how clarity and distinctness are known to be reliable guides to truth.

As Descartes will soon observe, human thought in itself "does not impose any necessity on things" (7:66). And yet he has asserted that the mind's innate ideas tell him (and the meditator) what the world can be or is like, what properties things can or do have. Why should ideas in the human mind correspond to, or accurately represent, the actual or possible properties of mind-independent things?

The type of answer given to this question depends on the sort of role he envisions for a divine guarantee of human ideas. He might be appealing to God for deep validation of the correspondence between human ideas and the true and immutable natures of things; or perhaps he saw no need for deep validation but had a presumption in favor of the accuracy of intellectual ideas. On either scenario, his claim remains strong: that the human mind is innately stocked with ideas that reveal the essences of things.

Ontological argument (7:65–8)

Descartes' presentation of the ontological argument begins as follows:

> Certainly, the idea of God, or a supremely perfect being, is one which I find within me just as surely as the idea of any shape or number. And my understanding that it belongs to his nature that he always exists is no less clear and distinct than is the case when I demonstrate of any shape or number that some property belongs to its nature. Hence, even if it turned out that not everything on which I have meditated in these past days is true, I ought still to regard the existence of God as having at least the same level of certainty as I have hitherto attributed to the truths of mathematics. [7:65–6*]

This passage asserts that the meditator has a "clear and distinct perception" of a connection between God's "nature" and his existence. Perception of this connection is offered as proof of God's existence. In this initial presentation, the proof is over quickly. The passage continues by repeating the apparent fall-back methodological position, equating the certainty of this proof with the usual certainty ascribed to mathematics.

The remainder of the Meditation is divided about equally between the ontological proof and methodological reflections arising from it. The full force of the proof is developed by responding to various objections to the brief version just stated (7:66–8); this process continues in the Replies. Descartes then purports to remove any remaining doubt about the truth of past days' meditations by again deriving the truth of clear and distinct perception from the existence of God.

Ontological argument defended

The "ontological argument" is so-named because it proves God's existence by considering his "essence," or the necessary properties of his "being." The Greek root *ontos* simply means "being." The Latin form is *esse*, from which the word "essence" derives. Thus a thing's "essence" is the "what it is" of the thing, that is, those properties that are inseparable from its being. The core of any ontological argument is the allegedly necessary connection between God's essence and existence. The original argument is attributed to the eleventh-century Benedictine monk Anselm of Canterbury. Various versions of this argument (and objections to them) were well known in Descartes' day (although not under the name "ontological argument," which is due to Kant). This type of argument is contrasted with a cosmological argument, which argues that God must be posited as a cause for the existence of finite or contingent beings in the world. The Third Meditation arguments from "effects" are forms of cosmological argument.

Descartes' first presentation, quoted above, distills the argument into the single insight that "it belongs to [God's] nature that he always exists" (7:65). Existence is a property inseparable from God, that is, from a "supremely perfect being." When baldly stated, the argument has the form of contemplating one's idea of God and finding that it represents the necessary existence of the deity. As with the ideas of geometrical objects, it may here be a case of bringing the meditator to notice something in the idea of God that she hadn't noticed before. Still, the bare statement of that presumed insight may not immediately overwhelm the meditator. So Descartes elaborates the argument by having her consider three objections.

She first considers an objection arising from a standard position among scholastic Aristotelians: that existence is separable from essence. This means that questions of existence and essence must be answered separately (7:66). (While Aristotelians routinely held that knowledge of essences depends on knowledge of existing things, they also held that the question of whether a thing exists is distinct from the question of what that thing is, or its essence.) The meditator has in fact already found a distinction between essence and existence in her ideas of geometrical essences, for she was readily able to suppose that actual existence was not part of the essence of such objects (7:64). If actual existence is always separable from essence, then God's existence cannot follow from his essence.

Descartes responds by suggesting that this objection vanishes upon careful consideration of the idea of God:

> But when I concentrate more carefully, it is quite evident that existence can no more be separated from the essence of God than the fact that its three angles equal two right angles can be separated from the essence of a triangle, or than the idea of a mountain can be separated from the idea of a valley. Hence it is just as much of a contradiction to think of God (that is, a supremely perfect being) lacking existence (that is, lacking a perfection), as it is to think of a mountain without a valley. [7:66]

In effect, he asks the meditator simply to consider closely her idea of God, and he describes the expected result: she will find that existence is included in her idea as an intrinsic property of God. The parenthetical remarks expand upon the original argument by repeating that God is a supremely perfect being and noting (or claiming) that existence is a perfection. Both of these claims will subsequently be challenged. But, in this first response, Descartes has clarified the argument by connecting existence to God's essence through the notion of perfection. A being that did not exist would lack a perfection (viz., existence), but God is supremely perfect, hence he must have that perfection. Or so the idea of God allegedly reveals.

Assuming that the meditator has reached the desired insight by investigating her idea of God, Descartes' second objection questions the significance of this result. Even if existence is inseparably bound up with God's essence in the meditator's idea, surely her thought "does not impose any necessity on things" (7:66). Hence real existence cannot be concluded from the idea: "it does not seem to follow from the fact that I think of God as existing that he does exist." Indeed, "just as I may imagine a winged horse even though no horse has wings, so I may be able to attach existence to God even though no God exists" (7:66). There are apparently two stages to this objection.

The objection first asks whether it would follow simply from the fact that the meditator thinks of God as necessarily existing that he must exist. The continuation then suggests what is behind this objection. If the connection between the essence and existence of God in the meditator's idea were a mere construct or a fictitious composite, like imagining wings on a horse, then the idea would have no bearing on reality.

Descartes' response concedes that mere human thought could not entail the existence of God, and then denies that the meditator is dealing merely with her own composite idea:

> From the fact that I cannot think of a mountain without a valley, it does not follow that a mountain and valley exist anywhere, but simply that a mountain and a valley, whether they exist or not, are mutually inseparable. But from the fact that I cannot think of God except as existing, it follows that existence is inseparable from God, and hence that he really exists. It is not that my thought makes it so, or imposes any necessity on any thing; on the contrary, it is the necessity of the thing itself, namely the existence of God, which determines my thinking in this respect. For I am not free to think of God without existence (that is, a supremely perfect being without a supreme perfection) as I am free to imagine a horse with or without wings. [7:66–7]

This response answers both stages of the objection at once (or else it conflates them). The meditator is to determine that she is perceiving a true and immutable nature by examining whether she can separate existence from her idea of God. Descartes here again appeals to the principle, suggested in the earlier consideration of geometrical ideas, that fictitious connections are subject to the meditator's will. What she has arbitrarily joined, she can put asunder, as with the horse and wings. But what has an intrinsic connection will resist all efforts to resolve the ideational connection, and therefore is conjoined by necessity. She finds that the connection between God's essence (including his supreme perfection) and his existence cannot be sundered. Nor, indeed, can the connection between mountain and valley (assuming that "valley" here means the lower area of a mountain – although it is interesting that this example is of a presumably empirically obtained idea). Both are therefore cognized as necessary. This necessity is not, Descartes maintains, imposed by the meditator but is discovered in her ideas.

The third objection questions whether this alleged necessity should be recognized as a special form of "hypothetical necessity." With a hypothetical necessity, one makes a supposition, say, that all triangles are right-angled triangles, from which it would then follow that all triangles are subject to the Pythagorean theorem (which in fact holds only for right-angled triangles). The conclusion, that all triangles are Pythagorean, follows necessarily *given* the hypothesis or supposition that all triangles are right-angled. But in fact all triangles are not right-angled. (If they were, the conclusion would follow with unrestricted necessity.) The supposition is not true and so certainly not necessarily true. Although it follows from the supposition that all triangles are right-angled that they are all Pythagorean, truth cannot be established through mere supposition or hypothesis.

The text of this third objection runs as follows:

> while it is indeed necessary for me to suppose God exists, once I have made the supposition that he has all perfections (since existence is one of the perfections), nevertheless the original supposition was not necessary. [7:67]

The objection suggests again that the meditator's idea is a kind of construction. That is, it suggests that the meditator is merely assuming, without there being any reason that necessitates this, that God has all perfections. It is then granted that, given this supposition, it would necessarily follow that God exists, since existence is a perfection and God has been assumed to have all perfections. But such necessity would be merely hypothetical. According to the objection, there are no grounds for believing that the supposition that God necessarily contains all perfections is true and therefore no reason to believe that the necessity is unrestricted.

Descartes' answer again directs the meditator to her innate idea of God, where she is to find that the idea necessarily attributes all perfections to God, not by way of supposition, but intrinsically.

> Admittedly, it is not necessary that I ever light upon any thought of God; but whenever I do choose to think of the first and supreme being, and bring forth the idea of God from the treasure house of my mind as it were, it is necessary that I attribute all perfections to him, even if I do not at that time enumerate them or attend to them individually. [7:67]

The intrinsic content of the idea of God (it is maintained) necessarily attributes all perfections to him. In this way, it contrasts with fictitious ideas, such as that all triangles are right-angled, or, to use Descartes' own example, that all quadrilaterals can be inscribed within a circle (when some cannot). Such fictitious ideas can enter into hypothetical necessities, but these hypothetical connections contain no inner necessity. By contrast, the idea of God has this inner necessity, of the same sort that obtains between the idea of a triangle and the property of having three angles.

Thus far, Descartes' response to the third objection does not move beyond the response to the second, in which he also (in effect) claimed that the idea of God is not fictitious. But he goes on to add something new. He further claims that the idea of God has the mark of a "true idea" and is "an image of a true and immutable nature" (7:68). The mark of a true idea is the clear and distinct perception of the necessary connection between God's perfection and the property of existence. As in the earlier discussion of the essence of matter, clear and distinct perception of a necessary connection is taken as evidence for its truth. Furthermore, again as with the geometrical ideas, he has the meditator find that the idea of God is fecund. Other properties of God, such as his uniqueness, follow from the innate idea, just as they do in geometry (7:68). If the meditator does find that these other properties follow from her idea, even though she had not thought of them before, that counts as evidence that they were discovered in the idea and not imputed to it by her. These aspects of the idea would, then, be independent of the meditator's will, hence not fictitious.

When all is said and done, there remains the question (broached in the second objection, above) of how the human idea of God can be known to reveal the essence of a mind-independent reality. Thus far, Descartes has rested this part of the argument on two claims: first, the meditator's clear and distinct perception that the idea of God includes necessary existence for God; and, second, her discovery that the idea itself has an innately given true and immutable nature and so is not fictitious – a discovery that also relies on her clear and distinct perception of the connections among properties, such as perfection and existence.

If the argument relies on clear and distinct perception, what role, if any, does the presumed innateness of the idea play? The quick answer is that neither Descartes nor his Aristotelian (or generally empiricist) opponents could conceive of a clear and distinct idea of God that arose from the senses. God, it was agreed, is an immaterial being. Immaterial beings are not spatial and do not fall under the senses. Hence the idea of the immaterial being cannot be received through the senses. Although painters may show God as a white-haired man, those images reveal nothing of the infinite, immaterial being of God.

A more extended answer would involve the notion that the innate ideas discussed in the Fifth Meditation are intellectual ideas, and that the human intellect is an instrument of truth. This deeper connection between truth and the intellect is exactly what Descartes takes up in further methodological reflections, subsequent to the ontological argument.

Further objections and replies

Before turning to those reflections, let us consider some objections to the ontological argument posed in the Objections and Replies.

Gassendi raised several objections concerning the relation between essence and existence. To begin with, he refused to acknowledge that essence and existence can be separated. He reasoned that if a thing doesn't exist, it has no essence either, since essences can't exist apart from their instances (7:319–20, 324). (In fact, he considered notions of essence to be mere empirical generalizations from similarities among things [7:320–1].) Hence he rejected Descartes' claim that actual existence pertains to some essences but not others. He also argued that existence cannot be a perfection present or absent in the essence of a non-existent thing, since what doesn't exist can have no perfections, from which he concluded that all existing things equally share the perfection of existence; hence God, if he exists, doesn't differ from other things on this score (7:323). These objections reflect disagreements over the very idea of there being true and immutable essences or natures that can be cognized apart from things, and as containing more or less perfection; it marks a larger metaphysical and epistemological disagreement, not peculiar to the ontological argument.

The most famous of Gassendi's objections is his assertion that existence is not a predicate that can be differently related to God and to other things. Either existence isn't a predicate, or it is equally contained in the conception of all things (7:322–3). One way of putting the point is that all things, when they are thought of, are thought of as existing. He adopted Descartes' examples of a mountain and a winged horse. Presumably we can't think of a winged horse without wings, or a mountain without a slope, just as we can't think of God without attributing knowledge and power to him. But existence is a different matter. Here Gassendi objects that Descartes could not "explain how it is possible for us to think of a sloping mountain or a winged horse without thinking of them as existing, yet impossible to think of a wise and powerful God without thinking of him as existing" (7:324).

One way to interpret this point is that any representation of a thing represents it as it would be if it did exist. In representing mountains or winged horses, there is nothing we add to or subtract from the representation in thinking of them as existing. Hence, in the cases of God, a mountain, and a winged horse, our bare ideas represent them as existing. But if this is true of all ideas, it is not peculiar to the idea of God; and since we don't infer from mere thinking of them that a specific triangle or a winged horse exist, we should not infer from our idea of God that he exists. Stated in this way, Gassendi's point is similar to Hume's and Kant's later objections that existence is not a predicate or property. Effectively, they say that imagining a thing as existing is no different from simply imagining a thing: the thing "looks the same" in both cases. Therefore, thinking of the thing as existing adds nothing to it; hence existence is not a predicate or property. To imagine a thing *is* to imagine it as existing.

Now, in fact, Descartes granted Gassendi's (and so Hume's and Kant's) point that when we imagine or represent things we represent them as existing, but he disagreed with their conclusion. Descartes, unlike Gassendi (in the Objections), held that thought cannot be reduced to images. Descartes contended that thought is able to grasp abstract relations and properties, including possibility and necessity, which can therefore enter into the content of a judgment. In the case of existence, he claimed that we are able to understand the difference between a thing with merely possible existence, and one that exists necessarily. In both cases, in thinking of the thing we would think of it as it would be if existing. But in the one case (say, a geometrical figure) we recognize it as a merely possible existent, whereas in the case of God we cognize his existence as necessary.

Here is how he puts the point in the First Replies:

It must be noted that possible existence is contained in the concept or idea of everything that we clearly and distinctly understand; but in no case is necessary existence so contained, except in the case of the idea of God. Those who carefully attend to this difference between the idea of God and every other idea will undoubtedly perceive that even though our understanding of other things always involves understanding them as if they were existing things, it does not follow that they do exist, but merely that they are capable of existing. [7:116–17]

He allows that our ideas represent things as existing but denies that Gassendi has fully described the content of the various thoughts involved (7:383). According to Descartes, the content can include various relations between the thing represented in thought and its existence: its existence can be perceived as merely possible (a thing like this can exist), as necessary (this thing must exist and so does exist), or as impossible, as in the case of chimeras or impossible animals (things like this cannot exist).

We are not in a position to settle this dispute between Descartes and Gassendi on the theory of thought, its content, and its implications for reality. But it should be noted that neither one obviously carries the day, so that Gassendi's objection against the ontological argument, based on his denial that existence is a predicate, begs the question about the structure, content, and implications of our thoughts.

A more telling objection was raised by Caterus in the First Objections:

> Even if it is granted that a supremely perfect being carries the implication of existence in virtue of its very title, it still does not follow that the existence in question is anything actual in the real world; all that follows is that the concept of existence is inseparably linked to the concept of a supreme being. So you cannot infer that the existence of God is anything actual unless you suppose that the supreme being actually exists; for then it will actually contain all perfections, including the perfection of real existence. [7:99]

Caterus objects that the necessity by which we include existence in the concept of God has no force in relation to the actual existence of God. He in effect asks whether human concepts accurately reveal extramental reality. He concedes that if a God (defined as a supremely perfect being) exists, he exists necessarily. But this is simply to say that if something exists that in fact corresponds to our concept, then of course it has the properties found in our concept. (That just *is* what it is for something to exist corresponding to our concept.) And if one of those properties is necessary existence (following from supreme perfection), then the thing will have necessary existence. But the more important thing to be determined is whether anything exists corresponding to our concept, and that cannot be determined from our concept alone. Or so Caterus argues.

Descartes responded at length and made several interesting points (7:115–20). Of primary interest here is that Descartes takes Caterus to be raising a form of his second objection (above), that the idea of God is a fiction, cobbled together by the human mind (7:116–19). That is, he takes Caterus to be questioning whether the idea of God ineluctably imputes necessary existence to God. But in the above quotation, Caterus grants that it does when he allows that "the concept of existence is inseparably linked to the concept of a supreme being." For Caterus, the question is not whether the idea of God is fictitious in the sense of being put together by the human mind (as opposed to being discovered as an innate idea with its own intrinsic unity); rather, it is whether such an idea actually informs us of real necessities in the world outside the mind, in this case of a really necessary, because supremely perfect, being. It is a matter of whether the human intellect, with its innate ideas, is adjusted to, and so accurately reflects, the structure of extramental reality. (Descartes was privy to this issue [7:150–1, 226] and explicitly asserted that human concepts do reveal the truth about things [7:162, def. IX].)

To illustrate what is at stake, let us return to geometry. Descartes argued that the human mind innately contains the ideas of geometrical figures, and that these ideas determine the real possibilities of material things. That is, he believed that the geometrical structures perceived by human thought determine what spatial properties matter can have. Let us grant for a moment his claim that the mind has geometrical ideas of the sort he describes. With hindsight, we know that they do not impose a necessary structure on matter or space. The structure of physical space is not accurately described by Euclid's geometry (on a cosmic scale or a microscopic scale); rather, various non-Euclidean geometries are needed. Even if it were true that the human mind innately represents spatial structures as Euclidean, that would not prove that physical space has that structure. The fact that an idea is innate may mean that it is not fictitious in the sense of being cobbled together, but what we need to be shown is that it is not fictitious in the sense of being false.

We are thus brought back to the fundamental principle of Descartes' metaphysical epistemology: that the innate ideas of the human intellect, insofar as they provide clear and distinct perceptions, reveal the truth about the nature of extramental reality. We are still looking for a satisfactory demonstration that this is so.

Clear and distinct perception as sole method found (7:68–9)

At the end of the ontological argument, Descartes makes a sweeping methodological pronouncement:

> whatever method of proof I use, I am always brought back to the fact that it is only what I clearly and distinctly perceive that

completely convinces me. Some of the things I clearly and distinctly perceive are obvious to everyone, while others are discovered only by those who look more closely and investigate more carefully; but once they have been discovered the latter are judged to be just as certain as the former. [7:68]

This statement emphasizes the "conviction" and "certainty" that comes from clear and distinct perception but so far does not mention truth; but Descartes immediately reasserts the truth of such perceptions in discussing God's role in banishing the doubt. The quoted statement also offers an important methodological hint for the reader undergoing (or not undergoing) the epistemological conversion experience of the *Meditations*. It says that truths that are not immediately obvious can become so upon more careful investigation. Belief in the Pythagorean theorem results from such investigation, but once the theorem is seen, it is believed "just as strongly" (7:69) as simpler mathematical results. Finally, Descartes claims that the ontological argument possesses this same clarity, even if at first obscured by preconceived opinions (7:69).

The comparison of the ontological argument with the proofs of geometry has been a theme of the Fifth Meditation. As invoked at this juncture, its role is to remind the reader of the need to turn away from "preconceived opinions" and "the images of things perceived by the senses" (7:69) in order to comprehend the argument. But the comparison was used earlier (7:65–6) to support the ontological argument by comparing its perceived certainty with that of mathematics – which had been, prior to the *Meditations*, the paradigm of certainty for the meditator (7:65).

How does the relation between the ontological argument and the proofs of geometry work? If the meditator is now inclined to accept mathematical results as true despite the doubts of the early Meditations, as Descartes has implied she might (7:65–6), then the comparison could serve as a justification for Descartes' method of clear and distinct perception. Such a justification would use the accepted status of mathematics to confer legitimacy on other uses of clear and distinct perception. Suppose that the meditator is prepared at this juncture to grant mathematics its own cognitive force. If the ontological argument achieves the same standard of conviction, then the meditator might be expected to grant it the same cognitive force. Descartes would have gained her agreement that the proofs of mathematics and metaphysics have the same cognitive footing. On the surface, at least, this strategy provides a way to avoid the nagging problem of the circle, for it permits a proof for the existence of God to derive its cognitive legitimacy from the comparison with mathematics, not from a divine validation of clear and distinct perception.

We will return to this strategy in discussing the circle. For now, we must note that Descartes, at this juncture of the Fifth Meditation, apparently takes the opposite tack and argues that even the truths of mathematics cannot be known without first knowing that God exists.

Knowledge of God needed to banish doubt (7:69–71)

Despite recent statements of the certainty and evidence of mathematics, Descartes now asserts that all knowledge, even of geometry, depends on God (7:69). We may be convinced by geometrical demonstrations while attending to them (they "compel our assent," as in Meditation 4), but when not attending to those demonstrations, we can recall arguments such as those from the First Meditation, which offer general reasons for doubting our cognitive faculties. And these general doubts undermine our confidence even in the demonstrations of geometry, so long as we are not at that moment closely considering the demonstrations.

One might think it sufficient for saying we "know" geometrical truths that we understand and assent to geometrical demonstrations when presented with them. But Descartes claims that unresolved general doubts about knowledge, posed when we are not directly considering those demonstrations, can undermine our knowledge of geometry even if we can correctly construct every proof in Euclid. His argument can be understood if we consider his conception of knowledge. In the First Meditation, he spoke of seeking something in the sciences "that was stable and likely to last" (7:17). In the Fifth Meditation, he argues that without a knowledge of God, we would "never have true and certain knowledge about anything, but only shifting and changeable opinions" (7:69). As he makes clear in the Second Replies, he is not denying that even an atheist can "cognize" or understand the Pythagorean theorem and be convinced of it (7:141*). But the atheist, without knowledge of God, will be subject to skeptical challenges such as those of the First Meditation; he does not have knowledge (something stable), because his opinion can be dislodged. As Descartes puts it, "no act of cognition that can be rendered doubtful seems fit to be called knowledge" (7:141*). Those who know God can counter such doubts, so they can possess (stable and lasting) knowledge.

The basic form of Descartes' argument is clear. He presents a conception of knowledge according to which the thing known must be true, must be accepted for good reasons, and must not be subject to known objections. He then suggests that prior to recognizing that God exists and is no deceiver, we can undermine even our knowledge of geometry by raising skeptical doubts about the general reliability of our cognition. Once God's existence and goodness have been proved, we can remove the doubts, and now the "good reasons" we have for believing geometrical demonstration (that we clearly and distinctly perceive them) remain a stable basis for knowledge. (Even if skeptical doubts arise again, we can now easily turn them back by considering our proof for the existence and goodness of God.)

God and the circle

The fact that Descartes appeals to clear and distinct perception to prove the existence of God (7:69) and then appeals to God to support the truth of clear and distinct perception (7:69–70) resulted in Arnauld's charge of circularity (7:214). In Chapter 5, we considered "remove the doubt" and "presumption in favor of the intellect" strategies for avoiding the circle, as opposed to a "strong validation of reason" strategy, which seemed to make the circle inevitable. What we need to know now is whether, in the Fifth Meditation, Descartes is appealing to God's existence and goodness merely to remove a ground for doubt without positively validating the intellect, or whether he is appealing to God for direct validation of the intellect (as seemed the case in Meditation 4). If the former, then the sense in which all knowledge "depends on God" would be comparatively weak: it would depend on our investigating the deceiving-God hypothesis and finding it wanting, so as to remove the doubt and be left with our otherwise presumptively true clear and distinct perceptions. If the validation strategy is in play, then the sense in which all knowledge "depends on God" would be quite strong: we would need to know of God's existence and goodness in order to have a reason to trust that our clear and distinct perceptions are true.

The question of which strategy fits the text of the Fifth Meditation depends in part on what sort of challenge to the intellect Descartes intended to address there. If he was simply responding to the "slight" and "metaphysical" doubt raised by the "long-standing opinion" that there is an all-powerful God who might be a deceiver, then the remove-the-doubt strategy (as paired with presumption) appears to avoid circularity. Descartes would simply be arguing that as long as one hasn't considered the deceiving-God hypothesis carefully, one is subject to this ground for doubt. (Indeed, the atheist remains permanently subject to it.) Anyone who followed the procedure of Meditations 1 and 2 and came to appreciate clear and distinct perception might then use such perceptions to remove what turn out, against the standard of such perceptions, to be slight and metaphysical grounds for doubt. If a presumption in favor of the intellect is in place, then removing the doubt leaves us with our usual trust in the truth-detecting powers of our cognitive faculties when used properly.

In favor of the view that Descartes appeals to such a presumption, recall his several comparisons of the ontological argument with geometrical demonstration. In our discussion above, these comparisons initially seemed to provide a fall-back position. That is, Descartes would be saying that even if the arguments of Meditations 3 and 4 about God and deception fail, the ontological argument still achieves the same cognitive force as geometrical demonstration. But if the meditator is operating under the presumption that the transparent perceptions of the intellect are true, then these comparisons could support the truth of the ontological argument by putting it in an epistemic class with mathematical knowledge. (The question would remain of whether the arguments merit the comparison.)

However, there is a fly in the ointment. Another ground for doubt is in play besides the deceiving-God hypothesis. This is the defective-origins proposal from the First Meditation (a version of the defective-design hypothesis). This challenge surely cannot be removed simply by using clear and distinct perception to prove that God exists and is no deceiver, for it trades on the assumption that there is no God and that the human intellect is therefore the product of chance causes and may be naturally defective. Let us consider whether there is any way to answer this challenge without begging the question or arguing in a circle.

Defective origins

In the latter part of the Fifth Meditation, Descartes presents two grounds for doubt about such evident matters as the geometrical demonstration that the three angles of a triangle equal two right angles:

> as soon as I turn my mind's eye away from the demonstration, then in spite of still remembering that I perceived it very clearly, I can easily fall into doubt about its truth, if I am unaware of God. For I can convince myself that I have been made by nature so as to go wrong from time to time in matters which I think I perceive as evidently as can be. This will seem even more likely when I remember that there have been frequent cases where I have regarded things as true and certain, but have later been led by other arguments to judge them to be false. [7:70*]

The meditator dismisses the second ground, that she accepted some things as true and later judged them to be false, by saying that previously she was ignorant of the rule that clear and distinct perceptions are true "and believed these things for other reasons which I later discovered to be less reliable" (7:70). Prior to undergoing the process recorded in the *Meditations*, the meditator (as, earlier in life, Descartes himself) did not know how to recognize clear and distinct perceptions and so formed her beliefs on other grounds (such as sensory experience or the authority of a teacher).

The first ground, that she has "been made by nature so as to go wrong" in (at least some cases of) clear and distinct perception offers the real challenge, by reinvoking the defective-origins hypothesis. It is this ground for doubt, not the deceiving-God hypothesis (ostensibly already removed in Meditations 3–4), that the meditator now purports to banish through her knowledge that God exists. Here is what she says:

> Now, however, I have perceived that God exists, and at the same time I have understood that everything else depends on him, and that he is no deceiver; and I have drawn the conclusion that everything which I clearly and distinctly perceive is of necessity true. Accordingly, even if I am no longer attending to the arguments which led me to judge that this is true, as long as I remember that I clearly and distinctly perceived it, there are no counterarguments which can be adduced to make me doubt it, but on the contrary I have true and certain knowledge of it. [7:70]

God's existence by itself would not counter the defective-origins hypothesis. Two further considerations are needed: God's goodness (non-deceptive nature) and the fact that, as the passage says, "everything else depends on him." Descartes seems to be reprising a line of thought from the Fourth Meditation. Our clear and distinct perceptions are true because God made us, and in particular, he made our intellect (and will), and he would be a deceiver if clear and distinct perceptions, to which we are compelled to assent, were ever false. In this way, God's creation of our cognitive faculties provides strong validation for those faculties.

The defective-origins hypothesis concerns the origin of the meditator's cognitive faculties: have they been fashioned by chance developments in a godless universe, or have they been created (hence designed) by God? According to the above argument, they have been designed by a non-deceiving God. But a familiar problem arises. Our only reason for believing that God exists and created our minds is that we clearly and distinctly perceive it to be the case. And the defective-origins hypothesis challenges the reliability of such perception. Either the question is begged, or the circle closes again.

229

Let us consider more fully the situation of the meditator to see if there is a way out, or at least a way of mitigating the problem. In order to evaluate the defective-origins hypothesis, the meditator might compare the competing explanations for the origin of her intellect. If she had to prove that one of the explanations is true before proceeding, she would indeed be stuck in a circle. But suppose for a moment that she actually considered the defective-origins hypothesis to offer an even more "slight" and "metaphysical" ground for doubt than the deceiving-God hypothesis. She might think that the basic presumption in favor of the intellect entitles her to use her intellectual faculty in evaluating the (so far ungrounded) possibility of defective origins. Or she might appeal to the extraction argument (reviewed in Chapter 5) in support of clear and distinct perception. She would then use her intellect to find the best explanation of the origin of her intellectual faculty. In the course of Meditations 3–5, she has (allegedly) found three good arguments for the existence of God, and one for his goodness. She finds that the defective-origins hypothesis is merely speculative, and in fact she cannot conceive that a conscious human mind could arise from chance conglomerations of matter. Hence, she accepts the creation hypothesis as the best explanation for the origin of her cognitive faculties.

Descartes surely would have considered the defective-origins hypothesis to be comparatively weak. In his day, there was general disagreement over whether a purely material being could have sensation and thought. Furthermore, there was very little support for the notion that a thinking being might develop in nature through chance interactions of matter, unguided by a creator. Descartes presumably reflected his own judgment of the implausibility of this hypothesis when he characterized as "exaggerated" (7:226) all the doubts of the First Meditation that relied on ignorance of God (which must include both branches of the defective-design argument). He no doubt thought it unlikely or impossible that thought could arise from matter by chance processes. Of course, to be effective in this context he must not rely merely on opinion but on a reasonable assessment of the real possibility of this happening. Today we conjecture that consciousness and thought can evolve by natural processes (although at present there is no complete explanation of how mind could evolve). Hence, we are unlikely to grant to Descartes that his creationist hypothesis is stronger than the alternative.

In any event, even by Descartes' own lights, for his creationist hypothesis to be able to *rule out* alternatives, the metaphysical method of intellectual perception must be able to establish some strong metaphysical conclusions: that God exists, is no deceiver, and is the creator of the human mind. Suppose that in order to avoid making any initial claims about God or creation, Descartes first appealed to the extraction argument in support of clear and distinct perception, and he subsequently used that method to decide for creation over natural origins. Such a move would beg the question about whether clear and distinct perception can be trusted. As we observed in Chapter 5, those perceptions must be used in assessing the extraction argument itself. The extraction argument might, for instance, simply involve a mistaken act of over-generalization from the certainty of the *cogito*. If clear and distinct perception cannot already be trusted, how would we decide? A presumption in favor of the intellect fares no better; it also begs the question about whether the intellect can be trusted to reveal the real natures of things, and hence the existence and creative tendencies of God.

More generally, one would not need to embrace the defective-origins hypothesis to question whether the human mind is able to limn the essences of things and establish that God exists and has furnished us with intellects adequate to the tasks of *a priori* metaphysics. The defective-origins hypothesis is only one version of an opposing, naturalistic account of the origin of thought. One might assert that the human mind has arisen from nature, and that it is not generally defective in design, but that it lacks the innate ideas or intellectual perceptions of God and matter that Descartes claims to find in the Fifth Meditation. Or one might allow that the mind has ideas of God and of the essence of matter but question whether those ideas actually reveal the essences of things.

Such challenges to the existence or reliability of Descartes' intellectual perceptions move beyond the circle to address his system more generally. We will return to them in Chapter 10.

The circle and the aim of the Meditations

An underlying question frames our consideration of the circle. This is the question of whether, in the *Meditations*, Descartes intended, or needed, to provide a deep challenge to the reliability of human cognition, or merely wanted to use the skeptical process to direct the reader to clear and distinct perceptions and then on to the first principles of metaphysics and physics. (This question was raised at the ends of Chapters 2 and 3.)

Evidence can be found on both sides. Less than two years after the *Meditations* appeared, Descartes wrote to Princess Elizabeth that he tried "never to spend more than a few hours a day in the thoughts which occupy the imagination, and a few hours a year on those which occupy the intellect alone" (3:692–3), detached from imagination and sense. The feel of the letter (discussed further in Chapter 10) is that one should engage in metaphysics long enough to perceive the existence of God and the essences of mind and matter, and then get on with the business of natural philosophy (having come to a new understanding of the senses, as in Meditation 6).

If Descartes' aim was simply to introduce the method and results of clear and distinct perception and get on with things, then talk of a presumption would be understandable. Descartes would indeed be out to discover some truth, not about the question of whether human minds can know truth but about the main topics of metaphysics (God and finite beings). He wanted to help the reader to see what good reasons for adopting a metaphysical thesis are like, and then to direct her to some conclusions based on good reasons. He did not intend to pose some very deep question about whether the human mind is capable of truth at all. He wanted to help some human minds to perceive clearly and distinctly the truths that he had already seen for himself. He did not argue in a circle, because he never intended to offer a strong validation in the first place. In this connection, it is interesting to note that in the Geometrical Arguments he did not attempt to validate clear and distinct perception but simply appealed to "self-evident" propositions and arguments (7:162–3).

On the other side, it seems that given his metaphysical ambitions, Descartes both should have wanted to, and did, pose deep questions about the relation between the human intellect and the real order of things. He was after all not out just to achieve an "all things considered" best theory of the world. He was after the one true metaphysics.

We have seen that Descartes knew the deeper challenge could be posed. In the passage from the Fourth Replies quoted in Chapter 5, he acknowledged that one may ask whether "the order in which things are mutually related in our perception of them" matches "the order in which they are related in actual reality" (7:226). There he suggests that the question can be favorably resolved by removing the "exaggerated doubts" of the First Meditation. But it is not clear that once the matter has been raised it can be disposed of so easily. In another place, the second objectors (7:127) reprised Caterus' query (7:99) about whether our human concepts or ideas should be thought to reveal the real essences and existence of things, as in the ontological argument; they urged that God's existence depends on the real possibility of his essence, not on human concepts. In response, Descartes distinguished two sorts of possibility. The first sort coincides with "whatever does not conflict with our human concepts" (7:150). He took that to be the common meaning and even offered it as a definition in the Geometrical Arguments: "When we say that something is *contained in the nature or concept* of a thing, this is the same as saying that it is true of that thing, or that it can be asserted of that thing" (7:162). However, he was aware that the claim that human concepts reveal real possibilities (or, in the ontological argument, real actualities) might be challenged. He acknowledged that the second objectors might be asking about a sort of possibility "which relates to the object itself" (7:150). But in the Replies he refused to take seriously the position that human concepts do not match the objects in themselves, for otherwise "all human knowledge will be destroyed, though for no good reason" (7:151). Given that he acknowledged the question of whether our concepts match reality, there is plenty of material in Meditations 4–5 to suggest that he did take the question seriously and answered by offering a divine guarantee for human (metaphysical) cognition.

This second aim, of deeply challenging reason and providing deep foundations in response, is not incompatible with the first (methodological) aim, of helping the reader to uncover and use the faculty of pure intellect. But that first sort of aim does not require the second. It can be evaluated on its own, by whether the reader finds the promised clarity. The first aim meshes nicely with the methodological bent of the early seventeenth century. The second aim engages more fully the metaphysical tradition. Previous metaphysicians had attempted to explain how human cognition could achieve knowledge of essences – whether through Platonist direct apprehension of separate Forms, or the Aristotelian intellect, which distills essences through sensory contact with things. Descartes' doctrine of the creation of the eternal truths offers its own explanation of how human concepts could (innately) be aligned with the very natures of things. Perhaps Descartes was caught between these two aims: of simply putting forward the best arguments he had for the first principles of his new science (something he could do without circularity, but with no guarantee of ultimate truth), and of offering an ultimate explanation for why his best arguments must reveal the one true theory (where his efforts appear question-begging or circular).

The several readings of Descartes' aims and strategy offered here are intended to help readers to develop their own positions on the circle in conjunction with further reading of the relevant texts. That position might be one of those described, some combination of them, or a further strategy. One of the intriguing features of philosophical texts is that they repay close study and interpretive work. The problems surrounding the circle and Descartes' metaphysical method are rich and complex. Final assessment remains with the reader.

References and further reading

For introductory discussion of Descartes on innate ideas see Kenny, ch. 5, and Cottingham, *Descartes*, ch. 6. Flage and Bonnen, ch. 2, consider innate ideas in the context of Cartesian method. The articles by Gaukroger and Marion in the *Cambridge Companion* examine Descartes' work in mathematics and his argument about matter's essence. Menn, *Descartes and Augustine*, ch. 8, sec. B, discusses the essence of matter. Several articles on Descartes' mathematics and its relation to his physics may be found in S. Gaukroger (ed.), *Descartes: Philosophy, Mathematics and Physics* (Brighton, UK: Harvester, 1980).

For additional discussion of Descartes' version of the ontological argument, consult Kenny, ch. 7, B. Williams, ch. 5, and Dicker, ch. 4. J. Barnes, *The Ontological Argument* (London: Macmillan, 1972), examines the logical structure of the argument, and G.R. Oppy, *Ontological Arguments and Belief in God* (Cambridge: Cambridge University Press, 1995) surveys the history of the argument.

References on the circle are provided at the end of Chapter 5.

Chapter 8

The natural world and the mind–body relation

Meditation 6: The existence of material things, and the real distinction between mind and body

The Fifth Meditation initiated the meditator's return to the material world. Having disavowed matter and the senses in the First Meditation, she was directed in the Fifth to contemplate the essence of material things – although still without using the senses. Now in the Sixth (and longest) Meditation, she will consider the senses and their objects. This Meditation rehabilitates the senses, but with limitations not recognized in the meditator's original sense-based epistemology. The material world is regained as well, but under a new conception.

The first half of the Meditation (7:71–80) is devoted to the question "whether material things exist" (7:71). It begins with a merely "probable" argument for their existence, then reviews the sensory doubt, and finally offers a proof that material things exist. The second half (7:80–90) concerns the embodied mind, including the origin and function of the sensations, emotions, and appetites arising from embodiment. The meditator considers how the senses and appetites function in the whole human being (consisting of mind and body) to preserve health and well-being, and how the nerves and brain operate to produce sensations and feelings.

Many philosophical discussions of this Meditation focus on the second titular topic, "the real distinction between mind and body." In Descartes' technical terminology (derived from the scholastics), a "real distinction" is a distinction between two substances (7:13, 162; see also 8A:28–9) – in this case, between two substances having mutually exclusive essences (thought and extension). The argument for this distinction occupies a single paragraph (7:78), the penultimate paragraph in the long discussion of the existence of material things. In the flow of the text, the argument reads simply as the initial step in the coming proof that material things exist. Nonetheless, the distinction holds a central place in Descartes' metaphysics, and it conditions his theory of sensation and appetite as manifestations of mind–body union and interaction.

The Sixth Meditation completes Descartes' analysis of the human cognitive faculties. It situates sense, imagination, and memory in the theory of the faculties by describing them as modes or acts of the intellect (7:78). But these acts are distinguished from "pure intellect" because they depend on bodily processes (although Descartes elsewhere posited a purely intellectual memory [3:48, 84]). This dependence plays a role in the two arguments offered for the existence of body.

Intellect versus imagination (7:71–3)

The initial (merely probable) argument for the existence of material things relies on a phenomenal distinction between imagining something and perceiving it by the pure intellect (7:71–2). Appealing to an (alleged) experiential difference between these two acts, it contends that the phenomena are best explained by supposing that, when imagining something, the mind interacts with the body. In this context, as in the Second Meditation, "imagining" and "imagination" are technical terms arising from a standard classification of the cognitive faculties shared by Descartes and the Aristotelians. As we have seen, to imagine something meant literally to form and experience a mental image of it. The term "image" readily suggests a visual image, but any type of remembered or constructed sensory representation could count as an image, whether visual, auditory, gustatory, olfactory, or tactual.

Descartes directs the meditator to consider the difference between imagining certain geometrical figures and perceiving them through the intellect alone, without forming an image. He has her notice that in the case of a chiliagon (a thousand-sided figure), we can understand such a figure and its properties, even if we cannot distinctly imagine all its thousand sides. Indeed, he suggests, any image we form in thinking of a chiliagon would not differ from the image we might form in thinking of a myriagon (a ten-thousand-sided figure). But we clearly understand, or intellectually perceive, that the myriagon and chiliagon are different. Hence, the real work is not done by images but by the intellect operating on its own (the pure intellect). For simpler figures, such as a triangle or pentagon, we may indeed form a well-defined image, but here as well the meditator notices a difference between imagining the figures and understanding them without an image (also 7:387, 389).

Descartes illustrates this crucial phenomenal difference using the pentagon:

> I can of course understand the figure of a pentagon, just as I can the figure of a chiliagon, without the help of the imagination; but I can also imagine a pentagon, by applying my mind's eye to its five sides and the area contained within them. And in doing this I notice quite clearly that imagination requires a peculiar effort of mind which is not required for understanding; this additional effort of mind clearly shows the difference between imagination and pure understanding. [7:72–3]

Imagining the pentagon involves an "additional effort," which produces an image of the pentagon, five sides bounding a closed area. Does pure understanding (or pure intellection) of the figure involve any sort of image, perhaps one devoid of sensory qualities such as color? Descartes does not say explicitly, but the quoted contrast between understanding and imagining the figure suggests that intellectual perception of the pentagon does not involve imagery of any sort. Exactly what it would then be is unclear, but presumably it would involve non-imagistic cognition of the various essential properties of the pentagon, including its spatial structure and the relations among its parts.

The argument through which the meditator infers the (probable) existence of the body unfolds in two further steps. First, she notes that imagination is not essential to mind or pure intellect. From this, she infers that the faculty of imagination requires something besides the mind (i.e., a body) for its operation. She reasons as follows:

> I consider that this power of imagining which is in me, differing as it does from the power of understanding, is not a necessary constituent of my own essence, that is, of the essence of my mind. For if I lacked it, I should undoubtedly remain the same individual as I now am; from which it seems to follow that it depends on something distinct from myself. And I can easily understand that, if there does exist some body to which the mind is so joined that it can apply itself to contemplate it, as it were, whenever it pleases, then it may possibly be this very body that enables me to imagine corporeal things. So the difference between this mode of thinking and pure understanding may simply be this: when the mind understands, it in some way turns towards itself and inspects one of the ideas which are within it; but when it imagines, it turns towards the body and looks at something in the body which conforms to an idea understood by the mind or perceived by the senses. [7:73]

The first point, that the pure understanding is essential to the self or thinking thing, was suggested in the Second Meditation. That Meditation also listed imagination and sense experience as acts of mind. Imagination is now classified as inessential to the mind. This conclusion may well be a result of the procedure of Meditations 3 and 4, in which the meditator abandoned the senses and imagination

entirely (7:34, 53) and yet retained integrity as a thinking (and intellectual) thing. Indeed, at this point the thinking thing – although
known only as a substance of unknown type – is *conceived* as a non-
extended mind (7:53) with the faculties of (pure) intellect and will.

The second point, that because imagination is not essential to
mind it depends on something else, is new. It apparently relies on the
assumption that all the properties that the thinking thing possesses on
its own must be entirely explicable through an essential property, in
this case, pure understanding. Given traditional Aristotelian notions
of substance and essence, this is an odd point. An Aristotelian would
think that substances have some properties that are instances of their
natures or essences and other properties that are "accidents." For
example, rationality would be considered essential to human beings,
and individual acts of reason as instances of that essential property.
But skin color would be viewed as "accidental" or non-essential, yet
all human beings possess on their own some color or other.
Nonetheless, the quotation evidently concludes that since the imagination is not essential to the thinking thing, it must depend on both
the thinking thing and something else.

The assumption that all the properties that a thing has on its own
must depend on essential properties is related to a position discussed
in Chapters 5 and 7 in connection with Descartes' notion of
substance. There we learned (in the language of the *Principles* [8A:25],
but consistent with this Meditation [7:78]) that all modes or properties of substances depend on or presuppose a principal attribute, or a
specific essence through which they are conceived. For ease of reference, let us call this position "constitutive essentialism." Since at this
point we don't yet know whether the thinking thing has just one principal attribute, in the present case the doctrine simply implies that
every mode or property of the thinking thing must be a mode of some
essential attribute or other of that thing. All its modes would have to
be conceived or understood through an essential attribute.
Consequently, since imagination is a mode of thought (as affirmed in
the Second Meditation and reaffirmed below [7:78]), it must be understood through the attribute of thought.

The above passage now adds a new wrinkle to constitutive essentialism. We learn that if a whole class of modes is not essential to a

thinking thing, we must invoke both the thinking thing (as the thing of which they are modes) and something else to explain their occurrence. Acts of pure intellection are, as a class, essential to the mind. Acts of imagination are not. Presumably, what isn't explicable through one thing acting on its own must be explained as the result of interaction between two or more things or substances. Acts of pure intellect involve ideas that the mind can produce by itself, out of its own latent structure (as constituted by God), including purely intellectual ideas of God and the essence of matter. But the images of imagination are not essential and so require something else for their explanation.

The meditator speculates that if the mind were "joined" to a body, imagination could be understood as arising through mind–body interaction. In order to produce images, the mind would engage the body. The need to "turn toward" the body presumably accounts for the special effort involved in imagination. The language in the quotation, of the mind "inspecting" or "looking at" something in the body, is quite striking but ought not to be read literally (see Chapter 9). We may speculate that in these cases the mind is supposed to interact with a structure in the body that actually possesses the imagined shape: that in imagining a triangle, the mind interacts with (but does not literally look at) a triangular figure in the brain. On this reading, the non-essential modes arise through causal interaction with a body distinct from mind.

Descartes has the meditator conclude that it is "probable" that the faculty of imagination requires mind–body interaction, hence probable that the body exists. Presumably, the argument is merely probable because other explanations for imagination have not been ruled out. Since the meditator wants a "necessary inference" (7:73) that body exists, she presses on to find a "sure argument." She now considers some ideas she has been ignoring for some time, the ideas of the senses, including sensory ideas of shape, size, position, and motion, and of "colors, sounds, tastes, pain and so on" (7:74).

Review of doubt about senses (7:74–8)

Descartes adopts the strategy of having the meditator review her previous beliefs about the senses, and her reasons for calling them into doubt, before deciding what she should now believe about the senses (7:74). Although the review would not be required for the ensuing argument that material things exist, Descartes devotes two long paragraphs to it (7:74–7). These paragraphs serve a double function. They contrast the previous beliefs about the senses that the meditator will retain with those to be rejected. Further, they explain how the to-be-rejected beliefs would have precluded the meditator from discovering the truths of the *Meditations* if she hadn't engaged in the process of doubt.

The meditator considers the various sensory beliefs that were put in doubt (in Meditations 1 and 3), some of which will be rehabilitated:

1   the existence and properties of external objects;
2   the thesis that something in external objects "resembles" the qualities found in experience (such as color); and
3   the "teachings of nature," according to which one should avoid pain and eat when feeling hungry.

With respect to 1, Descartes rehearses the grounds for doubting the senses from Meditation 1. These are cases of sensory deception, as when square towers appear round in the distance; the dream argument; and the defective-design argument. The latter two also undermine 2, for sensations can't resemble external objects if those objects don't exist. In 3, the "teachings of nature" are invoked to explain why we find pain distressing, or are inclined to eat when we have the feeling called hunger. Descartes suggests that the bare sensations of pain or hunger are not intrinsically distress-producing or food-oriented. Rather, nature teaches us to *judge* that pain is to be avoided, and that when feeling hungry we should eat (7:76). The reason given in Meditation 3 (7:39) for questioning such teachings is reprised: "since I apparently had natural impulses towards many things which reason told me to avoid, I reckoned that a great deal of confidence should not be placed in what I was taught by nature" (7:77). If the teachings of nature can lead us astray in some instances, how can we ever trust them? (Recall the parallel argument from sensory fallibility in Meditation 1.)

Of factors 1 to 3, only 2, the resemblance thesis, will be rejected outright as part of a revised attitude toward the senses. Descartes will soon give arguments for both the existence of external things and the general reliability of the teachings of nature regarding bodily benefits and harms (7:83). He will also reaffirm that the senses provide information about the properties of external things. Early in the present review, the meditator reports having sensations "of light, colors, smells, tastes and sounds, the variety of which enabled me to distinguish the sky, the earth, the seas, and all other bodies, one from another" (7:75). She will subsequently reaffirm that such sensations do allow us to distinguish among bodies (7:81), but she will reject the notion that our sensory ideas are fully like images that resemble the "real properties" of material things. More precisely, she will reject the resemblance thesis for color, sound, odor, and the other so-called secondary qualities while allowing that, when used appropriately, our senses do inform us of real sizes, shapes, and other primary qualities (7:80–1).

Among the "previous beliefs" now in doubt, Descartes includes an empiricist theory of knowledge. The meditator previously embraced the resemblance thesis because she relied on sensory ideas alone in forming her conceptions of things: "Since the sole source of my knowledge of these things was the ideas themselves, the supposition that the things resembled the ideas was bound to occur to me" (7:75). But the Fifth Meditation has revealed a source other than the senses for our ideas of bodies; namely, clear and distinct intellectual ideas of the geometrical properties of things. Prior to that insight, the meditator (as, earlier, Descartes himself) had been an empiricist:

In addition, I remembered that the use of my senses had come first, while the use of my reason came only later; and I saw that the ideas which I formed myself were less vivid than those which I perceived with the senses and were, for the most part, made up of elements of sensory ideas. In this way I easily convinced myself that I had nothing at all in the intellect which I had not previously had in sensation. [7:75–6]

The theory of knowledge in this quotation fits that presented by Hobbes and Gassendi in their Objections and held by subsequent empiricists such as Locke and Hume. Descartes distinguishes between the "vivid" ideas of the senses and "less vivid" ideas formed through reasoning. Furthermore, he says that these less vivid ideas were "for the most part" composed from sensory ideas. This qualification may allow for truly creative imaginary constructions (as in the painter's analogy), for idealization or extrapolation from sensory ideas, or for awareness of emotions and volitions (which he did not classify as specifically sensory). But the meditator previously hadn't permitted the intellect any content of its own (such as innate ideas), for she had accepted the Aristotelian theory that there is nothing in the intellect "not previously had in sensation."

Descartes presents the meditator as naturally inclined toward empiricism and the resemblance thesis. This portrayal accords with the account of childhood prejudices due to sensory immersion given in the *Principles* (8A:35–7) and reviewed in Chapter 3. It also meshes with the methodological claim that the meditative processes of the *Meditations* are needed to help to withdraw the mind from the senses and discover pure intellection. This newly discovered cognitive resource is now available for proving that bodies do indeed exist, although perhaps not with the properties previously ascribed to them by the meditator.

The argument begins by offering the grounds for moving beyond the just-reviewed doubts: "now, when I am beginning to achieve a better knowledge of myself and the author of my being, although I do not think I should heedlessly accept everything I seem to have acquired from the senses, neither do I think that everything should be called into doubt" (7:77–8). How can her improved knowledge of self and God counter the doubts about the senses? She has discovered in herself an ability for clear and distinct perception, which provides the basis for the proof. As for God, the Fourth Meditation has demonstrated that he would not give us a nature that would lead us to falsehoods we couldn't correct.

The first step in the proof pertains to mind–body distinctness. Once it has been shown that mind and body are distinct, external bodies are posited to explain the causal origin of the mind's sensory ideas.

Mind–body distinction (7:78)

The primary proof for mind–body distinctness occupies all of one paragraph (although a second argument is later sketched [7:86]).

Descartes had offered a proof in the *Discourse*, which is now to be stated more rigorously (7:8). Later, in the *Principles* (8A:25–32), he explains the distinction at length, although he reduced the argument itself to a summary.

The Discourse *argument*

In the *Discourse* the argument for mind–body distinctness comes after the *cogito* reasoning but precedes the extraction of the truth rule and the proof for God's existence. It runs as follows:

> Next I examined attentively what I was. I saw that while I could pretend that I had no body and that there was no world and no place for me to be in, I could not for all that pretend that I did not exist. I saw on the contrary that from the mere fact that I thought of doubting the truth of other things, it followed quite evidently and certainly that I existed; whereas if I had merely ceased thinking, even if everything else I had ever imagined had been true, I should have had no reason to believe that I existed. From this I knew I was a substance whose whole essence or nature is simply to think, and which does not require any place, or depend on any material thing, in order to exist. [6:32–3]

That mind is a substance distinct from body allegedly can be "known" (or "recognized," French *connaitre*) from the fact that the existence of the material world can be doubted, while one's own existence, as a thinking thing, cannot be doubted (at least while one is thinking).

As critics immediately pointed out (in letters to Descartes now lost), this argument is fallacious. It is an argument from ignorance. The fact that one can doubt the existence of the body while being unable to doubt the existence of the thinking self does not prove that mind and body are distinct. For it is possible that the thinking self and the body are actually identical, and the reasoner is ignorant of that fact. If so, he could doubt the existence of body (including his own body) while affirming his existence as mind alone, simply through ignorance of his real identity.

To see that the argument is fallacious, consider a parallel argument concerning the identity of a masked man who is pursued by the captain of a garrison of troops. Suppose the captain were to argue as follows:

1   I cannot doubt the existence of the masked man, Zorro, for he is here before me.
2   I can doubt the existence of the young nobleman, Don Diego; for all I know, he may have died suddenly.
3   Therefore, Zorro cannot be Don Diego.

The captain's argument does not work, for it remains epistemically possible that Zorro is Don Diego. The argument simply reveals that the captain is ignorant of Zorro's true identity – that, in fact, he is Don Diego. If he knew Zorro's identity, then upon correctly identifying that Zorro was present he would know that Don Diego stood before him. Of course, even if Zorro were actually Don Alexandro, the above argument would not rule out Don Diego as the masked man, for it does not speak to Zorro's identity. Hence, whether mind is actually distinct from body or not, the *Discourse* argument fails.

Descartes responds to such criticisms in the Preface of the *Meditations*. He admits that the argument would be fallacious if it relied merely on the fact that "the human mind, when directed toward itself, does not perceive itself to be anything other than a thinking thing" (7:7–8). But he denies that he had actually intended to assert the real distinction in the *Discourse* passage – even though the above quotation leaves little doubt that he *did* draw that conclusion.

Descartes' unwillingness to admit an error is less important than his granting that the *Discourse* argument, if taken as an argument for the real distinction, would not work. He promises to show that a close relative to it does work – that is, to show "how it follows from the fact that I cognize nothing else [besides thought] as belonging to my essence, that nothing else does in fact belong to it" (7:8*). How does saying that he "cognizes nothing else" in his essence besides thought differ from saying that he cannot doubt he is thinking but can doubt that the body exists? The Synopsis answers this question by comparing the meditator's epistemic position in Meditations 2 and 6 (7:13). In Meditation 2, the meditator cannot doubt that she exists as a thinking thing but can doubt the existence of body. From this she concludes that her *concepts* present mind and body as distinct, but she cannot rule out that mind and body might, unbeknown to her, still be identical (see 7:27). Once it has been proved (in Meditation 4) that "everything that we clearly and distinctly understand is true in a way which corresponds exactly to our understanding of it" (7:13), the meditator can (in Meditation 6) argue from distinct concepts of mind and body to the real distinction. It is (allegedly) no longer an argument from ignorance, for her concepts are now seen to portray accurately the real natures of mind and body.

The argument in Meditation 6

As we have seen, the meditator did more in Meditation 2 than simply discover that she could doubt bodies but not her own existence as a thinking thing. She purportedly discovered that she was essentially a thinking thing whose nature included intellection – even while admitting that thinking might actually be a bodily activity. The meditator will now consider an argument to show that she can exist as a substance really distinct from bodies and their activity. (This implies that she is an "immaterial substance," a phrase used rarely by Descartes [e.g., 9A:207].)

Recall that a substance is "a thing capable of existing independently" (7:44), or apart from everything else (except God, who preserves everything in existence [7:49; also 8A:24–5]). Given this definition, we can imagine two different goals that Descartes might have set for himself in establishing mind–body distinctness. In one scenario, he might simply want to show that the self and its body are distinct in the way that any two individual substances might be, such as individual tables and chairs; self and body can exist apart from each other, as a chair can be moved back from the table. (This sort of numerical distinction between individuals is all that is required by the scholastic term "real distinction" [see 8A:29].) On this reading, his appeal to the differing essences of mind and body (viz., thought and extension) would merely be a way of establishing that the self and its body are numerically distinct independent things – but he would not be setting out purposely to show that mind and body are different kinds of substance. Their differing essences would serve as premises, incidental to the conclusion of individual distinctness. In the second scenario, Descartes would intend from the start to demonstrate that mind and body are different in kind (in an especially strong way). They are not merely different kinds of substance (as we ordinarily might think oil and water differ), but they have no attributes in common whatsoever (save the generic ones, existence, duration, and number). This sort of strong difference in kind fits Descartes' conception that each kind of substance is characterized by a distinct principal attribute through which its modes must be conceived (a conception thus far left tacit in the *Meditations* but invoked just after the present argument [7:78] and in the First Replies [120–1]). Indeed, Descartes suggests elsewhere that such attributes must be logical opposites, or mutually exclusive (9A:349).

Although some construals of Descartes' argument proceed along the first line, we will adopt the view that he was aiming from the start to establish a distinction in kind between mind and body. He needed a distinction in kind for the argument for immortality sketched in the Letter (7:13–14). More importantly, the distinction in kind is a central conclusion of his metaphysics. While the actual wording of the argument can suggest the first reading – indeed, the argument as worded concludes with a distinction between the individual self and its body – it is naturally read as aiming to distinguish two kinds of substance having nothing in common, which is how Descartes later described its conclusion (8A:25; 9B:348).

As developed in Meditation 6 (and explained in the Replies), this goal requires three conclusions, which may be regarded as conditions for a real distinction of kind. It must be shown that mind is a substance whose sole essence is thought, that body is a substance whose sole essence is extension, and that the two are mutually exclusive and so distinct. Adapting Descartes' own terminology, let us call the first two points the "complete-being" conclusions and the third point the "mutual-exclusion" conclusion.

The three conditions may be set out as follows:

1   *Complete being*: a thinking thing can exist as a substance whose sole essence is thought.
2   *Complete being*: body can exist as a substance whose sole essence is extension.
3   *Mutual exclusion*: mental substance has no bodily modes, and bodily substance has no mental modes.

Despite first appearances, 1 and 2 do not already imply 3, except with specific assumptions or added premises. Under an Aristotelian conception of substance, thought might serve as the essence of a substance lacking a body (e.g., an angel), but that need not preclude that some thinking substances (such as human beings) are in fact naturally and essentially conjoined with bodies and cannot naturally exist or operate independently of such bodies. So to establish his point for an Aristotelian audience, Descartes must show both 1 and 3. Moreover, even on Descartes' own "constitutive-essence" conception of substance, all three points are needed. On this conception, a substance's modes must all be understandable through its essence. This assumption, together with 1 and 2, can yield 3 only if it is already shown that thinking essentially includes no modes of extension. Otherwise, mind and body might each be substances but might also each exhibit the modes of the other (some or all minds might be extended; some or all bodies might think). Hence, to prove a real distinction of the intended kind, the "mutual-exclusion" point is needed.

With these points in mind, let us consider the text. The relevant paragraph, divided into three parts for easy reference, runs in full:

[A] First, I know that everything which I clearly and distinctly understand is capable of being created by God so as to correspond exactly with my understanding of it. Hence the fact that I can clearly and distinctly understand one thing apart from another is enough to make me certain that the two things are distinct, since they are capable of being separated, at least by God. The question of what kind of power is required to bring about such a separation does not affect the judgment that the two things are distinct.

[B] Thus, simply by knowing that I exist and seeing at the same time that absolutely nothing else belongs to my nature or essence except that I am a thinking thing, I can infer correctly that my essence consists solely in the fact that I am a thinking thing.

[C] It is true that I may have (or, to anticipate, that I certainly have) a body that is very closely joined to me. But nevertheless, on the one hand I have a clear and distinct idea of myself, insofar as I am simply a thinking, non-extended thing; and on the other hand I have a distinct idea of body, insofar as this is simply an extended, non-thinking thing. And accordingly, it is certain that I am really distinct from my body, and can exist without it. [7:78]

Questions arise concerning each part, and their relations. What role is played by the appeal to God's power in A? Does B by itself present the basic argument for a distinction in kind, or is it achieved only in C? Or is C an elaboration of B in response to an objection implied in the first sentence of C? Let us consider each part in turn.

God and possibility

Passage A may seem to argue that because God can do anything, he can separate mind from body, so they really are distinct. That would be a weak argument, because it would appeal to the incomprehensible power of God to prove something about the created world. If it required the miraculous power of God to separate mind from body, no conclusion could be drawn about their *natural* relations in ordinary circumstances.

Passage A is not about miracles but pertains to the *real possibilities* of the natural (created) world. The notion of possibility in Descartes is complicated by his doctrine that God freely created the so-called eternal truths – including the truths of mathematics and the very essences of things – and could have created them otherwise than he did. But Descartes did not conclude from this doctrine that the human mind cannot know real possibilities for the world as created. As we will see in Chapter 9, he held that God created some unchanging eternal truths and adjusted our minds to them. Hence, as

discussed in Meditation 5, our clear and distinct intellectual perceptions reveal the real possibilities of things. God need not be
mentioned here; it would be enough to recall that our clear and
distinct perceptions inform us of real possibilities. Indeed, the quotation says that "the kind of power needed" to effect the separation is
irrelevant to our judgment of a real distinction (see also 7:170).
Descartes in fact believed that the mind separates from the body when
the latter stops functioning (7:153). Hence, under the natural circum-
stance of death the two substances separate. Such circumstances
could not be mentioned here, because the notion of a well-functioning
human body enters the Sixth Meditation only later.

We can now see that passage A does two things. First, it reaffirms
clear and distinct perception as a guide to real possibility. Second, it
provides a criterion for a real distinction. If two things can exist apart,
then they are really distinct. But the criterion of possibility tells us
that two things can exist apart if "I can clearly and distinctly understand one thing apart from another." The conditions for such
understanding are given in points 1 to 3 above. And, indeed,
Descartes describes this very set of conditions, including the mutual-
exclusion conclusion, in explicating his argument for Caterus
(7:120–1, quoted below).

Clear and distinct understanding

Passages B and C rely on clear and distinct perceptions, the first
tacitly, the second explicitly. Passage B reports two facts: that one
knows one's own existence (the initial *cogito* conclusion); and that one
"sees" (or "notices," Latin *animadvertere*) that "absolutely nothing
else belongs to my nature or essence except that I am a thinking
thing." From these facts, the inference ensues "that my essence
consists solely in the fact that I am a thinking thing." (Here the "I" is
restricted to the self as conceived in previous Meditations [7:78, 81];
Descartes will subsequently argue that this "I" forms a whole human
being by being conjoined with the body, and that this union is essential to a whole human being [7:88, 228; see also 8B:351].)

Passage B excludes everything from the essence of the self or the
"I" except thinking. Does it thereby preclude the "I" from being a

process of a body, or from having corporeal attributes? That depends on whether it follows from the fact that the self's *essence* is thinking that it is distinct from body and lacks bodily attributes. The assumption of constitutive essentialism might help here. If thinking is the essence of the self, and if the concept of thinking includes no modes of the body, then constitutive essentialism implies that the self lacks all bodily attributes. (Descartes presents no argument for constitutive essentialism, but he may have considered it apparent to the "natural light" upon a full analysis of the notion of a "mode" as simply a modification of the essence or being of a thing – hence a thing's essence should provide the basis for all its modes [7:79; see also 8A:25, 8B:348–9, 355, and 5:404–5].)

Of course, it must be established that the meditator has a clear and distinct idea of herself as only a thinking thing. Here some previous results can be brought to bear. In Meditation 2, the meditator learned to conceive of herself independently of body through the thought experiment of doubting the existence of all bodies and the resultant discovery that she could cognize herself as a thinking thing and could achieve an understanding of herself if and only if she ignored all bodily attributes. Descartes now asks the meditator to affirm that this conception of the self as a thinking thing is a clear and distinct perception of an essence – akin to the clear and distinct conception of extension achieved in Meditation 5. Earlier in Meditation 6, she has affirmed that sense and imagination, which seem to require a body as their cause, are not essential to a mind. She can be a mind even if she lacks sense and imagination, with their required relation to a body. Finally, passage B claims that the meditator perceives that "absolutely nothing" belongs to her essence except thinking, which presumably is meant to exclude the attributes of body. If she finds that these points do describe her conception of herself, then, on the assumption that clear and distinct perceptions reveal the real possibilities of things (and assuming constitutive essentialism), she knows that a purely thinking substance can exist, and that it has no bodily attributes.

Even if this reading of B is correct, it relies on an assumption (constitutive essentialism) and implied assertion (that the phrase "absolutely nothing" is meant to exclude bodily attributes) that are not spelled out. Descartes might have felt the need to make the points explicitly, or to add an additional argument.

The argument in C

The core of C is the claim to have clear and distinct ideas of the self as a thinking, non-extended thing and of body as an extended, non-thinking thing. From these ideas, the conclusion is drawn that the "I" or mind is "really distinct" from body (and so from its body).

Passage C offers the following clear and distinct ideas:

i   The self is simply a thinking and non-extended thing.
ii   Body is simply an extended and non-thinking thing.

These points suggest that mind and body are conceived differently and mutually exclusively. If accepted, they support the mutual-exclusion conclusion. But that by itself does not entail that mind and body are distinct substances. For that conclusion to follow, it must be shown that each can be a substance. For i and ii to yield an argument for real distinctness between substances, we need to know that mind can exist on its own independently of body (and vice versa). We need the complete-being conclusion.

We can now bring passage B into play again, this time without needing constitutive essentialism. B asserts that each of us knows we exist as a thinking thing whose sole essence is thought. It asserts the complete-being condition for minds; Descartes may have assumed that conclusion would be accepted for bodies. If so, then we have grounds for thinking that each can exist as a complete being, and so, together with points i and ii, we have met conditions 1 to 3 above.

Putting the three passages together, A provides the criterion for a real distinction between substances (capability of existing apart); it also offers clear and distinct perception as the method for determining whether the criterion is met. B affirms that a thinking thing can exist on its own. C affirms that this thinking thing has no properties peculiar to bodies. But if it can exist as a thing that has no bodily properties, it can exist apart from bodies. Which, by the criterion in A, means that mind is a substance really distinct from body.

The argument as a metaphysical insight

Described in this way, Descartes' argument takes the form of a metaphysical insight into mind and body. Meditation 2 prepares the meditator for thinking of mind independently of body, that is, for having a clear and distinct idea of mind unalloyed with any concept of body. The affirmation, in Meditations 3–5, that clear and distinct ideas are true, gives the meditator license to assert that the world is the way she clearly and distinctly perceives it to be. Meditation 5 offers a clear and distinct perception of the essence of body. Then Meditation 6 draws these previous insights together and asserts that mind and body are substances with mutually exclusive essences. Substances with nothing in common are really distinct.

In the Synopsis, Descartes described the *Meditations* as leading to just such an insight. He assigned the various Meditations their roles:

Meditation 2: "form a concept of the soul [or mind] which is as clear as possible and is also quite distinct from every concept of body."
Meditation 4: come to "know that everything that we clearly and distinctly understand is true in a way which corresponds exactly to our understanding of it."
Meditations 2, 5, 6: "have a distinct concept of corporeal nature."

From this it is inferred, in Meditation 6, that "all the things that we clearly and distinctly conceive of as different substances (as we do in the case of mind and body) are in fact substances which are really distinct one from the other" [7:13].

The argument in Meditation 6 adds little to this summary. The First Replies explicate the notion of a substance as a "complete being" (7:120–1). The *Principles* develop the technical terminology further, describing thought as the "principal attribute" of thinking substance, through which all its "modes" are understood (8A:24–30). Beyond such explications, Descartes did not add any new elements when restating the argument in the Geometrical exposition (7:169–70) or *Principles* (8A:28–9). The argument consists of metaphysical insights into the mutually exclusive real natures of mind and body and the possibility of their existence as really distinct substances. (A second argument [7:85–6] contends that mind is indivisible and body is divisible, and concludes they are really distinct, presumably because each has a property that the other cannot have.)

A persistent objection

Several of the objectors pressed Descartes on how he knew that a thinking thing or mind could not in fact be identical with certain "corporeal motions" in the body (7:100, 122–3, 200; 9A:207). They were in effect asking him how he could be sure he wasn't still arguing from ignorance about the real identity of thought with bodily processes.

In the First Replies, Descartes responds by invoking the notion of a "complete being" and then arguing for mutual exclusion:

> I have a complete understanding of what a body is when I think that it is merely something having extension, shape and motion, and I deny that it has anything which belongs to the nature of a mind. Conversely, I understand the mind to be a complete thing, which doubts, understands, wills, and so on, even though I deny that it has any of the attributes which are contained in the idea of a body. This would be quite impossible if there were not a real distinction between the mind and the body. [7:121]

The problem with this answer is that Caterus (and the second objectors, 7:122–3) wanted to know how he excluded the possibility that his perception of mind as capable of existing separately from body was in fact incomplete, even though it seemed complete. (Incomplete, on the possibility – which is exactly what is under dispute – that mind really is a bodily process.)

Arnauld developed this objection in detail (7:198–204), summing up his main point by offering a counter-example (an argument allegedly parallel to Descartes' in all relevant respects, but producing a clearly false conclusion):

> I clearly and distinctly understand that this triangle is right-angled, without understanding that the square on the hypotenuse is equal to the squares on the other sides. It follows on this reasoning that God, at least, could create a right-angled triangle with the square on its hypotenuse not equal to the squares on the other sides. [7:202]

One can have a clear and distinct perception of a right-angled triangle without knowing everything about it, including not knowing the Pythagorean theorem. But, Arnauld observes, it does not follow that the unknown properties, such as the Pythagorean relation between the squares on the sides, are not actually properties of the triangle. So perhaps thought really is a bodily process, even though one can conceive of mind without thinking of body.

Descartes pointed out several problems with this argument (7:224–7). First, even if a triangle can be regarded as a substance, "the property of having the square on the hypotenuse equal to the squares on the other sides is not a substance" (7:224). Fair enough. Arnauld's objection does not really parallel the mind–body argument, which asserts that both mind and body can exist on their own. Second, Descartes claimed that if we clearly and distinctly understood the Pythagorean property, we would see that it does belong to a right-angled triangle. But, he asserted, if we clearly and distinctly understand the property of extension, we see that it does not contain thought. Third, he argued that we cannot deny that the Pythagorean theorem applies to right-angled triangles while having clear and distinct perceptions of both. But, he argued, we can do this for mind and body, from which he concluded that if mind and body weren't distinct kinds of substance, we wouldn't be able to have a clear and distinct perception of each independently of the attributes of the other.

In the end, these responses all boil down to two claims: that we have a clear and distinct perception of mind as a distinct kind of substance from body (and vice versa), and that our clear and distinct perceptions tell us how the world is (or could be). If either claim is denied, the argument fails. It could, for instance, be true that we have distinct concepts of mind and body, and that we find each

257

concept to be (in some sense) "complete." But if it were not also true that our concepts reveal the underlying structure of the world, the argument would fail. It also fails if we are mistaken that our concepts of mind and body clearly and distinctly present them as capable of existing apart. Equally, however, if both claims are true, the argument works.

Mind as intellectual substance (7:78-9)

In moving toward the conclusion that external objects exist, Descartes examines further the essential properties of mind itself. He has the meditator again consider whether various mental faculties and modes of thought are essential to her existence as a thinking thing:

> I find in myself various faculties for certain special modes of thinking, namely imagination and sense perception. Now I can clearly and distinctly understand myself as a whole without these faculties; but I cannot, conversely, understand these faculties without me, that is, without an intellectual substance to inhere in. This is because there is an intellectual act in their formal concept. [7:78*]

Descartes here characterizes the thinking thing as "an intellectual substance" (see also 7:12, 9A:207). This accords with our finding in Meditation 2, that intellection is the essential feature of thought. The passage further claims that sensation and imagination are not essential to mind. The point is not that sensation and imagination are not types of thought that must exist in a mind; indeed, according to the passage they each require an "intellectual substance" in which to inhere. Sense perception and imagination are kinds of perception, and as such are species of intellectual act. (As explained in the *Principles*, perception *is* simply the operation of the intellect [8A:17], so any kind of perception is a kind of intellectual act.) But the meditator concludes that she could exist as a thinking thing without having such acts. Presumably, she is able to conceive of herself as a pure intellect who contemplates God, the mind itself, and the objects of geometry but has no sensations or appetites. Descartes would ascribe those three objects of cognition to a disembodied mind, as the meditator now conceives herself to be.

In Chapter 4, we considered whether thought, or the thinking thing, has a core essential feature. Some philosophers interpret Descartes as making consciousness the essence of thought. But he does not say that directly, and here he characterizes mind as "intellectual substance." He also classifies all instances of intellection as perception; sense perceptions and imaginations are instances of intellection only in so far as they are perceptions. In Chapter 5, we found that his comparison of ideas with images suggests that ideas always represent. Indeed, in Meditation 3 he affirms that "there can be no ideas that are not as it were of things" (7:44). If this means that all ideas represent "individual things," this statement is difficult to reconcile with Descartes' appeal to "concepts" and "simple notions" (Chapters 4, 5) through which we grasp properties or essences common to many things (assuming, as seems natural, that such concepts are a type of idea). His statements in the *Meditations* do, however, suggest that all ideas represent in some way (but see 8A:35). It thus appears that for Descartes, intellection (perception, or representation) is the central feature of thought.

In Chapter 6, we saw that will is a feature of mind distinct from intellect, and that intellect and will are both required for judgment. In the *Principles* (8A:17), Descartes says that all modes of thinking may be divided into acts of either intellect (perceptions) or will (volitions). The fact that he considered the will to be a distinct faculty of mind may seem to challenge the interpretation that intellection is the core essential feature of thought.

If we scour Descartes' writings, we will find few direct statements concerning what makes both intellect and will count as mental faculties and their operations as instances of thought. However, there is an intriguing passage in the Sixth Replies that speaks to their relation. There Descartes explains that understanding and volition have a special "affinity and connection," and that "the thing that understands and the thing that wills are one and the same in virtue of a unity of nature" (7:423). What might this unity of nature be? Both will and intellect are faculties whose operations are instances of thinking. That they both produce thoughts might provide the unity, yet this answer offers little insight into their "affinity." Instances of both volition and intellection are accessible to consciousness, and if consciousness was the nature of thought, that would provide a "unity of nature." The fact that both types of act are conscious again does not entail a special affinity between them; it simply ascribes a common feature to them. However, if we take intellection as the core feature of thought, it does provide a unity of nature. We saw in Chapter 5 that an act of will requires an idea or object. But ideas with representational content are operations of the intellect; consequently, will, too, presupposes intellection in its conception. The converse does not seem to be required; intellection or representation can be understood without will. Perhaps because intellection or representation is more basic than will, it counts as the essential feature of the thinking thing and explains why the mind is denominated an "intellectual substance." (We will return to the relation between consciousness and the nature of mind in Chapter 10.)

External objects exist (7:78–80)

Because acts of imagination and sensation are not essential to the self conceived simply as a thinking thing, the meditator wants an explanation for why such acts occur in her own mind. She now notes a feature that distinguishes sense perceptions from the acts of imagination described earlier in the Meditation. Imaginings are under the control of the will; one may choose, or not choose, to imagine a pentagon. But her sensory ideas "are produced without my cooperation and often even against my will" (7:79). Hence, she reasons, these ideas must be produced by "another substance distinct from me" (7:79). The question then becomes, given that we have sensations, what produces them in us (that is, in our minds).

The meditator considers three options. Our sensations might be produced in us by bodies, by God, or by some other created being "more noble than body" (such as, presumably, an angel). She assumes that if our sensations are caused by bodies, that cause "will contain formally and in fact everything which is to be found objectively or representatively in the ideas" (7:79). But if God or an angel caused our sensory ideas, those beings would contain the content or objective reality of the ideas "eminently." The notion of "eminent" containment was introduced in Meditation 3 and further explained in the Geometrical Arguments (7:41, 161); in the present context, it means that God or an angel can cause ideas of shape in us, even though they are not bodies and hence do not possess shape. Meditation 5 has established that bodies can be shaped, and it is now assumed that if a body causes a sensory idea in us, that body will contain "formally and in fact" what is found "objectively" or "representatively" in that idea.

This contrast between the idea–body causal relation and the idea–God/angel relation provides the crux of the argument. Our sensory ideas seem to present us with shaped bodies. We naturally believe that such ideas present the actual properties of bodies. We have no faculty to tell us that God or angels cause the ideas in us. The meditator therefore reasons: "I do not see how God could be understood to be anything but a deceiver if the ideas were transmitted from a source other than corporeal things." And it has already been established that God is no deceiver. Therefore, "it follows that corporeal things exist" (7:80).

The argument as given is compressed, and it raises some questions that are answered only later. It asserts that if a body causes a sensory idea in us, the idea reveals properties that really are in the body, whereas if God or an angel causes a sensory idea in us, it does not. But why should we believe that, when a body acts as cause, our ideas present it as it is? Why should the effect represent, or accurately portray, the properties of the cause? Gassendi raised this question, observing that "an efficient cause is something external to the effect and often of a quite different nature" (7:288). A cause need not resemble, or contain formally, something found in its effect (see 7:39). (Indeed, Descartes held that God creates an extended universe but is not himself extended.) Although Gassendi's objection contained errors in interpreting Descartes' position (and received only a perfunctory reply, 7:366), the basic question is on target. It cannot be assumed that bodies in fact have a certain property simply because they cause an idea of that property when affecting a mind.

Descartes knew that he needed an explanation here, for he himself sharply distinguished cases in which bodies cause sensory ideas of shape and other geometrical properties in minds from those in which bodies cause ideas of color, sounds, and so on. In the latter cases, we have a natural inclination to affirm the resemblance thesis, which is false. In the conclusion of the argument that bodies exist, Descartes was sensitive to the difference between the two classes of cause:

> They may not all exist in a way that exactly corresponds with my sensory grasp of them, for in many cases the grasp of the senses is very obscure and confused. But at least they possess all the properties which I clearly and distinctly understand, that is, all those which, viewed in general terms, are comprised within the subject matter of pure mathematics. [7:80]

Although Meditation 5 has established that properties of the bodies are modes of extension, the present argument does not concern purely intellectual ideas of possible matter but sensory ideas of actual bodies. It requires that these sensory ideas present some properties that bodies actually have, else God is a deceiver. And given what was said in Meditation 4, it would also seem to require that if some of our sensory ideas lead us to affirm that properties exist in bodies that aren't there (such as color as a real quality), we should be able to correct our mistake. These requirements are (thus far) unexplained.

We seem to be missing a premise. It is supplied in the subsequent paragraphs, which examine more generally the reliability of the senses.

Descartes affirms straight away that the senses tell us things such as that "the sun is of such and such a size or shape" (7:80). Sensory ideas do, or can, inform us of the actual shapes and sizes of bodies (that is, specific geometrical properties of individual bodies). But he also affirms that there is something "true" in his sensations of "light or sound or pain." He relates both types of perception, of shape and light or color, to what one "is taught by nature." But nature "in its general aspect" is "nothing other than God himself, or the ordered system of created things established by God" (7:80). God has set up our sensory apparatus. He has given us a tendency to believe that things are as they appear. By itself, that might lead us to think that bodies are both shaped and colored (in the "real quality" or "resemblance" sense of being colored). But he also provided us with purely intellectual perceptions of the essence of matter. Hence we should be able to trust our senses to reveal to us, at least sometimes, the properties that we already know particular bodies can have, such as size and shape. (Further discussion is needed to describe the "truth" in the sensations of color or pain.)

The additional premise is that sensory ideas function to inform us of the properties of objects in the environment. Accordingly, sensory ideas will inform us of some properties bodies actually have. Moreover, if some sensory ideas present bodies to us as having properties they actually have in the way presented (as size or shape), and some present properties which are not in bodies in the way presented (as color), we should be able to correct the resulting erroneous beliefs (such as the resemblance thesis) – or at least suspend judgment in unfavorable circumstances. But the faculty of pure intellect (allegedly) informs us that bodies actually can have the properties of size and shape. Therefore, we should believe that the senses will, under favorable conditions, reveal the true sizes and shapes of particular bodies.

Most of the remaining Meditation elaborates the conception that sensory ideas function to inform perceivers of their environments. This role for the senses is contrasted with the role of the intellect in revealing the essences of things. The discussion begins with a basic feature of Descartes' theory of sensation, the view that sensory ideas and appetites arise from mind–body union and interaction.

Mind–body union (7:80–1)

The teachings of nature are judgments arising in connection with mind–body union. These judgments concern sensations, including those that pertain directly to bodily states, such as pain, hunger, and thirst, as well as those pertaining to external objects. Examples of such judgments were mentioned earlier in reviewing the doubt, including the judgment that pain is distressing, or that the feeling of hunger means that we need food (7:76).

Bodily sensations and mind–body union

Descartes first considers teachings that concern the sensations that pertain to the human body itself. He has the meditator reason:

> There is nothing that my own nature teaches me more vividly than that I have a body, and that when I feel pain there is something wrong with the body, and that when I am hungry or thirsty the body needs food and drink, and so on. So I should not doubt that there is some truth in this. [7:80]

My own nature is bestowed on me by a non-deceptive God, so I should be able to trust it. But how do we know when to trust it, and when not? Descartes suggests that (at least some aspects of) judgments concerning our vivid sensations can be trusted. Pain, hunger, thirst, and other bodily appetites are strong elements of our experience and lead to immediate judgments. At the same time, Descartes will soon argue that the natural judgments we form concerning other strong elements of our experience, such that color sensations resemble something in bodies, are not trustworthy. So there must be something besides the vividness of these sensations that certifies our natural judgments. Presumably, the added factor is that the considered judgments of the intellect provide us with no reason to think that pain, hunger, and so forth are generally misleading concerning our bodily state.

The internal sensations teach the meditator not only that she has a body but also that she (qua mind) is closely united with it so as to form a unit (a whole human being):

> Nature also teaches me, by these sensations of pain, hunger, thirst and so on, that I am not merely present in my body as a sailor is present in a ship, but that I am very closely joined and, as it were, intermingled with it, so that I and the body form a unit. If this were not so, I, who am nothing but a thinking thing, would not feel pain when the body was hurt, but would perceive the damage purely by the intellect, just as a sailor perceives by sight if anything in his ship is broken. [7:81]

The evidence for mind–body union comes from the existence of sensations such as hunger or thirst. The argument for the union takes the form of contrasting hypotheses about what our experience would be like, given the presence or absence of a genuine union between mind and body. If there were no real union, when the mind received information about the state of its body it would have the perspective of a sailor who observes his ship. The sailor sees that the ship has damage, but he doesn't feel it directly (or, if he has sympathetic reactions, they are not equal to felt pain). By contrast, we feel pain when our body is damaged. The pain doesn't take the form of a detached observation that, say, a knife has sliced the skin next to the thumb. Instead of simply surveying damage to our body (like the sailor), we experience a "confused sensation" (7:81). Presumably, pains are confused just because, although drawing attention to the damage, they do not fully portray its nature and extent. Otherwise, the science of medicine would be easier, for we could have direct and detailed knowledge of our body's damaged or diseased states through our internal perceptions.

External objects and the teachings of nature

Having earlier proved that bodies exist, Descartes has the meditator consider what nature teaches her about such bodies:

> I am also taught by nature that various other bodies exist in the vicinity of my body, and that some of these are to be sought out and others avoided. And from the fact that I perceive by my senses a great variety of colors, sounds, smells and tastes, as well as differences in heat, hardness and the like, I am correct in inferring that the bodies which are the source of these various sensory perceptions possess differences corresponding to them, though perhaps not resembling them. [7:81]

The first teaching of nature, that other bodies exist, has been established previously through explicit argument. The second teaching, that some of the surrounding bodies should be pursued and others avoided, is now accepted on the grounds that the teachings of nature ultimately derive from God, so must be trustworthy. The third teaching, that objects have differing properties, corresponding to the various types of sense perception they produce in perceivers, is apparently backed by the same general considerations about the function of sense perception. That is, even confused sensations, such as various colors or smells, correspond to real differences in the bodies that produce them.

Descartes will subsequently qualify these claims by noting cases in which the teachings lead to error and by putting restrictions on the types of thing that sense perceptions reveal. But he affirms that the senses are generally to be trusted where bodily benefit or harm is at stake.

Objections to mind–body union and interaction

In the various passages quoted above, Descartes makes two sorts of claim: first, that various internal and external sense perceptions are reliable guides to bodily preservation; and, second, that such perceptions arise through mind–body union. The first claim did not meet objections, and indeed, skeptical challenges to the senses typically did not question their general reliability in everyday use. The second claim, about mind–body union, was challenged. Descartes was committed to a two-way interaction between mind and body: body affects mind in sensation, and mind affects body in voluntary action. (He mentioned the mind's effects on body only incidentally in the *Meditations* [7:84].)

Gassendi asked whether two substances completely different in kind, and sharing no properties, could causally interact (7:337–45), but Descartes said little in reply (7:387–90). A powerful challenge on this point came from Descartes' friend and correspondent Princess Elizabeth. Having read the *Meditations*, on 16 May 1643 she wrote to Descartes:

> I beseech you to tell me how the soul of man (since it is but a thinking substance) can determine the spirits of the body to produce voluntary actions. For it seems every determination of movement happens from an impulsion of the thing moved, according to the manner in which it is pushed by that which moves it, or else, depends on the qualities and shape of the surface of this latter. Contact is required for the first two conditions, and extension for the third. You entirely exclude extension

from your notion of the soul, and contact seems to me incompatible with an immaterial thing. [3:661*]

Elizabeth refers to Descartes' doctrine that bodily movements are controlled, physiologically, by subtle matter known as "animal spirits." So if the mind directs the voluntary movements of the body, it must control the direction (or "determination") of the spirits. But these spirits are material and so have only the properties of extension (size, shape, position, and motion). Now, she asks, if mind is unextended, how can it direct the spirits? For, she confesses, the only way she understands that something could alter the direction of another thing is by pushing it, or channeling it with its surface. But pushing requires contact, and channeling requires a surface, so both require extension. How could an unextended mind have a surface, or make contact with a body?

Descartes soon answered (21 May), and at some length. He explained that in thinking about such questions, three things must be kept distinct: our concept of mind, of body, and of mind–body union (3:665). In the *Meditations*, he had focused largely on the first two notions, and hence on mind–body distinctness. However, he referred her to the Sixth Replies, where he had compared mind–body union to the relation between gravity and extended bodies (7:441–2). Gravity, he observed, is attributed to a whole body, even though it can be regarded as acting from a single geometrical point (the "center of gravity"). Accordingly, just as we believe that a body's heaviness can cause a body's motion without itself being extended, so too we should think of mind as able to act on body even though it is not extended (3:667–8).

Elizabeth immediately saw the weakness of this response (letter of 20 June). As Descartes had admitted to her (3:668), he did not believe that gravity is a real quality acting on extended matter. Rather, he held that gravity results from the contact of rapidly moving, minute particles on the surfaces of the larger bodies that fall to earth. Elizabeth found herself unable to comprehend why comparison with a false notion of gravity should speak to her problem. With dry humor, she proposed that the distractions of being a princess must have dulled her mind, accounting for her stupidity in being unable to comprehend, from what you had previously said concerning weight, the idea by which we should judge how the soul (non-extended and immaterial) can move the body; nor why this power, that you have then under the name of quality falsely attributed to it as carrying the body toward the center of the earth, ought to persuade us that body can be pushed by something immaterial. [3:684]

Elizabeth rightly thought that the fault lay with Descartes' response, not her comprehension. So she pressed her point, confessing that "it would be easier for me to concede matter and extension to the soul, than the capacity of moving a body and of being moved, to an immaterial being" (3:685).

Eight days later (28 June), Descartes acknowledged the weakness of his previous effort and tried again. He now described the three "primitive notions," of mind (or soul), body, and mind–body union, in relation to the cognitive faculties by which they are known:

The soul is conceived only by the pure intellect; body (i.e. extension, shapes and motions) can likewise be known by the intellect alone, but much better by the intellect aided by the imagination; and finally what belongs to the union of the soul and the body is known only obscurely by the intellect alone or even by the intellect aided by the imagination, but it is known very clearly by the senses. [3:691–2]

There is no surprise in his saying that the mind is known by pure intellect alone, for he made clear from the Second Meditation onward that imagination is of no help in grasping thought as a property or attribute. Similarly, it is no surprise to find him saying that extension can be grasped by pure intellect as well, even though he allows here that shapes are more easily known with the help of imagination (at least, that would be true for triangles and pentagons, as opposed to chiliagons and myriagons). However, it is surprising for him to say that mind–body union is known "only obscurely" by the intellect (or intellect and imagination) but "is very clearly known by the senses." This statement is odd because, formally, Descartes held that the senses do not know anything. Like his Aristotelian predecessors, he held that the senses do not judge (7:43, 438), only the intellect (in conjunction with the will). So how are we to understand his point?

Descartes has conceded that he could not offer (or even form) a clear conception of mind–body union and interaction. He fell back on an argument by elimination. He continued to trust his metaphysical conclusion – perceived with clarity and distinctness – that mind and body are distinct substances, each understood apart from the other. With substance dualism firmly in place, he inquired about mind–body union and interaction. Then "the senses" – or rather, the fact of sense perception – tell him that mind and body must interact. For how else could sense perception arise if it was not caused by the body? (Here, he could appeal to his proof for the existence of bodies.) Similarly, given the fact that decisions result in voluntary bodily motions, we must accept that mind can influence body. Once the mind–body distinction is in place, a theory of mind–body union and interaction becomes necessary. Descartes' response does not elucidate how the interaction occurs but proposes that it must occur since mind and body are distinct and yet we do sense and act. (In fact, Descartes' followers, and perhaps even Descartes, ultimately concluded that God mediates all mind–body interaction, just as he is the cause of all motion, so that no genuine mind–body interaction is required.)

Elizabeth was not buying. Responding three days later, she wondered whether there might not be "unknown properties" in her mind that would reverse Descartes' immaterialist conclusion and explain mind–body interaction. In her view, Descartes had not really shown that thought and extension are incompatible, even if his arguments showed that thought does not *require* extension. But although pure thought may not require extension, sensing and voluntary motion seem to. Hence she was prepared, at least provisionally, to suppose that the mind is extended in performing these functions (4:2). She did not accept that the argument for mind–body distinctness had really ruled out the possibility that mind is extended.

Descartes' argument from elimination stands or falls with his argument for substance dualism. The denial of dualism, while not resolving all questions about mind–body relations, would change the framework for thinking about interaction.

Role of senses versus intellect (7:82–3)

Having rehabilitated the senses for everyday use, Descartes now draws the crucial contrast that separates his theory of the senses from that of the Aristotelians. This contrast separates the legitimate teachings of nature from certain "ill-considered judgments" that the meditator has made since childhood. The legitimate teachings of nature concern bodily benefits and harms. The prejudices of childhood go beyond such judgments in formulating a tacit theory about the nature of sensory qualities, or they draw conclusions from perceptions obtained in less than optimal conditions.

Cases of childhood prejudice include the following:

> the belief that any space in which nothing is occurring to stimu-late my senses must be empty; or that the heat in a body is something exactly resembling the idea of heat which is in me; or that when a body is white or green, the selfsame whiteness or greenness which I perceive through my senses is present in the body; or that in a body which is bitter or sweet there is the self-same taste which I experience, and so on; or, finally, that stars and towers and other distant bodies have the same size and shape which they present to my senses, and other examples of this kind. [7:82]

The prejudices include three cases of forming an errant theory about the existence or qualities of bodies and one case of drawing conclu-sions about object properties under conditions known to yield error. In his physics, Descartes denied that there are any truly empty spaces; he held that a fine matter, known as æther, fills in where larger bits of matter are not found (8A:42–51). Yet some people believe otherwise. Why so? They have leapt to this conclusion in their childhood and retained the prejudice! Similarly, Descartes held that bodies contain particles that have various sizes, shapes, and motions, but he denied that they have the Aristotelian "real qualities" of color or taste (as in the resemblance thesis). Why do people believe otherwise? Prejudice again! And finally, someone might believe that stars or distant towers are actually very small. But, as the meditator noted even in

Meditation 1, such errors result from not taking into account the known limitations of the senses. We should, for instance, not judge the size of very distant things from their appearance alone but should realize that we have to draw closer, or make measurements, to determine their true size.

There is a problem here. Both the legitimate teachings of nature and the prejudices of childhood produce a current inclination to make a judgment – that pain is to be avoided, or that a color sensation resembles something in objects. How are we to tell which impulses result from a legitimate teaching and which from childhood habits? That is where the intellect comes in. Speaking of his nature in so far as he is a mind–body unity (as opposed to his nature as a mind alone, or the nature of his body alone), he writes:

> My nature, then, in this limited sense, does indeed teach me to avoid what induces a feeling of pain and to seek what induces feelings of pleasure, and so on. But it does not appear to teach us to draw any conclusions from these sensory perceptions about things located outside us without waiting until the intellect has examined the matter. [7:82]

The intellect must, then, provide some teachings of its own that allow us to sort out legitimate teachings from prejudices. The quoted statement that we should not draw "any conclusions" about external bodies is an exaggeration – we can conclude that those that induce pain should be avoided, and so on. Rather, we should avoid drawing any conclusions about the *essences* of external things until the intellect has been consulted. And the intellect will tell us to reject the resemblance thesis about color (see Chapter 9).

Descartes compared the roles of the senses and intellect as follows:

> The proper purpose of the sensory perceptions given me by nature is simply to inform the mind of what is beneficial or harmful for the composite of which the mind is a part; and to this extent they are clear and distinct enough. But I misuse them by treating them as reliable touchstones for immediate judgments

about the essence of the bodies posited outside us, which essence they signify only very obscurely and confusedly. [7:83*]

The senses tell us about benefits and harms. For that purpose, our sensory ideas are clear and distinct enough, which presumably means they allow us to tell objects apart, to keep from running into things, to distinguish food from rocks, to avoid open fires, and so on. Beyond that, as was mentioned earlier, they also allow us to determine facts about the world, such as the size and shape of the Sun. (Reasoning might be involved in working out the true size, but it will be reasoning based on sensory observation of the Sun.) But the senses do not reveal the essences of things.

Here is the crux of Descartes' cognitive revolution. The essences of things are not revealed through sensory experience but through the intellect. An Aristotelian could accept that statement, but he would mean something different by it. To the Aristotelians, the intellect operates on sensory materials to extract the essences of things. For Descartes, knowledge of essences comes from the intellect operating on its own, independently of the senses. In his view, the Aristotelian method leads to the entrenchment of childhood prejudices, such as the resemblance thesis. His method bypasses the senses altogether to grasp extension as the essence of matter. The senses then assume the role of informing the knower of dangers and opportunities, and of providing information about the specific shapes, sizes, positions, and motions of individual things. The intellect cannot discover such dangers and opportunities, or such facts about the world, without sensory help.

Analysis of sensory error (7:83–9)

In the Fourth Meditation, Descartes asked how the existence of any human cognitive error could be reconciled with God's goodness. Now he asks how certain deceptions of the senses can be reconciled. These deceptions arise when the internal senses, although properly functioning, still lead to a harmful result or a false conclusion. Such deceptions are not prejudices that can be corrected by the intellect. Rather, they are cases in which usually trustworthy teachings of nature go wrong.

Descartes gave this problem the lengthiest treatment of any topic in Meditation 6. Part of his interest was surely to reconcile the goodness of God – which he has invoked on numerous occasions – with the fact of occasional sensory deceptions that cannot easily be avoided. But part of his interest was surely to present his novel theory of the human body as an intricate machine.

Sometimes the teachings of nature lead us to do things that are not beneficial, as when someone ill with dropsy desires drink when drinking would be harmful. Or they may deceive, as when someone feels pain in a place with no injury, such as an amputee who seemingly feels pain in her missing hand (7:77). In these cases, the teachings of nature about the need for drink, or the location of bodily damage, are incorrect. The dropsical man shouldn't drink, even though his thirst makes him want to. And the amputee has no damage to her fingers (she has no fingers), although her feeling of pain can make her believe her finger is hurting (see 1:420).

Descartes first considers a means for explaining away such errors, by attributing them to a disorder in the body alone. He offers a comparison with a badly made clock. Clocks are for telling time. When they tell time badly, they depart from their intended function. Even though the spring, pendulum, and gears follow the laws of nature (7:84), the clock's operation does not accord with the clockmaker's intention. Now consider the human body. Let us say that in a non-diseased state, it is like a well-made clock. It does what it is "supposed" to do. In the diseased state, it is like a poorly made clock. Its parts still follow the laws of nature as laid down by God, but it malfunctions. Following this line of thought, the fact that the dropsical man wants to drink may be excused because the body is broken, and God presumably can't be held responsible for a broken bodily machine. (In the nature of things, anything with parts can break, for matter is intrinsically divisible.)

Descartes rejects this answer, saying "a sick man is no less one of God's creatures than a healthy one, and it seems no less a contradiction to suppose that he has received from God a nature which deceives him" (7:84). His rejection turns on an analysis of what counts as the "nature" we are given by God in this case. The nature in question is not the body considered alone, but the particulars of mind–body union and interaction. He rejects appeal to a broken bodily machine, because the body by itself contains no standard of well functioning and hence no standard for error (at least in relation to the teachings of nature, which are the current topic). As he put it, the comparison of a sick man and a badly made clock is merely "a label that depends on my thought" and is "extraneous to the things to which it is applied" (7:85). Although this part of the text is somewhat obscure, it clearly asserts that the notion of defect, in the case of errant teachings of nature, arises only in connection with mind–body union. It is only because the mind reacts to bodily states in a certain way that an error can be said to arise. God is (potentially) culpable because he instituted the mind–body relation.

Descartes is caught between using God's perfection and goodness to underwrite the general reliability of the senses and wanting to avoid the conclusion that God is responsible for errors in our design that should have been avoided. He adopts the solution of (1) making God responsible for the errors in question, since he arranged the laws of mind–body union, and (2) providing an argument that God did the best that could be done in setting up those laws.

Preferably, God would arrange things so that the brain state that causes thirst, or a feeling of pain in the foot, arises only when drinking would be good for us, or when the foot was really damaged. But, Descartes explains, God was constrained by the fact that the mind interacts only with the brain, at a central location. All information about the body's own states and about external bodies must be conveyed there by the nerves. Why this had to be Descartes does not say. Is it because the mind, being simple and unextended, cannot interact with the whole body and be directly affected by damage in the foot, or by the need (or lack thereof) for liquid in the stomach and intestines? But why should that be a rule for mind–body interaction? Descartes already describes the (unextended) mind as "turning toward" extended patterns in the body (e.g., in imagining a triangle), so what prevents it from interacting with the whole body rather than only a part of the brain? He does not appeal to metaphysical necessity but to empirical evidence in supporting this aspect of his theory. He affirms that the fact that mind–body interaction occurs only in the brain "is established by countless observations, which there is no need to review here" (7:86; see also 6:109 and 8A:319–20).

Because mind–body interaction occurs only in the brain, the mind must rely on "signals" arriving there from the nerves (7:88). These signals are motions set up in the nerves and brain (vibrations or other characteristic motions). The nerves are made of matter, which is by nature extended. A motion at the brain end of a nerve might have more than one cause. Suppose that normally a jab in the foot causes motion R in the brain. The motion in the nerve from the foot must be transmitted up the leg, through the spinal cord, and into the brain. Now suppose that this nerve is caused to vibrate by a blow to the upper leg, or the back. It is possible that motion R, which signals pain in the foot, would result. A person would feel pain in the foot, even though there was no jab, and no tissue damage there. Similarly, conditions in the stomach might jiggle the nerves in ways that make the person want to drink, even though the total state of the stomach and intestines is such that drinking is harmful. And so on for other signals.

Given that God decided to join a mind to a body and to place the body in a complex world, he was faced with the fact that nerves could be jiggled midstream, or jiggled in an amputated arm, yielding a misleading signal. Why must this be so? Because the best design for joining mind and body assigns a fixed meaning to brain signals. As Descartes explained:

> any given movement occurring in the part of the brain that immediately affects the mind produces just one corresponding sensation; and hence the best system that could be devised is that it should produce the one sensation which, of all possible sensations, is most especially and most frequently conducive to the preservation of the healthy man. [7:87]

Usually, when we feel a pain in the foot, there is a problem in the foot. Usually, when we feel thirsty, we need to drink. Sometimes, we feel pain where there is no damage, or feel thirsty when it is not good to drink. These are real errors of nature, because they follow from our nature (7:88). But they arise in the "best system" of mind–body interaction that could be devised for beings such as ourselves. God goes with the usual case. Usually, the nerve from the foot will be jiggled by damage to the foot, for it is deeply encased in bone and flesh everywhere else.

To the complaint that God could somehow have arranged it so that our sensations never misled us, Descartes might repeat the Fourth Meditation point that God decided to create a variety of beings, including ones like us, warts and all.

Leaving the question of theological justification aside, this long passage reveals that Descartes considered the empirical study of human beings to include study of mind–body interaction. The theory that mind–body interaction occurs in the brain, just as the claim that mind and body do interact, is in the end established by facts of sense. Descartes considered many things about the nature of mind and matter to be settled by metaphysical investigation, independently of sensory evidence. But the existence and character of mind–body inter-action was, for him, fully an empirical matter.

Removal of dream doubt (7:89–90)

The message of the second half of Meditation 6 has been that the senses are generally to be trusted in matters concerning the well-being of the body. The final paragraph teaches that the senses can be trusted more generally, at least if their reports are subjected to proper scrutiny using other faculties, especially memory and intellect. Now, at last, the "exaggerated doubts of the last few days" about the senses can be dismissed "as laughable" (7:89).

To establish the trustworthiness of particular sensory reports, Descartes prescribes comparing such reports among themselves, using memory and intellect to adjudicate conflicts and avoid error. Certain sorts of error, such as mislocated pain, are inevitable but rare. Even without careful checking, because God is no deceiver we know our pains usually reveal the proper location of damage. Even so, we can check the foot visually or by touch if need be. If the foot has been amputated, we know there is no damage, despite our feeling pain as if in the toe. In other cases, such as the famous bent stick in water, we can use the intellect to correct our habitual, tacit judgment that the stick is bent (7:438–9). (We might even learn always to double check partially submerged sticks to see whether they are bent.) In summary, the senses are generally reliable about practical matters, and sensory reports can be checked further for error.

The policy of checking sensory reports against one another yields a proposed criterion for distinguishing waking from sleeping:

> I now notice that there is a vast difference between [being asleep and being awake], in that dreams are never linked by memory with all the other actions of life as waking experiences are.... When I distinctly see where things come from and where and when they come to me, and when I can connect my perceptions of them with the whole of the rest of my life without a break, then I am quite certain that when I encounter these things I am not asleep but awake. [7:89–90]

If the senses, memory, and intellect confirm the continuity of our present experience with the past, then, since God is not a deceiver, "in cases like these I am completely free from error" (7:90).

In fact, we aren't free from error. Sometimes we awake from a dream believing it was real. Usually, within a few minutes we detect our error; but, despite what Descartes says, isn't the possibility of error always there? May we not dream that the criterion of continuity, proposed in the quotation, has been met, even though it has not?

Descartes admitted that, with "the pressure of things to be done" (7:90), we don't always have time to stop and check, so mistakes happen. He might also have admitted that in a dream we can have the illusion of checking when we haven't really checked. Do such possibilities undermine the trustworthiness of the senses? Perhaps they do establish that sensory experience cannot be trusted in all cases. But Descartes doesn't need to claim that it can be, and for two reasons. First, his main purpose in the *Meditations* has been to establish the truths of metaphysics, which don't rely on the senses at all. With respect to the primary truths of metaphysics (the existence of mind, the essences of mind and matter, and the existence and essence of God), the senses don't enter the picture. Second, for other purposes, Descartes only needs assurance that the senses are on the whole reliable, and that with sufficient cross-checking they will yield truth.

If Descartes meant that we should always be able to ascertain that we are free from sensory error, he asked too much. But he seems instead to have suggested that in the best cases we should trust our senses, because God is no deceiver and has given us no way to correct, and no reason to question, the best cases. In less than optimal situations, we can always suspend judgment, unless the needs of life force us to act.

The world regained

The world as regained in the Sixth Meditation is not the same as the one called into question in the First. But the difference, befitting the aim of the *Meditations*, is theoretical, not practical. While undergoing the process of meditation, the meditator was still to avoid oncoming carriages, eat food, drink liquids, sleep when tired, and engage in such social commerce as was needed for day to day living. As Descartes made clear from the outset, the aim of his doubt, and so of his cognitive search, was not "action" but "the acquisition of knowledge" (7:22). So what knowledge has (allegedly) been attained?

The new knowledge concerns the method of gaining knowledge, the existence and attributes of God, the natures of mind and matter, and the nature of the human being. Methodologically, the meditator no longer believes that what is most true is learned "from the senses or through the senses" (7:18). She now knows that pure intellect is the ultimate standard of knowledge. Using this faculty, she has discovered the essence of mind, the (true) idea of God, the resultant proofs of God's existence, the essence of matter, and the real distinction between mind and matter; as also (with sensory aid) the fact of mind–body union and interaction, and the proper attitude toward the senses. The senses do not provide material for knowing the essences of substances; but they are generally reliable for day to day living, and, when used with proper care, they can yield knowledge of the particular properties of bodies. The meditator has rejected her previous belief that bodies contain in them something resembling color, sound, and other secondary qualities. She now regards body as constituted through the modes of extension. Bodies must possess properties that cause color sensations (and other secondary sensations), but such properties are not described in the *Meditations* itself. The further description of the natural world is left to other works – the previously published *Discourse*, and the *Principles*.

We saw in Chapter 1 that Descartes intended his *Meditations* to support his new physics. In the next chapter, we will consider how. We will also consider whether the standard of absolute certainty used in the *Meditations* actually undermines Descartes' physics, at least where it must rely on experience. Descartes the physicist needs both senses and imagination as well as the intellect.

The whole human being who emerges at the end of the *Meditations* must re-enter the world in order to pursue physics as a natural science. He or she re-enters that world with a new appreciation of the power of the intellect and a new theory of the role of the senses. We must see if these findings can sustain the main objective of Descartes' philosophy, the construction of a new theory of the natural world, including the human mind–body complex.

References and further reading

Descartes' argument for mind–body distinctness has been frequently discussed; see Curley (ch. 7), B. Williams (ch. 4), and Wilson (ch. 6). Several of these treatments construe the argument as aiming for a distinction between individuals, for which the mutual-exclusion premise provides an unnecessarily strong basis. M. Rozemond, *Descartes's Dualism* (Cambridge, Mass.: Harvard University Press, 1998), thoroughly examines mind–body distinctness, union, and interaction, and the theory of the senses; she also lists references to the large periodical literature on these topics. M. Wilson, *Ideas and Mechanism: Essays on Early Modern Philosophy* (Princeton, NJ: Princeton University Press, 1999), includes essays on mind–body and the senses in Descartes.

Attention to Descartes' theory of mind–body union and interaction, and his theory of the senses, has been growing; see Cottingham (ch. 5), Kenny (ch. 10), Dicker (ch. 5), B. Williams (chs. 8, 10), Cottingham (ed.), *Cambridge Companion* (chs. 11–12), and Cottingham (ed.), *Reason, Will, and Sensation* (Part 4). Rodis-Lewis examines "Descartes and the Unity of the Human Being," in Oxford Readings, pp. 197–210. Essays in Gaukroger, Schuster, and Sutton (eds.), *Descartes' Natural Philosophy*, examine Cartesian physiology, the senses, and mind–body union and interaction (Parts 3–5). On the biological functioning of the senses in Descartes, see Hatfield, "Descartes' Physiology and Its Relation to His Psychology," in Cottingham (ed.), *Cambridge Companion*, pp. 335–70, and A. Simmons, "Sensible Ends: Latent Teleology in Descartes' Account of Sensation," *Journal of the History of Philosophy* 39 (2001), 49–75.

For an alternative view (to that presented here) on the relation between consciousness and thought in Descartes, see Simmons, "Changing the Cartesian Mind: Leibniz on Sensation, Representation and Consciousness," *Philosophical Review* 110 (2001), 31–75.

The "occasionalist" thesis that mind–body interaction is mediated by God was developed by Nicolas Malebranche in *The Search After Truth*. The question of whether Descartes was an occasionalist has been examined by S. Nadler, "Occasionalism and the Mind–Body Problem," in M.A. Stewart (ed.), *Studies in Seventeenth-Century European Philosophy* (Oxford: Oxford University Press, 1977), pp. 75–95, and D.M. Clarke, "Causal Powers and Occasionalism," in Gaukroger, Schuster, and Sutton (eds.), pp. 131–48.

Descartes' side of his correspondence with Elizabeth is translated in CSMK. Both sides of their correspondence are found in AT and translated in J. Blom (ed.), *Descartes: His Moral Philosophy and Psychology* (Hassocks: Harvester Press, 1978). On Elizabeth and other women philosophers in the seventeenth century, see E. O'Neill, "Women Cartesians, 'Feminine Philosophy', and Historical Exclusion," in S. Bordo (ed.), *Feminist Interpretations of Descartes* (University Park: Pennsylvania State University Press, 1999), pp. 232–57.

PART III

BEYOND THE *MEDITATIONS*

Chapter 9

The new science

Physics, physiology, and the passions

Descartes was a mathematician and natural philosopher before he was a metaphysician. From about 1630 on, he envisioned a new, comprehensive science of nature, the construction of and justification for which became his primary aim. The *Meditations* was to provide the promised metaphysical foundations for the new system.

To understand the role of the *Meditations* in establishing foundations for physics, we need to appreciate the scope of Descartes' physics. Physics today is far removed from "the world of nature," if under that term we imagine mineral formations, plants, and animals. The science of physics studies nature at very small (subatomic) or very large (astronomical or cosmic) scales. Other natural sciences, including chemistry and biology, study things at or near the scale of living things. The mental world is now often placed in opposition to the physical and natural worlds; psychology (the study of mental life) is only sometimes called a natural science.

In Descartes' day, "physics" or "natural philosophy" meant simply "the science of nature." "Nature" encompassed everything having a nature or essence (at least on the Earth), including human beings and human cognition. Aristotelian works on psychology (including *De anima*, "On the Soul," as well as works on dreams, memory, and the senses) were classed within physics. Descartes conceived of physics in this broad sense. He included animal and human physiology, and even the *Passions of the Soul* (11:326), within physics. While he wasn't clear on whether the human mind considered by itself fell within physics, he was clear that mind–body union and interaction were part of physics or the science of nature. Although affirming mind–body substance dualism, he did not take that position to imply that the embodied mind is somehow unnatural, or supernatural, or beyond natural science. It was not Descartes' intent to exclude mind from nature through his dualism.

All the same, Descartes' philosophy did realign the relation between mind and matter and offered a revolutionary conception of matter itself (by contrast with Aristotelian philosophy). It reduced matter to extension, leaving it no properties beyond the geometrical modes of extension: size, shape, position, and motion. This reconception changed the way living things could be conceived. Descartes thought of plants and animals as machines, denying them the active principles and cognitive powers found in Aristotelian physiology and psychology. In Descartes' mechanistic physiology, all bodily processes are viewed as interactions between particles according to the laws of motion. He extended the notion of lawful regularity to mind–body interaction, positing a permanent relation between brain states and the sensations, appetites, and emotions they produce in the mind. For him, there was no conflict between dualism and psychophysical laws.

In this chapter, we will examine Descartes' physics from its foundations as provided in the *Meditations* (and elaborated in the *Principles*). The broad conception of physics permits us to see how various Meditations provide foundations for physics that would not be apparent under the narrower, present-day conception. We can include among the "physical" topics not only the new concept of matter from Meditations 2, 3, and 5, and God's role in preserving that matter, but also the analysis of mental faculties from Meditation 2, and human physiology and mind–body interaction from Meditation 6.

Descartes' revolution in physics

The sixteenth and seventeenth centuries saw rapid intellectual change in Europe. The Aristotelian philosophy – dominant from the thirteenth through the sixteenth centuries – was replaced by new philosophies, including new philosophies of nature. Many factors contributed to this development. Aristotelianism itself had changed over the centuries and was challenged by the revival of Platonic philosophy in the fifteenth century. It survived the challenge, although in the sixteenth century syntheses of Plato and Aristotle became common. In medicine and physiology, Aristotelian viewpoints had been combined with Galenic anatomy and physiology (Galen was a second-century physician in Alexandria, Egypt). The Italian anatomist Andreas Vesalius revivified the study of anatomy through the publication of carefully prepared anatomical drawings based on dissection of human corpses. In astronomy, Copernicus combined the ancient standards of mathematical exactness with the desire for a coherent account of planetary motions, arguing that the Earth moves around the Sun (opposing the Earth-centered cosmos of Aristotle and of Ptolemy, a second-century Egyptian). In optics or the theory of vision, the geometrical, intromission theory of Ibn al-Haytham, an eleventh-century Islamic philosopher, was made available in a sixteenth-century Latin translation, which spurred new work. In natural philosophy proper, ancient Greek atomistic theories of matter were revived and discussed.

Early in the seventeenth century, demand intensified for a "new science" of nature, and for a new philosophy to frame it. Francis Bacon called for a reformed science, based on greater attention to direct observation of nature, including observations made by artisans and skilled craftsmen. Galileo defended the Copernican system in astronomy through arguments against the assumptions of Aristotelian physics and Ptolemaic astronomy, and with his telescopic observations of the moons of Jupiter (thus questioning Earth's uniqueness as a body about which other bodies revolve). He developed a new science of motion (including a law describing the acceleration of freely falling bodies). Kepler developed Copernican planetary astronomy and combined al-Haytham's optical theory with a new understanding of the internal anatomy of the eye. William Harvey proposed that the blood is pumped through the body so that it circulates several times per hour (as opposed to previous theories that blood slowly oozes and does not circulate).

These key developments in the "Scientific Revolution" all occurred prior to 1633, the year in which Descartes completed his *World*. Yet none of the authors mentioned proposed anything to rival the comprehensiveness of Descartes' new vision of nature, as presented in his *World* and *Principles*. The earlier innovators made important theoretical proposals in single areas of science, or, in Bacon's case, proposed a new method intended to generate, at some point, a comprehensive new theory of nature. Descartes, in addition to making individual discoveries and offering a new method, proposed a comprehensive new theory. He was the first to present a wide-ranging new system of nature, and that system was developed and elaborated by his followers for more than fifty years after his death before being displaced by Newton's physics.

Overview of Aristotelian physics

The radical nature of Descartes' proposals is best understood against the background of the prevailing Aristotelian physics. A common Aristotelian position held that natural bodies are a composite of form and matter, and that matter could not exist without form. The form of a thing determined its nature or essence. Forms were principles of growth and change; they literally made things "be what they are" by directing the development and activity of matter toward an end (hence away from any lack or "privation" of that end). Nature was divided into a variety of kinds of substance, each with its characteristic pattern of activity. All bodies were thought to be composed of the four elements: earth, air, fire, and water. In these elements, undifferentiated matter takes on the forms of the four basic qualities: hot, cold, wet, and dry. Earth is cold and dry, air hot and wet, fire hot and dry, and water cold and wet. Other qualities, such as color and odor, also exist as forms that can be transmitted from bodies to the sense organs.

Higher-level natural kinds were divided into mineral, vegetable, and animal. In complex or "mixed" bodies (mixtures of elements), the four elements served as the "matter," and a kind-specific form gave each type of thing its characteristic pattern of activity. Thus, crystals or metals derive their properties from their forms (of quartz, gold, etc.). The oak tree grows as it does because its form (contained in the acorn) directs that growth. Similarly for the various kinds of animals, including the human animal. Each has a characteristic form, introduced into the reproductive "matter" of the female by the male during procreation, which directs its growth and activity. Certain powers or activities of this form are similar across animal species – all animals have nutritive, locomotive, and sensory powers. The form of the human animal also possesses a rational power, as its defining or essential power. The forms of all natural things direct them toward their natural end, whether the center of the universe (in the case of the earthy element), or knowledge and wisdom (in the case of a human being, the rational animal). In this way, Aristotle's physics compared all natural processes to the biological process of growth.

Aristotelian physics strictly divided the heavens from the Earth. The natural tendency of the earthy element to seek the center of the universe fixes the Earth in that location. Water has the same tendency, although less strongly, and so collects on the surface of the Earth. Air and fire have upward tendencies, the second stronger than the first. These four elements are found in the region of change, extending up to the sphere of the Moon (which acts as a bubble around the Earth). The Moon, Sun, planets, and "fixed stars" (an outermost bubble) are carried around the Earth, embedded in crystalline spheres. These spheres are not composed of the four elements but of a fifth element, the quintessence ("quint" means fifth), which is unchanging. The region above the sphere of the Moon, including the Sun and planets, was considered to be unchanging, with the heavenly bodies revolving around the Earth in uniform circular motion (which did not count as "change" or "alteration" in an Aristotelian sense).

To account for the apparently irregular motions of the planets, uniform circular motions had to be compounded by adding additional spheres.

To gain acceptance for his own physics, Descartes needed to break the hold of Aristotelian physics on common sense. Aristotelian physics says that for a body to keep moving, force must be constantly applied. This accords with much of our everyday experience. Descartes' laws of motion say that a body moving in a straight line will continue in motion unless hindered. Aristotelian physics says that earthy matter naturally moves toward the center of the universe (and of the Earth). Descartes says that invisible subtle matter, swirling in a vortex around the Earth, pushes objects downward. Aristotelian physics says that each natural kind contains a substantial form that serves to produce its characteristic activities, including the growth and development of living things. Descartes says that the various natural kinds differ only in the sizes, shapes, positions, and motions of their particles, and that animal bodies are mere machines. Aristotelian physics says that objects have the properties they appear to have, in the manner in which they appear to have them – that color, odor, and so on are real qualities encountered in sensory experience. Descartes says that, in objects, these qualities are really configurations of corpuscles that, in the case of color, induce spin in particles of light and ultimately cause a color sensation in the mind.

Descartes sought acceptance for a (then) counter-intuitive picture of nature. We may find it difficult to appreciate the full force of his problem, since his vision of nature has been partly retained, and it informs today's common sense.

Descartes' new system

In developing his new physics, Descartes drew upon the empirical results and theoretical proposals of previous authors, including the optical work of al-Haytham and Kepler, the astronomical arguments of Copernicus and Galileo, the circulatory theory of Harvey, and the revival of ancient atomism. But he moved beyond these results by proposing a new conception of homogeneous extended matter governed by a few laws of motion.

Although Copernicus and Galileo had challenged ancient physics and astronomy, neither offered a new system of physics to encompass both heavens and Earth. Descartes' physics did just that, by appealing only to particles in motion to explain all phenomena throughout the material world – including the formation of the Sun and solar system, the revolution of the planets around the Sun (carried along by a whirling vortex of subtle matter), and, in principle, everything observable in the heavens and on Earth. Descartes used his new conception of matter in framing comprehensive and detailed theories to explain the known phenomena of light, heat, fire, weight, magnetism, various minerals, and the physiology of living things. His proposed explanations were often quite fanciful, such as the explanation of magnetism by corkscrew-shaped particles flowing out from the poles of the Earth, circulating north and south, and entering the opposite pole while passing through the threaded channels in any magnetic bodies encountered along the way – with left- and right-hand threading accounting for opposite polarity (8A:275–310). These explanations were unified in that they appealed only to the properties of size, shape, position, and motion. The role of Descartes' metaphysics was to show that these are the only properties of matter, and hence must frame all explanatory hypotheses concerning the material world.

We saw in Chapter 1 that Descartes developed his comprehensive new theory during 1629–33, as he composed his *World*. This period began with the "metaphysical turn" of 1629–30, during which he claimed to have discovered the foundations of physics while thinking about God and the soul (1:144). We can appreciate more fully how this might have happened by comparing two strategies Descartes used in justifying his new philosophy of nature. When offering a sample of his new physics in the *Discourse* and essays, he did not present a metaphysical justification for its basic principles. He put forward as a hypothesis that bodies are composed of particles having only the properties of size, shape, position, and motion. The *Discourse* argues that this corpuscularian hypothesis is confirmed by the wide range of effects it could explain (6:76). In effect, it offers an empirical argument from explanatory unity in support of the new physics.

During this same period, Descartes also promised a metaphysical demonstration for the basic principles of his physics (6:76). In letters from 1638, he further elaborated the empirical argument but refused to reveal the metaphysical demonstration (1:563–4, 2:199–200). He mentioned both types of argument in a letter to the French mathematician J.B. Morin, comparing his explanations with those of the Aristotelians:

> Compare my assumptions with the assumptions of others. Compare all their *real qualities*, their *substantial forms*, their *elements* and countless other such things with my single assumption that all bodies are composed of parts. This is something which is visible to the naked eye in many cases and can be proved by countless reasons in others. All that I add to this is that the parts of certain kinds of bodies are of one shape rather than another. This in turn is easy to demonstrate to those who agree that bodies are composed of parts. Compare the deductions I have made from my assumption – about vision, salt, winds, clouds, snow, thunder, the rainbow, and so on – with what the others have derived from their assumptions on the same topics. I hope this will be enough to convince anyone unbiased that the effects which I explain have no other causes than the ones from which I have deduced them. Nonetheless, I intend to give a demonstration of it in another place. [2:200]

On some occasions Descartes does not explicitly reject the forms and qualities of Aristotelian physics but merely observes that they need not be "mentioned" in his physics (6:239, 3:492). Here, he takes his argument from comparative simplicity and unity of explanation to be sufficient to convince an unbiased mind that various natural phenomena "have no other causes" than particles of various shapes – that is, that they do *not* have as causes substantial forms and real qualities. Such an argument might not convince an Aristotelian who doubted whether Descartes' explanations really were more successful overall. Recognizing that the argument was not a strict demonstration, he continued to speak of a metaphysical demonstration, which became the *Meditations*.

Foundations for physics

Another clue from 1638 can help us to see how Descartes thought contemplation of God and the soul could yield foundations for his physics, if we draw on Chapters 3–8. In letters to Mersenne and the Jesuit Vatier, he explained that he withheld the metaphysical demonstration from the *Discourse* because he didn't want to introduce radical skepticism into a popular work. Such skepticism was needed so that his readers might "withdraw the mind from the senses" (1:350–1, 560). From Chapter 7 we know that he put forth the pure intellect, devoid of sensory material, as the instrument for knowing not only the soul and God but also the essence of material things. He appealed to this same instrument to support his claim (Chapter 5) that God preserves matter in existence from moment to moment (according to the laws of motion).

On this interpretation, the metaphysical turn toward the pure intellect provided Descartes with a direct argument for core principles of his physics. Let us put this reading to work, considering first the foundations of Descartes' physics of the material world and then his physics of mind–body union and interaction.

Real qualities, extension as essence

Descartes' denial of real qualities may not seem particularly radical now. Everyone who is acquainted with basic physics or introductory psychology knows the modern analysis of color perception, which explains color in objects using wavelengths of light (a distant relative of Descartes' spinning particles). But to Aristotelians and others in his audience, the denial of real qualities would have seemed particularly difficult to accept. Let us put ourselves in their shoes to see why.

Aristotelian real qualities are given that name because in an Aristotelian account the qualities we sense are direct representatives, or instances, of a quality in the object. When we see a red tulip, the real quality of redness is transmitted to our senses and received by our sensory soul as a "form without matter." The form of redness is what makes the tulip red; this same form is expressed in the red we experience, in accordance with Aristotle's principle that like knows like. In between, the form is transmitted "without matter" through the air, into the eye, and down the optic nerve (conceived as a hollow tube). This received form accounts for the phenomenal red we experience in perceiving the tulip.

The Aristotelian account has common-sense appeal because it says that our visual experience reveals the actual or "real" qualities of things. In some ways, however, the account as given by Aristotle was incomplete. Especially, the notion of a form without matter transmitted through a medium had to be filled out by medieval and early modern Aristotelians. If the form of red makes the object red, why doesn't it turn the intervening air red when transmitted through it? But the air between the tulip and us does not appear red; nor does the eye turn red when we see a red thing. To explain these facts, mainstream scholastic Aristotelians in the thirteenth to seventeenth centuries taught that the form in the medium has a special kind of diminished existence, called "intentional being," and so they termed the transmitted form itself an "intentional species." The technical term "intentional" conveyed two things: first, that the species of color "tends toward," "points to," or "represents" the color in the object; and, second, that the species of color in the air has diminished being, does not exist as a full-blown quality, and so does not turn the air red. In this way, they sought to square Aristotelian doctrine with the observed facts.

In the *Dioptrics*, Descartes proclaimed that he had no use for the "intentional species that exercise the imagination of the philosophers" (6:85*). In his account, everything in the sensory process (up to mind–body interaction) is purely mechanical. The quality of red in the object, the transmission of light and color, and the effect of light and color on the nervous system all reduce to the size, shape, and motion of particles. On this view (which is similar to Galileo's position), color in the object consists simply in the geometrical features of its surface, which cause it to put one or another spin on the spherical particles of light. This spin is transmitted to the eye, where it affects the retinal nerves in one way if the object is what we call "blue" and in another way if "red" (6:91–2). These differing effects in the nervous system and brain then cause differing sensations in the soul. Descartes did not deny that objects are colored; rather, he denied that color is a real quality of the sort envisioned by the Aristotelians. Color in objects is a purely mechanical property that affects the nervous system, causing a sensation of red. The experienced red – the content of the sensation – has an arbitrary but lawful relation (established by God or nature) with the brain that causes it, and hence with the physical property in objects (6:130–1, 7:81).

As Descartes saw things, he needed to overcome the natural human prejudice in favor of the Aristotelian resemblance thesis (as discussed in Chapters 5 and 8) in order to gain acceptance for his own theory. His initial reason for doubting that sensations of color and other qualities resemble something in objects was that they are "obscure and confused" (7:43, 80, 83). To see how this observation could challenge resemblance, we must ask: obscure and confused by comparison with what? If we simply consider the sensory experience, of a red ball, say, it hardly seems that our perception of the ball's redness is any more or less confused than our perception of its roundness. Both seem equally "in focus," phenomenally speaking. We must therefore seek another standard, by comparison with which our perception of the ball's color is obscure and confused, whereas perception of its shape is not.

Meditations 3–5 provide the needed standard. Descartes could argue that sensory ideas of color are obscure and confused by comparison with a clear and distinct (purely intellectual) perception of shape. In Meditation 3, he observes that color and other qualities are thought of "in a very confused and obscure way, to the extent that I do not know whether they are true or false, that is, whether the ideas I have of them are ideas of real things or of non-things" (7:43–4; see also 7:83). This experience contrasts with the intellectual perception of extension and its modes in Meditation 5, from which the meditator concludes that material things "are capable of existing, insofar as they are the subject matter of pure mathematics, since I perceive them clearly and distinctly" (7:71). Ostensibly, shape and other geometrical modes are clearly perceived to be potential properties of any possible material thing, whereas color is not.

An argument for excluding real qualities might then go as follows. Extension is the essence of matter. My sensory ideas of shape, size, position, and motion therefore present properties that things can have. I may sometimes be mistaken about the precise sizes and shapes of actually existing things, but the economy of the senses as bestowed by God ensures that I will be right some of the time. By contrast, I do not clearly and distinctly perceive color to be a possible property of objects. Ideas of color arise only from the senses, but I should rely only on my clear and distinct intellectual perceptions to tell me what properties things can have. My sensory ideas of color do not meet that standard. Hence bodies do not have the "real quality" color.

This argument draws on points from Meditations 3–6. But it has a serious flaw. It can be interpreted as an argument from ignorance. Perhaps color is a real quality, and the human intellect simply fails to perceive it to be one. We know Descartes was unwilling to assert that we know "all the properties" that are in mind or matter (7:220). Maybe we simply can't say whether color is a real quality or not.

This raises a question of interpretation. Does Descartes claim to perceive that color *is not* a possible mode of extension, or does he merely *not claim* to perceive that it is a mode of extension, as he perceives the geometrical modes to be? Does our intellectual perception exclude the real quality from matter, or is the status of color simply unknown?

It seems clear that Descartes actually wanted to exclude real qualities from bodies. But if his argument rests entirely on a direct intellectual perception that the real quality color is not a possible mode of extended substance, discussion ends there. The exclusion would rely on an intellectual perception of the nature of matter, pure and simple. This one-step argument offers little help if we don't immediately come to the same metaphysical insight ourselves. In Chapter 8, we found Descartes appealing to a principle that could shore up his argument – the "constitutive essence" principle, according to which all the modes of a substance must be "perceived through" its principal attribute. If we think of extension as the intelligible object of geometry (as we are instructed to do), then it has no color or other sensory properties. It has only extension, which can be divided into parts having size, shape, position, and motion (7:63–4, 73–4). If we subsequently try to think of color as a mode of extension, we find only obscurity and confusion. Indeed, Descartes claimed in the *Principles* that "we cannot find any intelligible resemblance between the color which we suppose to be in objects and that which we experience in our sensation" (8A:34).

In the argument for mind–body distinctness, Descartes parried the charge of arguing from ignorance by observing that he had clear and distinct perceptions that both mind and body can exist as complete things, on their own, without the other. In the present case, he could not argue that color is "really distinct" from body, for that would make color a substance – and he held that physical color in bodies arises from the size and shape (modes) of their surfaces, and that experienced color is a mode of mind (an idea or sensation). However, he might (and in fact did) argue that we can conceive of extended matter as existing without color, or the other so-called secondary qualities. In Part 2 of the *Principles*, Descartes repeated the point from Meditation 6 that the senses are not for showing us "what really exists in things" but for telling us what is beneficial or harmful to the mind–body complex (8A:41). To know what really exists in things, we must "lay aside the preconceived opinions acquired from the senses, and in this connection make use of the intellect alone, carefully attending to the ideas implanted in it by nature" (8A:42). He continued:

If we do this, we shall perceive that the nature of matter, or body considered in general, consists not in its being something which is hard or heavy or colored, or which affects the senses in any way, but simply in its being something which is extended in length, breadth, and depth.

Considering the quality of hardness, he argued that if we never felt any bodies, hence never felt them as hard, they would not "thereby lose their bodily nature." He extended this thought experiment to the other merely sensory qualities:

By the same reasoning it can be shown that weight, color, and all other such qualities that are perceived by the senses as being in corporeal matter, can be removed from it, while the matter itself remains intact; it thus follows that its nature does not depend on any of these qualities. [8A:42]

As in the argument for mind–body distinctness, Descartes here claims to perceive body as a complete being while explicitly denying it the perceived quality of color. It is not that he simply doesn't think about whether color is in body. He asserts that it is not. Hence, assuming he is thinking clearly and distinctly, he can claim to perceive that body, possessing essentially only the geometrical modes of extension, can exist as a complete being without color (as a real quality). But if matter can be a complete being without color, and if the properties that things have on their own must be instances of their essence, then here is an argument for excluding color. This argument is not explicit in the *Meditations* but may be latent in the perception of the essence of matter (Meditation 5) and the discussion of the respective roles of the senses and intellect in knowledge of bodies (Meditation 6).

Descartes drew other physical conclusions from the theory that extension is the essence of matter. Famously, he inferred that there can be no space distinct from matter, hence that a vacuum is impossible and the universe is a plenum (8A:49). There is no void, only matter in motion. Motion does considerable work in Descartes' physics. Let us therefore turn to the laws governing it.

Immutability, laws of motion

In Descartes' metaphysical terminology, motion is a mode of extension. But extension, as the essence of matter, does not specify what laws, if any, motions follow, or even say what will happen when moving bodies collide. Two extended things cannot interpenetrate or coexist in the same place, so something must give when one body hits another. But the bare concept of extension offers no hint about the outcome. Descartes' concept of extended matter does not include the Newtonian notion of mass, with its implications for momentum and transfer of force upon impact.

Descartes conceived extended matter as intrinsically inert. It contains no activity, and it accrues no force in virtue of being in motion. Rather, all force and activity must be referred back to God, who preserves matter in existence from moment to moment, as in the Third Meditation.

The Third Meditation did not mention laws of motion, but it provided the foundation for such laws in God's preserving action. The laws themselves were set out in the *World* and *Principles*. God preserves the motions of bodies in accordance with laws governing their interactions upon impact (Descartes did not recognize laws for action at a distance). Both works portray the universe as possibly evolving out of a soup of particles, created by God with a certain quantity of motion (11:32–5, 8A:101; see also 6:42–4). This "quantity" is defined as the product of the speed of bodies and their volume of matter. (Descartes did not allow for matter of differing specific gravities; he explained the density in ordinary objects by hypothesizing that some are more porous than others.) He conceived of speed as a scalar quantity, which means that no change in the quantity of motion occurs when a body changes direction. He then sought to derive the laws of motion from God's immutability; in preserving the universe from moment to moment, he preserves the same quantity of motion as at creation.

Descartes purported to derive three laws from God's immutability. The first is "that each thing, as far as it is able, always continues in the same state; and so when it is once moved, it always continues on" (8A:62*). This law describes motion and rest as persisting states of things. The second is "that all motion, in and of itself, is along a straight line; therefore, those things that move in a circle always tend to move away from the center of the circle they are describing" (8A:63*). These two laws are similar to Newton's law of inertia (his first law of motion) but differ from it because Descartes did not treat motion as a vector quantity (which would mean that changes in direction alter the quantity of motion). The third law is "that one body, in colliding with a stronger body, loses none of its own motion; but in colliding with a weaker body, it loses as much of its motion as it transfers to that weaker body" (8A:65*). This law is implausible on the face of it, since it suggests that a snooker ball could never move the slightly larger balls used in pool, no matter how hard it was driven. Descartes tried to explain away such counter-examples by observing that in our matter-filled environment, the larger body is surrounded by the fluid of the air, allegedly making it easier to move (8A:70) – although presumably both bodies are surrounded in this way, so it is hard to see what differential effect there would be on their ease of motion.

Descartes offered as a ground for his first two laws "the immutability and simplicity of the operation by which God preserves motion in matter. For he always preserves the motion in the precise form in which it is occurring at the very moment when he preserves it, without taking any account of the motion which was occurring a little while earlier" (8A:63–4). The source of natural rectilinear motion is God's preserving power. This yields another difference between Descartes' law of rectilinear persistence and Newton's law of inertia. Newton's inertial law became explanatorily basic – a place where explanation stops. In Newtonian physics, the continued motion of bodies in a straight line no longer requires explanation, by contrast with the Aristotelian scheme, in which continuing motion requires a continuing cause. (Newton himself, at least for a time, regarded continuing motion as the product of an inertial force, but later Newtonians conceived of inertial motion as basic, without a continuing force.)

Descartes considered this picture, in which God preserves particles of matter from moment to moment according to their tendencies, to be certified by his metaphysics. Nonetheless, it has its problems. It may be objected that in a single instant a particle can have no tendency to move, since for Descartes (8A:53) motion is simply transference from one location to another (requiring finite time). The force of this objection depends partly on whether Descartes conceived of instants as merely vanishingly small or as dimensionless points. But it may also depend on whether God does book-keeping on the "tendencies" or directions of particles in motion. If God recreates the universe from point-instant to point-instant, then the notion of a continuous direction of motion would be entirely dependent on God's preserving action, not on any "tendency" internal to the moving body itself.

Another problem concerns the coherence of bodies. If bodies are composed of innumerable parts, how do these parts cohere to form a single unit? Apparently, he held that bodies form units because their parts are at rest in relation to one another (8A:71). In a moving body, the common motion of its particles would keep them together. The quantity of motion of a body is the product of the quantity of matter times speed. The quantity of matter is simply the volume of matter traveling together. Any impact between macro-level bodies involves the surface of one body, such as a cue ball, touching the surface of another body, such as the eight ball. The volume of the whole cue ball is used to determine how it will move the eight ball. But the balls are units only because their particles move together. As the lead particles make contact, their motion should be changed relative to the rest of the ball, breaking the unity. Why shouldn't a collision result in both balls dissolving into one another, like colliding puffs of cigar smoke? Perhaps because, as Descartes says, particles with irregular shapes catch on one another and hold together (8A:144). But how can infinitely divisible matter hold any shape at all? Presumably, because God so conserves it.

A further problem is that the three laws themselves do not define a determinate outcome for cases of impact. The third law says that one body loses as much quantity of motion as another gains. But it does not say how much each loses and gains. To address this question, Descartes provided seven rules of impact in the *Principles* (8A:67–70). Although these rules allegedly follow from the three laws, they are not strictly derivable. Moreover, as Leibniz later observed, when represented graphically they yield discontinuities when the sizes and speeds of bodies are only slightly altered. These problems led Malebranche, who generally tried to defend Descartes' physics, to admit the difficulty and reformulate the laws.

In practice, this last problem had little effect on Descartes' physics, for he did not refer to the rules of impact again in the *Principles*, and he only rarely mentioned the laws of motion themselves (8A:108, 117, 144, 170, 194). The explanatory work-horse in Descartes' physics was the mechanistic interaction of particles in accordance with their shapes and motions. This picture required that such interactions be governed in a regular way, a requirement addressed by the above laws. But in justifying various mechanistic models, Descartes appealed to analogies with ordinary cases of bodily interaction, not to precisely calculated exchanges of quantity of motion.

The significance of Descartes' laws of motion lies more in their overall conception than in any technical contribution to the analysis of impact. They offered the general vision of law-governed interactions of matter everywhere in the universe. The first and second laws described rectilinear motion as a natural state that does not diminish of itself and will continue for ever if unimpeded by other bodies. Although Galileo is sometimes credited with formulating a proto-version of Newtonian inertia, he in fact treated circular motion along the surface of the Earth as the "natural" state. He had no conception of straight-line inertia. Although Descartes' conception did not involve vector quantities, it was the historical precursor to Newton's law of inertial motion.

Matter, innate ideas, and eternal truths

The essence of matter is extension, whose properties are understood through geometry. The ideas of geometrical essences inhere (innately) in the human intellect. Descartes asked some fundamental questions about these essences: why are they what they are? That is, why is the essence of the circle what it is, the essence of the triangle what it is, and so on? Furthermore, how does the mind come to have its innate ideas of those essences? The answers to these questions refer to the creative power of God.

As mentioned in previous chapters, Descartes held that the geometrical essences, as the essences of all created things, are free creations of God (1:145–6, 149–53, 7:380, 432, 435–6). God did not look to any standard or model, either independent of or internal to himself, in creating the essences; he simply made it the case that the radii of a circle are all equal to one another, and the angles of a triangle are equal to two right angles. He could have created other mathematical rules, so that the radii are not equal (1:152). Since our minds use the truths that actually were created, we may be unable to conceive such possibilities. (Descartes had no inkling of non-Euclidean geometry.) Nonetheless, he held, the mathematical essences (and others) are free creations of God's will.

The doctrine that the so-called eternal truths are God's free creations might seem to threaten human knowledge. What if God were to change them? On Descartes' view, nothing about the current set of essences required God to create them instead of others. If he reconsidered his act of creation, today's geometrical truth might be tomorrow's falsehood.

In fact, Descartes held that his doctrine provided a secure basis for human knowledge. On his theory, along with the eternal truths, God created the material world and various minds, with their respective essences, and he implanted innate knowledge of those essences in human intellects. God therefore adjusted the human intellect to the essence of matter (and, presumably, of mind). Moreover, since he is immutable, the threat of changing essences does not arise. Truths about essences remain "eternal truths" because once willed they are fixed for ever by God's immutability (1:149, 152).

In Descartes' context, this doctrine might actually have improved the theological palatability of his claim to know the first principles of physics. In the metaphysical theology of mainstream scholastic Aristotelians, knowledge of the essences of things implied an under-standing of the absolute limits on God's creative power. These Aristotelians held that the essences of created things, such as a rabbit or an oak tree, depend on God for their existence. But that did not imply to them that God freely chose the essences things have. On their view, God could not create a rabbit that wasn't an animal, or that violated the essence of rabbithood in any other way. The essences are therefore eternal, because they are grounded in God's (eternally determined) creative power. God understands the essences by understanding what he can and cannot create. On this view, a natural philosopher claiming to know the essences of things – and especially claiming to know possible essences *a priori*, as did Descartes – would be claiming to have fundamental knowledge of God's power. Descartes' doctrine that the eternal truths are free creations permits the natural philosopher to claim such knowledge of essences without thereby claiming to comprehend the structure or limits of God's creative power. Since it was a tenet of Catholic theology that God cannot be fully comprehended, in this way Descartes could sidestep theological problems that might otherwise arise for his claim to understand "completely" what the essence of matter is. He could claim that the human mind's innate ideas are perfectly adjusted to the created world, not because the human mind is able to grasp the limits of God's power but because God has freely created the world with its essences and our minds with ideas of those essences.

A mechanical philosophy

Descartes envisioned the world as a grand machine. This machine was not filled with cogs and gear-wheels but with fluids and pressures, spinning particles, and bits of irregularly shaped matter interacting to produce the phenomena of nature. In the *Meditations*, this mechanistic vision appears in the description of the human body as "a kind of machine equipped with and made of bones, nerves, muscles, veins, blood and skin" (7:84; also 7:229–30, 602). It was extensively developed in the *Principles* (as, too, in the posthumously published *World*).

The terms "mechanism" and "mechanical" have several meanings that might fit the concept of a mechanical philosophy. Beyond the comparison with a machine (discussed below), the terms may imply the blind following of laws without the intervention of undetermined will or choice. In this sense, even a dualistic psychology can be mechanistic if soul-substance is governed by laws. (Descartes proposed that the human will follows the rule of always choosing the apparent truth or apparent good, exercising the freedom of indifference only when the intellect fails to present clear truth or goodness [7:432–3].) In Descartes' physics, both material nature and mind–body interaction are governed by exceptionless regularities. His vision of nature was mechanistic in this first sense. But, unlike Newtonian physics, Descartes' natural philosophy is not filled with derivations from quantitative laws. His only published successes in fitting quantities to empirical phenomena were the sine law of refraction (6:101) and the work on the rainbow (6:336–43). We have seen that his theory of impact was generally a failure in fitting quantitative laws to observed phenomena.

Another aspect of a "mechanical" philosophy of nature is the banishment of active principles, vital forces, and action at a distance from natural processes. Descartes rejected the Aristotelian vegetative and sensitive souls and their relatives, which previously had been thought to govern (with a kind of implicit intelligence) the organic processes of living things. Whereas many previous natural philosophers, including the English theorist William Gilbert, as well as Kepler, accepted animistic theories of magnetic attraction, comparing the pull of iron to magnet to the attraction between lovers, Descartes offered his purely mechanical theory of subtle magnetic fluid (tiny spirals) interacting with threaded channels in magnetic bodies. The heat of fire was reduced to particles in motion, the action of light to pressure in an ætherial medium, and so on. There is no action at a distance; all material interaction is by direct contact.

"Mechanistic" can also mean non-purposeful, or without a guiding teleology. Descartes is famous for rejecting final causes from physics on the grounds that the human mind cannot hope to discern God's plan (5:185, 7:374–5, 8A:15–16, 80–1). (A "final cause" is the purpose for which something comes into being or changes state.) The explicit target of this rejection is the view that all of nature has been organized for the benefit of humankind. Descartes' cosmos was populated by many suns with many planets; he felt it ludicrous for human beings to suppose that the Sun and stars were created expressly for their benefit (3:431). He also banished final causes from the laws of motion. Aristotelians thought that earthy matter moves toward the center of the universe as its end or final cause (although without attributing awareness or knowledge to it, contrary to Descartes' caricature [7:442]). Descartes admitted no such "ends" into material interactions or bodily motions.

However, Descartes did not banish all teleological thinking from natural philosophy. In describing the composite human being (mind and body), he spoke of God or nature having arranged the rules of mind–body interaction so that sensations tend toward the preservation of the composite being (hence toward the health of the body [7:80, 87]). This counts as invoking purpose, teleology, or final causes in analyzing the mind–body relation and the functioning of the senses. Similar teleology appears in his physiology, where he spoke of the "functions" of the parts of the body, or what they "serve" to do (7:374–5; 11:121, 154, 224).

A final sense of "mechanical" means machine-like, or pertaining to machines. The most basic notion of machine in Descartes' time derived from the ancient science of mechanics, in which the lever was regarded as a simple machine. Descartes invoked this notion in proudly proclaiming of his philosophy that, "like mechanics, it considers shapes and sizes and motions" (1:420), and he composed a brief treatise on mechanics (1:435–47). But his philosophy was mechanical in a broader sense, in that he compared natural phenomena and animal bodies to complex machines with interacting parts. Many of Descartes' mechanical explanations take the form of analogies with effects observed in ordinary experience (8A:324–6). They use analogies to characterize micromechanisms, which in turn (purport to) explain the known phenomena of nature. Descartes explained the properties of water by comparing its particles to eels, the viscosity of oil by comparing its particles to branchy bushes that can stick together, like tumbleweeds (1:423), and magnetism through screw-shaped effluvia and threaded channels (8A:275). His grandest comparison was between the human body and the hydraulically driven automata found in the royal gardens of Europe in his day (11:130–1). This comparison again evokes latent teleology, regarding the design or function of the parts of the machine.

Mechanized body, embodied mind

Descartes' mechanical philosophy rejected animism everywhere, save for the human body (joined with a mind or soul), and perhaps the world as a whole (where quantity of motion is preserved by God). From the perspective of twentieth-century naturalism, this seemed like two animisms too many. In that century, Descartes was accused of putting a "ghost in the machine" of the human body.

Emphasis on Descartes' dualism can mask the extent to which he promoted a naturalistic, anti-vitalistic materialism concerning living things. Aristotelians and other vitalists were "naturalists" about living things inasmuch as they considered plants and animals to be part of nature, and hence their powers and active principles to be natural. By the standards of twentieth-century materialistic naturalism, however, their list of natural powers was too liberal. On those standards, the vegetative and sensitive powers of the Aristotelians, as also Descartes' immaterial mind, were non-naturalistic. Despite its dualism, Descartes' philosophy promoted a materialistic naturalism toward living things by holding that plants, animals, and the human body are nothing but machines. Indeed, he extended that sort of naturalism to animal psychology generally and to much of human psychology, which he thought could be explained through bodily mechanisms alone, independent of mind.

Machine men

The most complete description of Descartes' mechanistic physiology is the *Treatise on Man*, although portions were discussed in the *Discourse*, *Dioptrics*, *Meditations*, *Principles*, and *Passions*. The basic vision is simple – human and animal bodies are machines that respond to their environments through sensory stimulation, seek food when they haven't eaten, form material memories, and learn in response to sensory stimulation. As he wrote in Meditation 6, one may consider the human body "as a kind of machine equipped with and made up of bones, nerves, muscles, veins, blood and skin in such a way that, even if there were no mind in it, it would still perform all the same movements as it now does in those cases where movement is not under control of the will or, consequently, of the mind" (7:84). Moreover, since he denied minds to animals, all of their behavior had to be accounted for mechanistically. Much of human behavior (all responses not affected by will, or requiring general intelligence) could, he thought, be explained in the same way (see also 6:56–9).

Descartes thought of human and animal bodies as powered by a "fire without light" that burns in the heart (11:202, 333). This fire heats and expands blood as it enters the heart, acting like a boiler in a steam engine. The blood exits the heart moving quickly, some proceeding to the brain. There, at the base of the brain, the "animal spirits" – the subtler and livelier parts of the blood – are filtered out and enter the central cavity of the brain through the pineal gland. Some of the spirits then proceed down the nerves (conceived as hollow tubes) to the muscles; on entering a muscle they cause it to inflate like a balloon, become taut, and contract. Muscle movement and hence behavior are determined by which tubules the spirits enter (11:129–43, 170–97).

A sensory-motor loop controls the dispersal of the spirits. Sensory nerves are filaments encased in the tubules. When a sense organ is stimulated, the filament jiggles in a certain way, which causes it to tug on the opening of the tubule in the central cavity, allowing spirits to enter and flow toward a muscle. The pattern of spirits leaving the pineal gland reflects the pattern of stimulation of the nerves, which has in turn been determined by the stimulation of the sense organ. In the case of vision, the image on the retina is conveyed to the pineal gland (the images from the two eyes merging to form one), where in minded humans a visual sensation arises (11:174–6). The material processes of sensation, which create outward-flowing animal spirits, are capable of producing muscle movements in both humans and non-minded animals independently of any mental guidance. Even in humans, much behavior is guided by purely material processes in which a pattern of stimulation directly causes a motor response.

Which response occurs to a given stimulus might be determined by several factors, some innate, some depending on memory and learning (11:192–3). Some of the plumbing is innately structured to produce a rapid response to a given stimulus, as when in falling we extend our hand to protect our head (7:230). In other cases, a response depends on changes in tubule plumbing elicited by previous sensory stimulation, as when a dog (or human) learns to be ready for food when it hears the food bag rattle or sees the refrigerator door open. If the animal hasn't eaten, the liveliness of the spirits is affected; lack of food causes the spirits to be widely dispersed among the nerves and the animal to rove about (11:195). In the presence of food, the pattern of stimulation on the sense organ can cause the animal to approach and eat it through nervous processes alone.

Descartes gave few details of how the mechanisms responsible for environmentally appropriate behavior are set up, but he had high hopes for what they could (in principle) explain. The automata in the *Treatise* were ascribed numerous functions, both physiological and psychological, without being joined to a mind. Those mindless human bodies respond to environmental circumstances and their own internal state (11:194–5). Such functions, he said, "follow from the mere arrangement of the machine's organs every bit as naturally as the movements of a clock or other automaton follow from the arrangement of its counter-weights and wheels" (11:202).

The (much later) *Passions* also contended that purely physiological processes could dispose the body to respond in many situations without mental intervention. When a person is in circumstances conducive to fear (a lion is present, say), the flow of the spirits will cause him not only to feel fear but also to run away, without the intervention of thought or will:

> the mere fact that some spirits at the same time proceed to the nerves which serve to move the legs in flight causes another movement in the gland through which the soul feels and perceives this action. In this way, then, the body may be moved to take flight by the mere disposition of the organs, without any contribution from the soul. [11:358]

Just as a sheep (mindless automaton) flees the wolf simply through the motions of its animal spirits (7:230), a human being will flee a dangerous situation through a wholly mechanical process.

Descartes sharply distinguished humans from other animals. When humans take flight, they are aware of doing so and may experience fear. On Descartes' theory, feeling, awareness, and sensation depend on the presence of an immaterial soul or mind. But even our passions, which are caused by the body affecting the mind, are tuned to the body's mechanistic physiology and psychology. The function of the passions is to dispose the mind to continue the responses started by the body alone (11:359). By the time we feel fear we should already be running, through bodily processes alone. The feeling of fear keeps us running. The mind may be able to direct or redirect our responses; we might override the natural tendency to run from a lion by recalling that it chases running prey but may not attack someone stationary. But it is not in our power simply to choose not to feel fear or not to feel like running. By imagining the consequences of a behavior, however, we may be able to counteract the normal bodily response, redirect the flow of spirits, and diminish the feeling of fear (11:362–70).

Laws of mind–body interaction

Descartes developed a hybrid psychology in which some psychological functions are carried out by the body alone, some by the mind alone, and some through mind–body interaction. In his correspondence with Elizabeth (discussed in Chapter 8), he avoided any claim to comprehend how mind and body interact causally. He came to admit that our knowledge of mind–body interaction is factual. In effect, he relegated study of mind–body interaction to empirical science.

The *Meditations* offers a basic principle governing mind–body interaction, which is that "any given movement occurring in the part of the brain that immediately affects the mind produces just one corresponding sensation" (7:87). This is a principle of psychophysical lawfulness. It means that God has established a constant relation between brain states and sensations (including internal sensations, and passions). Such a principle was invoked in the *Dioptrics* in the form of a "divine institution" relating various sensory nerves to kinds of sensation:

> regarding light and color...we must suppose our soul to be of such a nature that what makes it have the sensation of light is the force of the movements taking place in the regions of the brain where the optic nerve-fibers originate, and what makes it have the sensation of color is the manner of these movements. Likewise, the movements in the nerves leading to the ears make the soul hear sounds; those in the nerves of the tongue make it taste flavors; and, in general, movements in the nerves anywhere in the body make the soul have a tickling sensation if they are moderate, and a pain when they are too violent. [6:130–1]

One sort of jiggle (or pulse in the spirits) in one place yields phenomenal color, another yields a sensation of sound, and so on. Descartes posited several such psychophysical, or psychophysiological, correspondences. These included, for vision, not only light and color but also a direct mechanism for producing an experience of distance (6:137–8, 11:183) based on the accommodation and convergence of the eyes (although in other cases he described judgmental processes underlying size and distance perception [6:138–40, 7:438]).

In the cases mentioned so far, none of the properties of the spirit flow are "carried over" into the content of the sensation. One sort of vibration causes pain to be felt; another sort, tickling; another sort, red or blue sensations. The mind experiences these qualities but does not experience the actual properties of the spirits in the brain. In the case of shape perception, however, Descartes described another sort of relation between brain state and sensory content. In the sensory perception of shape, the pattern in the brain may possess, and provide the content of, the shape found in sensation. Descartes held that in vision a point-for-point copy of the retinal image is produced on the surface of the pineal gland. This shape enters sensation in the "second grade" of sensation (7:437). This second grade presents a pattern of "light and color"; indeed, Descartes speaks of the "extension of the color and its boundaries together with its position in relation to the parts of the brain" (7:437). The shapes presented in this second grade are not always the shapes we notice in our visual experience, for, as explained in the *Dioptrics*, the retinal and pineal images might "contain only ovals and rhombuses when they make us see circles and squares" (6:140–1). Indeed, the second grade of sensation is normally over-looked, because the mind (in accordance with the modern psychological principle of shape constancy) habitually and rapidly produces a perception of the actual shape of the distant object (circles and squares in the example).

However, the problem of mind–body interaction immediately concerns the second grade of sense, not visual experience arising after further psychological processes. We are focusing on the rela-tion between shapes on the pineal gland and shaped patterns of color in sensation. Earlier, we saw that the language of the Sixth Meditation (7:73), as that of the Sixth Replies, suggests an inspec-tion model – the mind "looks at" the pineal image. Indeed, in the passage above, the mind is said to consider a colored image in rela-tion to the interior brain surface – very odd, since color experience arises only in sensation (the mind would be comparing a sensation directly with the inside of the brain). This language suggests that, in some way, the shape of the brain pattern provides the content of the imagined or (second-grade) sensed shape. However, the notion of the mind literally "looking at" or inspecting the brain is unsatisfac-tory, for it invokes, in seeing or looking, one of the capacities that the entire account is intended to explain (see also 6:130).

The Fifth Replies offers a way of avoiding the inspection model while codifying a second principle of mind–body interaction, for the sensation or perception of shape. There, Descartes uses the term "corporeal species" and explains that in his theory (as opposed to an Aristotelian one) the mind uses the body to produce the content of sensation or imagination without "absorbing" a species or form:

> you ask how I think that I, an unextended subject, could receive the semblance or idea of a body that is extended. I answer that the mind does not receive any corporeal species; the pure understanding both of corporeal and incorporeal things occurs without any corporeal species. In the case of imagination, however, which can have only corporeal things as its object, we do indeed require a species which is a real body; the mind applies itself to this species but does not receive it. [7:387*]

Furthermore, although the mind does not *understand* extension "by means of an extended species," it does "*imagine* extension by turning to a corporeal species which is extended" (7:389*). Descartes' language suggests that his corporeal species – acting in this way like Aristotelian intentional species – provide content to imagination and sense perception. But in accordance with his real distinction between mind and body, the mind cannot accept these species into itself. Such species act like the corporeal images of the Second Replies and "give form to the mind itself, when it is directed towards that part of the brain" (7:161).

The appeal to corporeal or material species avoids the implication of the inspection model that the mind would actually see the small corpuscles of animal spirits pulsing out of the pineal gland. But such species still requires that God "institute" a rule relating spirit flow to experience. This rule must account for the fact that only the shape of the pineal pattern "informs" the mind so as to produce a shape sensation; the pulsing of the flow does not produce a sensation of pulsing but instead a sensation of light and color (for vision). Other sensory modalities, such as smell, presumably also yield a shaped pattern on the pineal gland (even if only one particle wide); in such cases, the mind does not experience the shape but only an odor.

The notion of empirically discoverable mind–body relations does not require substance dualism, and it has outlived the widespread acceptance of dualism. In the nineteenth century, Gustave Fechner transformed the notion into the science of psychophysics, an area of successful quantitative measurement in the new experimental psychology of that time. The question of the relation between shaped patterns in the brain and the contents of sensory experience also lives on, in discussions of mind–brain isomorphism.

Role of experience, experiment

The *Meditations* sets a standard of certainty for knowledge that apparently can be met only by the clear and distinct perceptions of the intellect. The *cogito* reasoning, the perception of the essences of mind and matter, and the proofs for the existence of God and of external objects allegedly meet that standard. Even after external objects are regained in the Sixth Meditation, sense perception of particular properties of things is beset by "doubt and uncertainty" (7:80). Yet Descartes recognized the need for appeal to the sensory observation and experience in investigating nature (6:65, 7:86, 87, 8A:101, 319).

The lowered degree of certainty associated with the senses, together with the acknowledged need for observation and experiment in natural philosophy, creates a tension in Descartes' epistemology. If experience is needed for physics but offers less certainty, it appears that Descartes must either exclude the experience-based parts of physics from legitimate knowledge or allow them a lowered standard of certainty.

Descartes used experience to support his physics in two ways. We have seen that before publishing the *Meditations* he offered an empirical argument for the fundamental principles of his physics (matter in motion). Second, in that period and later, he acknowledged that even with the full foundations for physics in place (including metaphysical support for the laws of motion, also adumbrated in the *World*), questions about the particular mechanisms underlying specific natural phenomena remain underdetermined (6:63–5, 8A:101). Given his basic principles, more than one mechanism might be imagined to explain magnetism, or the properties of salt, or the instinctual behaviors of animals. Observation and experiment are needed to decide which mechanisms actually occur in the world.

Both before and after the *Meditations* was published, Descartes was willing to say that decisions about which mechanisms exist, even though based on observation, could yield "demonstrative" knowledge (2:141–2, 198; 8A:327–8). But he recognized that the standard of certainty in such cases was reduced. In the *Principles*, he explained that his metaphysical foundations attained "absolute certainty," but his more particular claims might achieve only "moral certainty" (8A:328–9) – that is, "sufficient certainty for application to ordinary life" (8A:327). The laws of motion, the essence of matter as extension, and the denial of a vacuum were intended, we may suppose, to achieve absolute certainty. But specific micromechanisms were posited with only moral certainty.

Descartes compared the grounds for believing his specific hypotheses to those for cracking a code (8A:327–8). If a proposed solution to a code makes sense of numerous messages, it is accepted as true, even granting that another (unknown) solution might also work. Similarly, if a proposed explanation for magnetism or another natural phenomenon accounts for everything, it is accepted as true, even though other (unthought of) explanations have not been ruled out. In these cases, we should simply accept the "all things considered" best theory.

In the case of cracking the code of nature, however, Descartes intended to give us a big headstart. His metaphysical foundations were to limit dramatically the domain of possible solutions. In cracking the code of nature, only geometrical modes may be attributed to bodies. Active powers, real qualities, and other active principles have been excluded by his metaphysics. In that way, his metaphysics was to provide a permanent framework for all future science.

References and further reading

General discussions of and guides to the Scientific Revolution of the seventeenth century, including the work of Galileo, Descartes, and Newton, include A.R. Hall, *The Revolution in Science, 1500–1750*

(London: Longman, 1983), J. Henry, *The Scientific Revolution and the Origins of Modern Science* (New York: St. Martin's Press, 1997), and S. Shapin, *The Scientific Revolution* (Chicago: University of Chicago Press, 1996). On the growth and decline of Cartesian physics, see E.G. Ruestow, *Physics at Seventeenth and Eighteenth-Century Leiden* (The Hague: Martinus Nijhoff, 1973), and J.L. Heilbron, *Elements of Early Modern Physics* (Berkeley: University of California Press, 1982). Selections from Aristotle, Copernicus, Bacon, Galileo, Boyle, and Newton may be found in M.R. Matthews (ed.), *Scientific Background to Modern Philosophy* (Indianapolis: Hackett, 1989).

On Descartes' part in developing a new natural philosophy (or natural science), see D. Garber, "Descartes' Physics," in Cottingham (ed.), *Cambridge Companion*, pp. 286–334, Gaukroger, *Descartes*, and G. Hatfield, "Metaphysics and the New Science," in D. Lindberg and R. Westman (eds.), *Reappraisals of the Scientific Revolution* (Cambridge: Cambridge University Press, 1990), pp. 93–166. On God as the agency behind motion, see Hatfield, "Force (God) in Descartes' Physics," in Cottingham (ed.), *Oxford Readings*, pp. 281–310. On the laws of motion and the instant in Descartes, and Cartesian physics more generally, see Garber, *Descartes' Metaphysical Physics* (Chicago: University of Chicago Press, 1992). R.S. Woolhouse, *Descartes, Spinoza, Leibniz: The Concept of Substance in Seventeenth Century Metaphysics* (London: Routledge, 1993), discusses Cartesian matter theory and its problems. Gaukroger, Schuster, and Sutton (eds.), *Descartes' Natural Philosophy*, contains chapters on the background, analysis, and reception of Descartes' natural philosophy.

For a sample of Aristotelian physics from Descartes' time, see the selections from Eustace of St. Paul in R. Ariew, J. Cottingham, and T. Sorell (eds.), *Descartes' Meditations* (Cambridge: Cambridge University Press, 1998), pp. 80–92. D. Des Chene, *Physiologia: Natural Philosophy in Late Aristotelian and Cartesian Thought* (Ithaca, NY: Cornell University Press, 1996), provides a general overview; see also W.A. Wallace, "Traditional Natural Philosophy," in C.B. Schmitt (ed.), *Cambridge History of Renaissance Philosophy* (Cambridge: Cambridge University Press, 1988), pp. 201–35, and R. Ariew and A. Gabbey, "Scholastic Background," in Ayers and Garber (eds.), *Cambridge History*, pp. 425–53. In scholastic Aristotelian physics, natural agents need not "know" or "deliberate about" their ends (in expressing final causes); see Thomas Aquinas, "Principles of Nature," in his *Selected Writings*, R.P. Goodwin (ed.) (Indianapolis: Bobbs-Merrill, 1965), pp. 7–28 (at pp. 15–16).

On the creation of the eternal truths and mainstream Aristotelian metaphysics (especially that of Francisco Suarez), see Hatfield, "Reason, Nature, and God in Descartes," in Voss (ed.), *Essays*, pp. 259–87. Thomas Aquinas denied that even the blessed in heaven, who are permitted some direct knowledge of God through divine illumination, can know all that God can do (*Summa theologica*, Part 1, question 12, article 8).

On scholastic theories of sense perception, see A. Simmons, "Explaining Sense Perception: A Scholastic Challenge," *Philosophical Studies* 73 (1994), 257–75. On the perceptual theories of al-Haytham (also known as Alhazen) and Descartes, see G. Hatfield and W. Epstein, "The Sensory Core and the Medieval Foundations of Early Modern Perceptual Theory," *Isis* 70 (1979), 363–84. On Cartesian mechanistic psychology generally, see Cottingham (ed.), *Cambridge Companion*, chs. 11–12, Gaukroger, Schuster, and Sutton (eds.), *Descartes' Natural Philosophy*, Parts 3 and 5, and J. Sutton, *Philosophy and Memory Traces: Descartes to Connectionism* (Cambridge: Cambridge University Press, 1998), Part 1 (see also references to recent discussions of isomorphism in ch. 16). Some of these authors, as also Gaukroger, *Descartes*, pp. 276–90, argue (contrary to the position taken here) that Descartes did not deny sentience to animals.

On Descartes' philosophy of science and the role of experience, see D.M. Clarke, *Descartes' Philosophy of Science* (University Park: Pennsylvania State University Press, 1982), Garber, "Descartes' Method and the Role of Experiment," Oxford Readings, pp. 234–58, and Hatfield, "Science, Certainty, and Descartes," in A. Fine and J. Leplin (eds.), *PSA 1988*, 2 vols. (East Lansing, Mich.: Philosophy of Science Association, 1989), 2:249–62.

Chapter 10

Legacy and contribution

At the end of Chapter 1, we traced Descartes' influence in science, metaphysics, and epistemology over
the centuries. Having examined his philosophy in some
detail, we can now consider its legacy and contribution
more fully. His legacy includes all effects on subsequent thought, good and bad. His contribution is the
part that has been or is valuable. His work sometimes
left unsolved problems or even dead-end proposals,
and it sometimes advanced the discussion until new
theories – perhaps inspired by his work – made his
contribution obsolete. Where the problems he set
remain open, the problems themselves are his contribution.

Philosophical problems

Both Descartes' methods and his specific theories set
problems for subsequent philosophy, including his
cogito reasoning, proofs for God's existence, theory of
sensory qualities, and mind–body distinction.

Knowledge and method

Descartes contributed two methods, the method of doubt and the method of clear and distinct perception. For him, these were linked according to a third methodological idea, the analytic method, which aims to discover some simple and fundamental truths assumed to underlie, or permit, all other knowledge. These simple truths, which form the elements of knowledge, may come embedded in complex judgments or ideas and need ferreting out.

According to Descartes, the elements of knowledge exist in the human mind as innate ideas (or innate capacities for sense-independent thought) that would be recognized if directly experienced. The flood of sense perceptions initially prevents such experience. The method of doubt was designed for withdrawing from sensory experience to find purely intellectual ideas. The method of clear and distinct perception says that these purely intellectual ideas are true and can be recognized because they ineluctably compel the assent of the will.

Subsequent rationalist philosophers, including Spinoza, Malebranche, and Leibniz, sought to employ such intellectual intuitions to build a new metaphysics, but only Malebranche endorsed the method of doubt. All three held that the pure intellect reveals the one true theory of the natures of things, yet each arrived at a different substantive metaphysics. Eventually, these disparate results made it appear either that rational intuition does not exist, or that it does not hold the key to the one true metaphysics. Locke and Hume (among others) argued that human beings have no rational intuitions of substantive metaphysical truths. Kant examined the cognitive structure of the human mind and concluded that there are no rational intuitions of the real essences of things, effectively ending the rationalist metaphysical epistemology of pure intellect.

Apart from the search for purely intellectual perceptions, the method of doubt can be employed as a kind of filter for achieving certainty of any kind. Numerous philosophers, including Hume, used a method of doubt in seeking the limits of knowledge. In the *Enquiry Concerning Human Understanding*, he concluded that certainty extends only to abstract mathematics (i.e., mathematics not applied to the world) and the present contents of perception. He concluded that a thorough examination of the mind's contents shows that all such content arises from internal feelings and sensory perception. A similar position was adopted in the twentieth century, under the name of sense-data theory, which is sometimes characterized as the direct legacy of Descartes. In fact, in this case a method he introduced into modern philosophy eventually led to an opposing position, that sensory experience provides the only certain knowledge. Hume and the sense-data theorists abandoned any claim to know an external world distinct from actual or possible contents of sense perception.

Sense-data epistemology was unable to move beyond the immediate contents of experience to account for even ordinary knowledge of tables and chairs. Consequently, it too was abandoned. The philosophical moral is that the demand for certainty (which motivated the method of doubt) is too strict. We must accept that knowledge falls short of absolute certainty. Modern science relies on potentially fallible observations and measurements to support its theories. In its interplay of theory and observation, neither is placed beyond doubt. Perhaps if the hope of achieving the one true theory through purely intellectual perception is relinquished, the method of doubt should go too. Descartes' contribution would then be to have made prominent two methods, the first of which (clear and distinct perception) was pursued for a century until rendered obsolete by later philosophy, and the second of which (the method of doubt) lasted longer but is now in retreat.

The cogito reasoning

The single most famous argument in philosophy is Descartes' *cogito, ergo sum*. Although found in the earlier writings of Augustine of Hippo, Descartes framed the version that attained world historical prominence.

The transition from one's thought to one's existence is unassailable, at least under a sufficiently modest conception of what is thereby known of one's existence. The *cogito* reasoning demands assent. The interesting part is to decide what exactly it proves.

In Chapter 5, we examined Descartes' attempt to use the *cogito* to argue for the general reliability of clear and distinct perception as a profound truth presenter, yielding direct metaphysical insights into the essence of God, matter, and mind. The extraction argument we considered there is logically valid. But given that we now find Descartes' metaphysical results, including his conception of the essence of matter, to be faulty, we can well doubt its soundness. In retrospect, the extraction argument seems like an over-generalization from a single case. The assumption that the *cogito* reasoning exemplifies a general method of clear and distinct perception, able to yield substantive metaphysical truths across the domain of human knowledge, must be abandoned. The basis for the initial *cogito* conclusion may well be restricted to the immediately available, present contents of experience and so be unable to sustain a general *a priori* metaphysics.

The enlarged *cogito* argument, as examined in Chapter 4, engendered a new attitude toward the contents of consciousness in relation to the mental. By isolating the domain of thought through the method of doubt, it drew attention to the fact that sensing, imagining, feeling, desiring, and deciding all have (or can have) conscious aspects. In the Aristotelian theory of sense perception, as in the work of Ibn al-Haytham, there was no requirement that all acts of sensory perception be accessible at a central locus of awareness. The eye might be said to judge light and color, and the faculty of judgment to combine angular size with distance to yield a perception of true size. To the extent that such results were centrally accessible, they were said to be known by the "common sense." But earlier theorists did not require, as would Descartes, that all cognitive acts in principle be accessible to consciousness. Although, as we have seen, he did not take the empirically ludicrous stand that we are in fact reflectively aware of, or notice, all our mental acts (5:220–1, 7:438), he did formulate the metaphysically bold thesis that every truly mental act is conscious and hence in principle capable of being noticed (7:246). It is a separate question whether he made consciousness into the essence of thought, to which we will return below.

God and reason

From the time of Plato and Aristotle, philosophers have advanced arguments to prove the existence and attributes of a divine being. With the early medieval marriage of Greek philosophy and Christian theology, the project of giving a rational proof for the existence and attributes of God became a mainstay of Christian thought.

Metaphysical theology introduced a deep strain of rationalism into later medieval European thought. Within philosophy, the existence and attributes of God were to be investigated on rational grounds alone, without appealing to scripture or divine inspiration. Pursuit of purely rational demonstrations concerning God (an object of religious veneration) fostered a rational attitude toward the deity itself. Divine attributes such as infinity and perfection were to be investigated solely through reason or the intellect (whether starting from the senses or not). The resulting conception is sometimes called "the God of the philosophers."

This rationalization of God, presaged by theologians such as Aquinas and Scotus and developed by Descartes and others, was an early impetus toward the European Enlightenment. For if God was subjected to reason in order to prove his (or its) existence, then reason could also note the limitations or lack of success of those proofs. Reason was applied to scripture by Descartes' near contemporaries, Hobbes and Spinoza, among others. If the authority of scripture was discounted, reason became the only evidentiary ground for belief in God. But if God was to be known through reason alone, his attributes would be limited to those deriving from infinity and perfection. The result was the deistic conception of God as the first cause and rational orderer of the universe, who (or which) does not intervene in human history.

Descartes did not endorse a rationalistic approach to religion, for he acknowledged the light of grace (3:425–6, 7:148) and the authority of scripture (2:347–8, 7:2). But he limited philosophical claims about God to what could be established rationally. He was an instigator of what historians call the "early Enlightenment." He distinguished rational proofs for God's existence and attributes from doctrines founded on revelation and subject to theological authority (1:143–4, 8B:353).

Primary and secondary qualities

Galileo and Descartes made prominent the position that color and other sensory qualities do not directly reveal the basic physical properties of things. This position was canonized by Boyle and Locke as the distinction between primary and secondary qualities in bodies. Primary qualities coincide with the basic categories of physics – in Descartes' case, extension, size, shape, position, and motion. The secondary qualities depend on the primary qualities and are categorized according to the type of sensation they cause in perceivers. Thus, bodies with a surface configuration that causes light to be reflected so as to cause a sensation of color in a perceiver have color ascribed to them as a secondary quality. The sensation in the mind is considered to be an idea of the secondary quality in the body, even though, for example, the idea of red does not intrinsically *seem* to be an idea of the microstructure of a surface.

The position of Descartes, Locke, and others is sometimes paraphrased as saying that bodies "are not really colored." Neither author denied (physical) color to bodies. They denied color in bodies as an Aristotelian real quality that "resembles," or is an instance of, the phenomenal color we experience. They held that color sensations tell us that there is a certain physical property in bodies (its physical color), but don't reveal the physical structure of that property. Whereas on the Aristotelian account phenomenal color provides a sample or instance of the object property, for Descartes and Locke phenomenal color is a subjective effect of nervous stimulation by light particles.

On this scenario, light, sound, and the other secondary qualities are perceiver-dependent properties of objects. This means that bodies are classified as having color only because they have an effect on light that ultimately causes a sensation of color. If there were no perceivers, there would still be physical light and sound (light particles and vibrations in the air), but objects would not have secondary qualities conceived as powers to cause sense perceptions, since by hypothesis there are no perceivers for the light particles and air vibrations to affect. One might ask whether secondary qualities of color and sound could still exist in the counterfactual sense that if there were perceivers of a certain sort, they would experience color and sound if affected by bodies of the right sort (solution of this conundrum is left to the reader as an exercise).

Descartes' contribution was to realize that the senses do not directly present the fundamental physical properties of matter but remain useful guides to the environment. He argued in the Sixth Meditation that secondary-quality sensations serve to reveal the presence of some property in objects whose physical nature remains unknown to the perceiver (if she hasn't yet learned Descartes' physics). The perceiver can use the fact that the same objects regularly produce the same color sensations to tell objects apart. Recent research has suggested that in fact color perception evolved to allow animals to receive mating signals, to find food, and to make other biologically salient discriminations. Descartes' functional attitude toward the sensory qualities was on the right track.

Science and metaphysics

Prior to the rise of the new science, various active principles were ascribed to bodies, often understood through a biological analogy of guided growth and development. Descartes agreed with many other new philosophers that these active principles could not be clearly understood. Although his position that matter is pure extension was ultimately unsuccessful, his theory offered a coherent vision of the world as geometrically conceived matter in motion. Everyone agreed that geometry was a paradigm of intelligibility. Disagreement came over whether the basic properties of matter are exhausted by the geometrical modes.

Descartes' mathematically oriented approach to matter was successful in a more general way. As modified by Newton, it became standard. Descartes' laws of motion were surpassed and rendered obsolete by Newton. As physics has developed, it has become apparent that in reducing all corporeal properties to size, shape, position, and motion, Descartes was guilty of what Arnauld had charged (7:220) – that is, of making an "imperfect abstraction" from the actual properties and forces of the natural world.

Matter is not purely homogeneous extension. Modern science has uncovered ever more complex microstructure. Mass replaced Descartes' purely volumetric notion of the quantity of matter. Kinds of matter were sorted by specific gravity, depending on mass per unit volume. As eighteenth-century physics developed, force became more fundamental than extension, so Kant could claim that extension is conceptually dependent on a force of repulsion. Across the nineteenth and twentieth centuries, various fundamental forces and particles, including massless particles and cloud-like particles, were posited. Hard little particles having only size and shape came to seem like a quaint picture from the past.

However, Descartes did not think that the fundamentals of his physics were an "imperfect abstraction" from actual things but a clear and distinct perception of the real possibilities of things. He did not offer his metaphysical foundations as an "all things considered" best theory. He did not ascribe to those foundations the merely moral certainty of his particular mechanistic hypotheses but asserted them as the one true theory. If he had put them forward as simply the currently best theory, he would not have faced the problem of justifying the absolute truth-presenting status of clear and distinct perception. (In this case, the "presumption" strategy for avoiding the circle might well not beg the question, since less would be claimed for the products of clear and distinct perception.)

Since his time, the method of seeking *a priori* insight into the real natures of things has been abandoned. Modern science now moves back and forth between theoretical conjecture and empirical evidence. The notion that the human mind has innate access to the fundamental properties of physics is no longer viable. It is refuted, if in no other way, by the historical development of the physical sciences, which has seen the previously unimaginable theories of general relativity and quantum mechanics develop through the process of theoretical and empirical give and take (spiced by developments in mathematical representation).

The nineteenth-century Darwinian T.H. Huxley hailed Descartes as a physiologist of the first rank for advancing the general picture that animal and human bodies are machines. Descartes wanted to explain biological processes using the same physical principles that apply everywhere else in nature. On this view, living things differ from non-living things only in the organization of the matter they contain, not because of any special life force or principle of vitality.

The mechanistic approach to the body was a major conceptual contribution, but it also has limits. The comparison of the body to a machine leaves open the question of whether the body has a design. If it does have a design, then functions can be assigned to its parts based on their intended service. Descartes, in the *Treatise on Man* (11:120) and *Meditations* (7:80, 87, 374), wrote as if the machine of the body had been designed by God. Yet in the *Discourse*, *Principles*, and correspondence he offered the tantalizing hypothesis (rendered false, he allowed, because one must believe that God created animal and human bodies fully formed) that everything on Earth, including plants and animal bodies, arose from the primordial soup through the natural processes of matter colliding with matter (6:42–4; 8A:99–100, 203; 2:525), ruling out direct design.

With the rise of Darwinian theory in the nineteenth century, the notion that organisms were directly created by intelligent design was rejected by modern science. This still leaves us with the problem of accounting for our perception that the parts of organisms serve functions. Some philosophers suggest that evolution plays the role of the designer, crafting the organism through the process of "natural selection." Evolutionary pressures "select" successful structures, thereby building up design-worthy bodily structures. Others reject such explanations as mere metaphor. We are left with an open problem, resulting partly from the success of the mechanistic picture and partly from its incompleteness.

Mind and body

Descartes' most active legacy pertains to mind. His most famous position is mind–body dualism and belief in an immaterial substance. Those doctrines are now used primarily as stalking horses or straw men for opponents of substance dualism. His more general legacy concerns the description of mental phenomena and the problem of fitting the mental into the natural world. In these areas, Descartes made lasting contributions in the form of insightful descriptions and persisting problems.

Realism about the mental

Descartes was a realist about the mental. He was the ultimate realist because he posited a distinct mental substance. But leaving his two-substance ontology aside, he was a realist about mental phenomena themselves. Even before presenting any argument about the ontological basis of mental phenomena (whether they were, at bottom, immaterial or material), he affirmed the existence of thoughts, including feelings, sensations, imaginings, remembrances, desires, and volitions.

His argument for mind–body dualism relied upon the claim that the mental and the material form two distinct classes of phenomena. That claim does not itself entail dualism, and it remains under discussion today. During the twentieth century, many philosophers and scientists came to believe that mental phenomena are difficult to integrate into the natural world (often identified with the material world). On this view, mental phenomena are not natural phenomena in their own right. To be legitimately retained in a naturalistic picture of the world, they would have to be reduced to physical or physiological processes. Some, such as the psychologist B.F. Skinner and the philosopher W.V. Quine, believed that this aim was hopeless and recommended eliminating mental talk altogether. But many others now take it to be obvious that mental phenomena exist and must be included in any complete account of what there is, whether reduction proves possible or not. There are few substance dualists among philosophers today, but some endorse a property dualism, which acknowledges irreducibly mental properties in addition to physical properties. Others think of the mental as an aspect that some or all physical things have. They might be dual-aspect theorists (mental and physical are two aspects of one underlying reality), or pan-psychists (all material things have a mental aspect).

The problem of the ontological status of mental phenomena was not solved by Descartes and has not been fully solved today. Descartes posited that mental phenomena such as color sensations exist as modes of mind. The phenomenal red we experience was, on this view, the content of an idea. Yet he did not hold that the mind literally possesses the property of red, any more than he held that the (non-extended) mind is literally square when we sense or imagine a square. (Although in that case he may well have held that the pineal gland has a square pattern on it.) So the problem arises for his view of where phenomenal red can be if the mind is not literally red and red is not a real quality. His dualism did not solve the problem, for he never explained how a non-extended mental substance, even if united to and interacting with the body, can contain red as a content, or have the phenomenal experience of red. He simply stated that it happens. Similarly today, materialists argue that phenomenal red is just something that happens in the brain when certain patterns of ionic activity occur in the visual cortex. Despite knowing (up to a point) which patterns of activity cause which sensations, even now no one can explain how ionic activity can contain or produce the phenomenal experience of red.

Descartes' notion of psychophysiological laws remains useful in the study of mind. He argued that mental states can, through empirical study, be brought into correlation with brain states. Neither a dualist nor a materialist would be required to expect, *a priori*, that such correlations exist; any pattern of relations between brain states and mental contents might be imagined, prior to empirical study. But there are regular correlations, which are being studied under ever finer resolution. This empirical enterprise builds on Descartes' contribution in hypothesizing empirically knowable psychophysiological laws.

Consciousness, representation, and intentionality

In the Synopsis and Meditation 2, Descartes characterized the thinking thing as having an intellectual nature, and in Meditation 6 he argued that intellection was essential to other mental capacities, such as sense perception and imagination. In these places he did not make consciousness the essence of mind, although it is safe to say that consciousness figured prominently in the arguments of Meditation 2 as a feature he ascribed to all thought (7:246).

In Meditation 3, Descartes contended that all thoughts involve ideas, and that all ideas are "as it were of things" (7:44). All ideas have objects, or representational content. This suggests that representation, or what is now called "intentionality," is the essential feature in Descartes' account of mind. In Chapter 8, we found reason to think that Descartes considered intellection to be the essence of mind. All thoughts, even those involving other "forms" (7:37), such as volitions and emotions, are directed to an object. Intellection is perception, and ideas, as its modes, are essentially representational. Representation or intentionality may well have constituted the essence of the mental according to Descartes.

On such a view, consciousness might be regarded as something that naturally occurs in thoughts, because the essential feature of thought is perception. The perceptual and representational character of thought, together with the presumed simplicity of the mind as a substance, might entail that every idea must be perceived, or enter awareness, by its nature. Descartes may have suggested something like this to Mersenne: "What I say later, 'nothing can be in me, that is to say, in my mind, of which I am not aware,' is something which I prove in my *Meditations*, and it follows from the fact that the soul is distinct from the body and that its essence is to think" (3:273). If the essence of thought is consciousness, then this "proof" simply reasserts that essential property. But on the present view, the proof might run that in a purely mental substance whose essence is perception, there is no place for any thought to hide. (Which need not mean that all thoughts are made explicit objects of reflection.)

From some present-day perspectives, there need be no direct relation between consciousness and the mental. Consider several mental functions: representing the current environment (senses), detecting the presence of food (classification), representing previous states of the environment (memory), adjusting behavior in response to its outcomes (learning), representing possible states of the environment (imagination), and acting to achieve an end (volition). Some of these functions, under the general description given, take place in amoeba, most of them in flatworms, and all or most in cats and dogs. Although no one knows for certain whether amoeba and flatworms are conscious, let us suppose that at least amoeba are not. Yet they, in some sense, certainly detect the presence of food. In that case, a "mental" function would occur without being accessible to consciousness, even in principle. It can be debated whether food detection in amoeba counts as mental, but we may well be able to imagine that a non-conscious being, such as a robot, could be constructed that would perform all of the above-named functions (under a behavioral description of those functions). More generally, modern cognitive science posits various subpersonal and non-conscious, but nonetheless mental acts of information processing. (This position is not restricted to those modern cognitive scientists who deny that consciousness is real.) From one present-day perspective, there is no necessary connection between mentality and consciousness.

Sometimes it is claimed that Descartes' contribution of treating thought and perception as representational includes "veil of perception" skepticism, which says that no one ever knows the world because all they can know are their own ideas. But the issues are separate. Indeed, one need not invoke the language of ideas and representations in order to pose external world skepticism. One can simply unfold the brain-in-the-vat scenario, in which brains are suspended in vats of nutrients and connected up to a supercomputer that gives us just the perceptions and feelings we have now. We would then have the experience of being seated in a comfortable chair reading a book, even though we lack eyes and are in fact suspended in nutrients while receiving appropriate electrical impulses to our sensory nerves. More generally, Descartes' own use of skepticism was not aimed at investigating the veil of perception but at withdrawing from the senses in accordance with the analytic method. His legacy includes a skeptical problematic only to the extent that the arguments for doubt in the First Meditation are considered effective, while his later arguments for their removal are deemed failures.

Descartes advanced an "act" and "object" analysis of thought, according to which all thoughts have objects. All thoughts can be characterized by their content plus a further act in relation to that content, whether the act be perceiving, judging, desiring, willing, or what have you. His analysis fed one major stream of thought about thought. Empiricists such as Hume took the opposite tack, attempting (successfully or unsuccessfully) to reduce thought to bare impressions and ideas (considered literally as images) and the laws of their succession. More recent analyses of "propositional attitudes" into content and attitude reflect the earlier act–object analysis.

The wisdom of the body

In his metaphysical *Meditations*, Descartes focused first and foremost on the self as a thinking thing. After challenging the usefulness of the senses in Meditation 1, he ignored the body and the senses for nearly all of Meditations 2–5, reinstating them only in Meditation 6. As a consequence, Descartes is sometimes described as denigrating the body, the senses, and bodily feelings and emotions.

In fact, Descartes ignored the senses and body only for the purpose of achieving metaphysical knowledge. He had his readers consider the uncertainty of the senses because "in my view this is a prerequisite for perceiving the certainty that belongs to metaphysical things" (7:162). Descartes did not recommend that one adopt the attitude of the *Meditations* in ordinary life, or even in the extended pursuit of theoretical knowledge. He wrote to Elizabeth that it was his rule "never to spend more than a few hours a day in the thoughts which occupy the imagination, and a few hours a year on those which occupy the intellect alone" (3:692–3). He recommended in general that everyone should, "once in a lifetime," come to understand the principles of metaphysics (3:695; see also 10:395, 398). But he advised that "it would be very harmful to occupy one's intellect frequently in meditating upon [the principles of metaphysics], because this would impede it from properly attending to the functions of the imagination and the senses" (3:695*).

The intended exercise of the imagination and senses includes the pursuit of natural philosophy, and Descartes in fact undertook various observations for himself. His most sustained empirical investigations concerned animal bodies. During the 1630s, he spent much time dissecting animal parts he collected in the villages (1:263, 2:525). Upon returning to his physiological studies in the mid-1640s, he worked on but left incomplete the *Description of the Human Body* and composed the *Passions*, each of which discussed his theories of human physiology in some detail.

We saw in Chapter 9 that Descartes attributed significant "wisdom" to mindless animal bodies and to the human body acting without mental direction. The abilities he attributed to the body include all the psychological functions described above as potentially being performed without consciousness: sense, classification, memory, learning, imagination, and action. (One might question whether the imagination of possible states of affairs could be performed by the body alone on Descartes' theory; the textual evidence is scant, but it suggests that he believed that memory could interact with imagination to perform the task [11:177–85].) For Descartes, those psychological functions could be carried out without mind at all. Although the body alone has no genuinely mental wisdom, it does respond appropriately to environmental circumstances, naturally pursuing benefits and avoiding harms.

Descartes held that the human mind is naturally adjusted to the wisdom of the body. Mind–body union is constituted by God or nature so that the mind is led to want the things that the body has already undertaken for the sake of preservation. As Descartes explains in the *Passions*, the function of passions (or body-based emotions) is to "dispose our soul to want the things which nature deems useful for us, and to persist in this volition; and the same agitation of the spirits which normally cause the passions also disposes the body to make movements which help us to attain these things" (11:372). The mind is here yoked to the wisdom of the body, which has precedence. The spirits set the body in motion, to approach what is good and flee what is bad. This flow of spirits also causes the mind to want the good thing and to want to avoid the bad.

On Descartes' theory, we are naturally in touch with our bodies and bodily inclinations. Nonetheless, through rational reflection we can gain some control over those inclinations. This requires effort and cannot always be attained by a simple act of will (11:359–70).

Descartes' theory of hugging exemplifies the intimate connection between bodily response and conscious feeling. Hugging is elicited through physiological changes that occur when an object of love is near: "we feel some kind of heat around the heart, and a great abundance of blood in the lungs, which makes us open our arms as if to embrace something." This movement of the arms is thus far governed by purely mechanical causes. The state of the body also affects the mind, making it "inclined to join to itself willingly the object presented to it" (4:603*). Consequently, the mind will cause the body to close its arms around the beloved.

The love one feels on such occasions is, in Descartes' view, a confused and confusing sensation. He explained this by observing that our adult emotions are conditioned by early bodily experiences, including those in the womb. He theorized that we experience only four emotions in the womb; joy upon becoming united with a healthy body, love at receiving nourishment in the womb, sadness when nourishment is lacking, and hatred if unnourishing matter comes to us (4:605).

> Those four passions, I believe, were the first we had, and the only ones we had before our birth. I think they were then only sensations or very confused thoughts, because the soul was so attached to matter that it could not yet do anything else except receive various impressions from it. Some years later it began to have other joys and other loves besides those which depend only on the body's being in a good condition and suitably nourished, but nevertheless the intellectual element in its joys or loves has always been accompanied by the first sensations which it had of them, and even the motions or natural functions which then occurred in the body. [4:605]

Whether Descartes' description of the complex psychology of love drew mainly on his experiences with the cross-eyed girl of his youth (5:57), with the woman for whose honor he dueled in his late twenties, with the housekeeper with whom he fathered a daughter in his late thirties, or with feelings for the Princess Elizabeth around the time he was fifty, we do not know. When he wrote the above-quoted letter to Chanut, the French ambassador to Sweden, he was apparently then experiencing love, for he wrote that "to treat of this passion would take a large volume, and though its nature is to make one very communicative, so that it incites me to try to tell you more than I know, I must restrain myself for fear that this letter may become tediously long" (4:606–7). Presumably, it is not thinking about the theory of love that makes one communicative, but the feeling itself.

Descartes' contribution was to recognize that mind and body are yoked in complex ways, conditioned by early childhood experiences starting in the womb. This contribution, though often neglected in mid-twentieth-century accounts of the philosopher, is becoming better known as attention turns to his descriptions of mind–body union and interaction.

Descartes now

Descartes is with us in our methods, theories, problems, and questions. His achievements in mathematics and science have been either fully incorporated into ongoing thought or surpassed. His contributions to philosophy appear in different lights from different perspectives. His image is used for many philosophical and rhetorical purposes. These can't be summed up in a single slogan; nor should they be, for Descartes' legacy and contribution are ongoing.

Perhaps the single most salutary example Descartes can offer us today is the image of the philosopher as intellectually and culturally engaged. Descartes was on to the hot topics of his day. He was in the thick of developing the new science and mathematics, and of revising metaphysics and its epistemology. It is easy to think that philosophy cannot hope to achieve his grand ambitions today. And in fact it cannot. Once we've given up the attractive view that the fundamental theory of the universe can be perceived through the *a priori* insights of the pure intellect, we no longer have a method by which philosophy can in one step move to the frontier of all human knowledge. But even without that unattainable aim, philosophers can continue to work at the frontiers of knowledge, as participants in the continuing process of elucidating, criticizing, and revising the core concepts of the arts, sciences, and humanities, and engaging in critical reflection on human institutions and practices. Because philosophers can't claim special non-empirical access to those core concepts, or the structure of institutions, we must engage in the world of experience – not merely by reflecting on our own experience but also by keeping up with knowledge and practice in any subject matter that bears on the objects of philosophizing.

Descartes firmly believed that you can't do philosophy without knowing anything – and that philosophy could by itself come to know the basis for everything. Today, we are seeing again that you can't do philosophy without knowing anything. But we also know that the basis for everything can only be found in everything. We can no longer look inward to find it; philosophy must look outward. That, too, is part of Descartes' heritage, the combined legacy of a broadly aimed philosophy, deprived of its rationalist methodology. To pursue

Descartes' broad philosophical ambition we must replace the method of pure intuition with an immersion in, and engagement with, the achievements, uncertainties, and ongoing projects of our time. No one who understands the goals and failures of Descartes can still believe, as he did, that philosophy could change the intellectual world overnight from its resources alone. We can no longer hope to start over from scratch and reconstruct all knowledge on a single plan. We have to begin in the middle, even as the framework provided by current knowledge is moving on.

Starting in the middle for us means gaining understanding of current concepts and practices. One approach to such understanding is immersion in current knowledge, in all relevant fields. Another is study of the history of philosophy, the sciences, the arts and humanities, and human institutions and practices. Philosophy can no longer hope, as Descartes did, to gain intellectual distance by turning away (even if only momentarily, as he wanted to) from the senses and the past. Study of the history of problems, solutions, theories, methods, and concepts is a method for looking afresh at things today. Study of the history of thinking is a tool for seeing how to continue now. Study of Descartes, who wanted to make history irrelevant to philosophy, and of his *Meditations*, which was designed to tap into ahistorical intellectual perceptions, is one way into philosophy now. With no Archimedean point available, history can serve as both ballast and tool in relation to the present. But, with apologies to Descartes, for us there is no one true method toward knowledge, or even any one true theory of what knowledge is. Which leaves lots of philosophy to be done.

References and further reading

Many recent books evaluate Descartes' legacy, some positively, some negatively. D. and A. Hausman, *Descartes's Legacy* (Toronto: University of Toronto Press, 1997), praise Descartes' innovative theory of intentional ideas. S.R. Bordo, *Flight to Objectivity* (Albany: State University of New York Press, 1987), criticizes Descartes' flight from the "feminine" and the "organic" – although her critique is challenged in Bordo (ed.), *Feminist Interpretations of Descartes*. Rorty,

Philosophy and the Mirror of Nature, attributed many modern intellectual ills to Descartes. In response, see G. Hatfield, "Epistemology and Science in the Image of Modern Philosophy: Rorty on Descartes and Locke," in J. Floyd and S. Shieh (eds.), *Future Pasts: Reflections on the History and Nature of Analytic Philosophy* (New York: Oxford University Press, 2001), pp. 393–413.

On recent developments toward a fallibilist epistemology, see A.I. Goldman, *Epistemology and Cognition* (Cambridge, Mass.: Harvard University Press, 1986), and K. Lehrer, *Theory of Knowledge* (Boulder, Colo.: Westview Press, 1990).

On the change between an Aristotelian conception that sensory acts need not all be available to a central "common sense" (even if the common sense serves to unify sensory knowledge) and Descartes' theory that all acts of mind are in principle available to consciousness, see Hatfield and Epstein, "Sensory Core" (cited after Chapter 9).

Locke drew the distinction between primary and secondary qualities in his *Essay Concerning Human Understanding*, book II, ch. 8. P.M.S. Hacker, *Appearance and Reality* (London: Basil Blackwell, 1987), contends that the modern scientific distinction between primary and secondary qualities denied color to bodies and was based on a mistake. E. Thompson, *Colour Vision: A Study in Cognitive Science and the Philosophy of Perception* (London: Routledge, 1995), reviews modern color theory and work in comparative color vision.

T.H. Huxley praised Descartes' contribution to physiology in "On the Hypothesis that Animals Are Automata, and Its History," *Science and Culture* (New York: Appleton, 1884), pp. 206–52. R. Dawkins, *The Blind Watchmaker* (New York: W.W. Norton, 1986), argues that Darwin's theory of natural selection can account for the phenomena of design without positing a designer. For an introduction to debates over evolution, see K. Sterelny, *Sex and Death: An Introduction to Philosophy of Biology* (Chicago: University of Chicago Press, 1999).

On the hypothesis that the qualities of sensation, and consciousness itself, are not real, see Dennett, *Consciousness Explained* (Boston: Little, Brown, 1991), and the reply by O. Flanagan, *Consciousness Reconsidered* (Cambridge, Mass.: MIT Press, 1992). On current thinking about conscious qualities and the mind–body problem, see J. Levine, *Purple Haze: The Puzzle of Consciousness*

(Oxford: Oxford University Press, 2001), and W. Seager, *Theories of Consciousness: An Introduction and Assessment* (London: Routledge, 1999).

On Descartes' duel, and his relations with Hélène, the mother of his daughter Francine, see Rodis-Lewis, *Descartes*, pp. 58, 139.

Appendix

Arguments, demonstrations, and logical form

Arguments are an important means of generating conviction for philosophical positions. In philosophical texts from Descartes' time, arguments were presented in a series of sentences leading to a *conclusion*. Sentences that support the conclusion are called *premises*. In a *formal* logical argument, the premises *entail* the conclusion, which means that if the premises are true, then, in virtue of their logical form, the conclusion must be true. The logical form of an argument is the argument's abstract structure and, as can be seen in the example below, is independent of the truth, and even the content, of any particular premises.

In its bare-bones structure, an argument can be set out in numbered steps. In today's logic, an argument that has correct logical form is said to be *valid*. Here is an example of a logically valid argument:

A   All dogs have fleas.
B   This thing is a dog.
C   Therefore, this thing has fleas.

The structure of the argument, with a universal *major premise* (A) and a *minor premise* about a particular (B), which entail a *conclusion* (C), follows one of the logical forms found in syllogistic logic as first set down by Aristotle.

The fact that an argument is logically valid does not mean that the premises or conclusion are true. That is a separate question. The above argument is valid, which means that the conclusion "logically follows" from the premises; this would be so even if the premises, A and B, were false. If a given argument is both logically valid and has true premises, then in today's parlance the argument is said to be *sound*. This means that the conclusion is established as being true by the argument, in virtue of true premises and correct logical form.

What are the implications for an argument if the premises or conclusion are false, or if the argument is invalid? If the conclusion is false (this dog doesn't have fleas), then if the argument is valid, one or more of the premises must also be false. In the argument above, it might be (and in fact is) false that all dogs have fleas. But even if that premise were true, it might be that "this thing" is a cat, or a stuffed animal. If either premise A or B is false, then the truth of C is not established by the argument. When we know that one or more of the premises is false, the conclusion may still be true; a particular dog can have fleas even if it is not true that all dogs have fleas. In general, if an argument is valid but the premises are false (and the conclusion is not equivalent to one of the premises), then the argument does not speak to the truth of the conclusion. And if the premises are true but the argument is invalid, the argument again does not settle the truth of the conclusion.

As discussed in Chapter 1, Descartes was not fond of syllogistic logic and preferred to take mathematics as his model of reasoning. This meant that he wanted to reduce his reasoning to simple steps, each of which was evident on the face of it and so had no need to be formulated in the artificial mold of the syllogism (10:405–6, 8A:205–6).

There are forms of reasoning we now consider more basic than the syllogism, which mathematicians had long used and which

Descartes used. These include the simple reasoning, called *modus ponens*, which runs as follows:

If P then Q.

$$\frac{P.}{Q.}$$

In the schematic version given here, "P" and "Q" stand for sentences. The ruled line shown here is one way of indicating that Q is presented as a conclusion that follows logically from the premises above the line. In this book other devices have been used to mark the conclusion, such as the connective "therefore" (as in the example below).

An argument concerning the subject matter of the syllogism example can be rendered in *modus ponens* as follows:

1   If something is a dog, it has fleas.
2   This thing is a dog.
3   Therefore, it has fleas.

This form of the argument is logically different from the syllogistic form. In the syllogism, it is a condition on the truth of premise A, "All dogs have fleas," that there exists at least one dog. Premise 1, "If something is a dog, it has fleas," has no such requirement. It can be true even if there are no dogs. Modern logic distinguishes claims about universal connections between predicates from claims about the existence of individuals having those predicates. Syllogistic logic did not make that distinction.

In ordinary human reasoning *modus ponens* appears often. It is used whether one is explicitly aware of its logical form or not, just as the syllogistic forms might also be used. The fact that Descartes spoke out against the syllogism does not mean that he did not argue in a logical manner (7:455). It meant that he did not consider the explicit use of formal syllogistic structure to be central to good philosophical argument or to finding the truth. He was willing to accept transitions between steps in arguments without feeling any requirement or desire to fit the argument to an explicit logical schema. Thus, from A, "this thing is a dog," he might think we can immediately infer B, "this thing is an animal." One could require that a universal premise (U), "all dogs are animals," be supplied. However, Descartes believed that we can trust our intuitive sense that B follows from A without needing to make premise U explicit. He explained this attitude in his popular dialogue, *The Search for Truth*. Reflecting on arguments similar to the *cogito* reasoning of the Second Meditation, he has his mouthpiece, Eudoxus, say:

> I cannot but stop you here, not to lead you off the road but to encourage you and make you consider what good sense can achieve if given proper direction. For is there anything in what you have said which is not exact, which is not legitimately concluded, which is not correctly deduced from what has gone before? All these points have been stated and worked out not by means of logic, or a rule or pattern of argument, but simply by the light of reason and good sense. When this light operates on its own, it is less liable to go wrong than when it anxiously strives to follow the numerous different rules, the inventions of human ingenuity and idleness, which serve more to corrupt it than render it more perfect. [10:521*]

In speaking of "deduction" here, Descartes does not have in mind formal deduction according to rules of logic but rather the procedure, described in the *Rules* (10:369–79), of arriving at a conclusion by following steps of reasoning evident to "good sense" or the "light of reason." (Some of Descartes' contemporaries distinguished reason, as the faculty of transitions between steps in an argument, from the intellect, as the perceiver of individual propositions; Descartes did not adhere to such a distinction.)

Descartes' model of good argumentation was mathematics. One model of such argumentation that virtually all of Descartes' readers would have known (at first hand or through a textbook) was Euclid's *Elements*. It was structured with definitions, postulates, and axioms (or "common notions"). Some of the axioms have the form of premise 1 above; for example, "If equals be added to equals, the wholes are equal." Descartes accepted such axioms as self-evident (9A:206). In Euclid's *Elements*, the definitions, postulates, and axioms were used to demonstrate theorems. However, Euclid did not rely exclusively on logical structure in his demonstrations. In many cases, spatial relations exhibited in diagrams played an ineliminable role. Diagrams constructable with compass and straight edge were an essential part of Euclid's geometrical proofs. To give an example, when it was said to place a point on a line segment, between the two ends of the segment, the procedure was carried out by relying on the assumed spatial structure of the line segment. That is, it was taken as given that all points of the segment lie *between* the two end points. This meant that a point located anywhere on the segment was already known to be between the end points.

Euclid's use of diagrams and spatial structure became an object of criticism during the mathematical revolution of the nineteenth century. Appeal to drawn or imagined spatial structures in a proof was now considered "inexact." Euclid's original demonstrations were seen as incomplete or defective. The perspective from which they came to be so viewed was foreign to Euclid: it was a perspective in which arithmetic and algebra are more fundamental than geometry, and geometrical relations are translated into algebraic operations. In effect, the nineteenth-century revolution altered the subject matter of mathematics so as to make numerical structure (or, on some views, set-theoretic structure) primary. Euclid's methods were not suited to the new algebraic conception of geometry. In the case of betweenness and the line segment, the segment would now be treated as part of the real number line, its points as numerical values, and betweenness would be determined through the relations of "more than" or "less than." (This was not the procedure of Euclid, or even of Descartes.)

The nineteenth-century revolution was in part made possible by an area of mathematics that Descartes helped to create: analytic or algebraic geometry. But Descartes himself did not advocate a fully algebraic geometry, and he retained the spatially understood notion of "extension" as his primary mathematical notion. He considered spatial structures to afford a particularly clear means for representing different things of any type as distinct from one another (as in the diagrams in Rules 12 and 14 [10:413, 450]). And he admitted into his geometrical constructions various curves generated by the point of intersection between certain sorts of moving line (*Geometry*, 6:389). He also held that the various arithmetic operations (addition, subtraction, multiplication, and division) can be clearly and evidently represented through operations on line segments (10:464–8). When he stated a preference for self-evident reasoning over logical syllogisms, part of what he had in mind was the practice in geometry of reasoning from diagrams in a way that was not rendered logically explicit (and, we might note, could not have been with the syllogistic resources of the time), but which nonetheless had the force of proof. After the time of the *Rules*, Descartes adopted the view that the structure of extension can be grasped by the pure intellect, independently of images and imagination. However, this need not mean that he considered the spatial structure of extension any less important to geometrical reasoning; he now claimed that the structure of extension can be grasped by pure intellect (7:72–3). (The primacy of spatial structure in mathematics at this time can be understood by considering what Descartes could have meant by speaking of extension as "continuous quantity" (7:63); there was no numerical understanding of continuity at this time – continuous magnitude was represented by the geometrical line.) Even in this later period, he held that mathematical reasoning typically draws upon the imagination (3:692), that geometrical figures can be represented in imagination (7:72), and that extension can be distinctly imagined (8A:323).

Descartes considered mathematical reasoning, which proceeds by small steps, each of which seems evident, to be more indicative of true understanding than arguments that are supposed to convince simply by dint of formal structure. He did not himself discuss problems from Euclid's *Elements*, which was, after all, elementary (2:182) – even if, he ventured, it was not really understood by many scholastic philosophers (9A:210–11) – but he discussed many geometrical problems from other ancient authors, including Archimedes, Apollonius, and Pappus. As discussed in Chapter 2, in metaphysics Descartes preferred the analytic method of exposition over the synthetic method of Euclid's *Elements*, but the sense of "analytic" there is distinct from "analytic" or algebraic geometry, and so provides no challenge to the point made here about the fundamental nature of spatial extension in Descartes' conception of mathematical magnitude.

Descartes did not limit self-evidence to mathematics. He found it in other ideas or notions that were not geometrical, did not include spatial extension in their content, and therefore could not be imagined (represented in an image). Such are the idea of God as an immaterial being and the notion of causation applied to God as cause. Here, again, he claimed to find connections among ideas that were self-evident, not because they satisfied logical form but because the content of the idea or notion revealed an evident connection upon "mental inspection." An example is his own axiom or common notion that "Concerning every existing thing it is possible to ask what is the cause of its existence" (7:164). Presumably, this is supposed to be evident simply from considering the fundamental or primitive notions of *thing*, *existence*, and *cause*.

Descartes was not by any means opposed to logical argument. He held the syllogistic form to be artificial in relation to paradigmatic examples of human reasoning as found in geometry and mathematics. He was not committed to abstract logical form as the basic mode of justification in reasoning. He appealed instead to the intuitive certainty found in self-evidently true steps of reasoning. This mode of reasoning was familiar to him from geometry. Part of his methodological aim, as discussed in Chapter 2, was to find similar self-evident arguments using small steps in metaphysics. The extent of his success is something to be decided by evaluating his individual arguments. This will include not only the ones laid out in logical form but also those that rely on appeal to allegedly self-evident implications from primitive ideas or notions, such as those of *thing*, *existence*, *cause*, or even *thought*. In analyzing Descartes' arguments for ourselves, we may want to clarify their implicit logical structure by stating them as explicit, logically valid arguments. In doing so, we should aim to draw out the implicit structure on which Descartes relied in following "good sense" or "the light of reason."

References and further reading

The student seeking an acquaintance with modern logic might consult any of a number of introductory books, including G. Priest, *Logic: A Very Short Introduction* (New York: Oxford University Press, 2000), and I.M. Copi and C. Cohen, *Introduction to Logic*, 11th edition (Paramus: Prentice Hall, 2002), where notions of validity and soundness are discussed and elementary logical systems described. A brief introduction to the notion of logical form may be found in C. Menzel, "Logical Form," in E. Craig (ed.), *Routledge Encyclopedia of Philosophy* (London: Routledge, 1998), vol. 5, pp. 781–5.

On Descartes' non-formal notion of "deduction," see Clarke, *Descartes' Philosophy of Science*, appendix 1. On his achievements in analytic geometry, see H. Bos, "On the Representation of Curves in Descartes' *Géométrie*," *Archive for History of the Exact Sciences* 24 (1981), 295–338, and *Lectures in the History of Mathematics* (Providence, RI: American Mathematical Society, 1991), chs. 2–3. On the effects of the nineteenth-century revolution in mathematics, see Bos, *Lectures*, ch. 9. Original sources in nineteenth-century mathematics, including Felix Klein's discussion and criticism of the trend toward arithmetization, can be found in vol. 2 of W. Ewald (ed.), *From Kant to Hilbert: A Source Book in the Foundations of Mathematics*, 2 vols. (Oxford: Clarendon Press, 1996). The nineteenth-century criticisms of Euclid as "incomplete" were elaborated in Moritz Pasch, *Vorlesungen über neuere Geometrie* (Leipzig: Teubner, 1882) and are surveyed in H. Eves, *Survey of Geometry*, 2 vols. (Boston: Allyn & Bacon, 1963–65), sec. 8.1. On the mathematically sound use of spatiality and diagrams in Euclid's proofs, see L. Shabel, *Mathematics in Kant's Critical Philosophy: Reflections on Mathematical Practice* (London: Routledge, 2002).

Bibliography

Clarke, Desmond M., *Descartes' Philosophy of Science* (University Park: Pennsylvania State University Press, 1982).

Cottingham, John, *Descartes* (New York: Basil Blackwell, 1986).

Cottingham, John (ed.), *Cambridge Companion to Descartes* (Cambridge: Cambridge University Press, 1992).

Cottingham, John (ed.), *Reason, Will and Sensation: Studies in Descartes's Metaphysics* (Oxford: Clarendon Press, 1994).

Cottingham, John (ed.), *Descartes*, Oxford Readings in Philosophy (Oxford: Oxford University Press, 1998).

Curley, Edwin, *Descartes Against the Skeptics* (Cambridge, Mass.: Harvard University Press, 1978).

Des Chene, Dennis, *Physiologia: Natural Philosophy in Late Aristotelian and Cartesian Thought* (Ithaca, NY: Cornell University Press, 1996).

Dicker, Georges, *Descartes: An Analytical and Historical Introduction* (New York: Oxford University Press, 1993).

Flage, Daniel E. and Bonnen, Clarence A., *Descartes and Method: A Search for a Method in Meditations* (London: Routledge, 1999).

Frankfurt, Harry, *Demons, Dreamers, and Madmen* (Indianapolis: Bobbs-Merrill, 1970).

Garber, Daniel, *Descartes' Metaphysical Physics* (Chicago: University of Chicago Press, 1992).

Gaukroger, Stephen, *Descartes: An Intellectual Biography* (Oxford: Oxford University Press, 1995).

Gaukroger, Stephen, Schuster, John, and Sutton, John, (eds.), *Descartes' Natural Philosophy* (London: Routledge, 2000).

Guèroult, Martial, *Descartes' Philosophy Interpreted According to the Order of Reasons*, trans. R. Ariew, 2 vols. (Minneapolis: University of Minnesota Press, 1984–85).

Kenny, Anthony, *Descartes: A Study of His Philosophy* (New York: Random House, 1968).

Rodis-Lewis, Geneviève, *Descartes: His Life and Thought*, trans. J.M. Todd (Ithaca, NY: Cornell University Press, 1998).

Rorty, Amélie (ed.), *Essays on Descartes' Meditations* (Berkeley: University of California Press, 1986).

Rozemond, Marleen, *Descartes's Dualism* (Cambridge, Mass.: Harvard University Press, 1998).

Shea, William R., *The Magic of Numbers and Motion* (Canton, Mass.: Science History Publications, 1991).

Voss, Stephen (ed.), *Essays on the Philosophy and Science of René Descartes* (New York: Oxford University Press, 1993).

Williams, Bernard, *Descartes, The Project of Pure Inquiry* (London: Penguin, 1978).

Wilson, Margaret D., *Descartes* (London: Routledge & Kegan Paul, 1978).

Wilson, Margaret D., *Ideas and Mechanism: Essays on Early Modern Philosophy* (Princeton, NJ: Princeton University Press, 1999).

Index

345